How to be Happy
Though Young

How to Be Happy Though Young

Real Problems of Real Young People

BY GEORGE LAWTON

Author of "Aging Successfully"

THE VANGUARD PRESS, INC.
NEW YORK

Copyright, 1949, by the Vanguard Press, Inc.
Copyright 1939, 1940, 1941, 1942, 1943, 1944,
1945, 1946, by Scholastic Corporation. Reprinted
from Senior Scholastic by special arrangement with
the editor. All rights reserved.

Published simultaneously in Canada by
Copp, Clark Company, Ltd., Toronto.

No portion of this book may be reprinted in any form
without the written permission of the publisher, except
by a reviewer who wishes to quote brief passages in
connection with a review for a newspaper or magazine.

DESIGNED BY MARSHALL LEE

Manufactured in the United States of America
by H. Wolff, New York, N. Y.

To My Son Peter
And His Children To Be

Contents

FOREWORD: *For Adults Only*	xi
HOW IT ALL STARTED	xvii

Getting Along With . . .

. . . YOURSELF   1

Can We Manage Our Moods?	3
Memories That Are Too Real	5
Fears: Their Causes	9
So You Are Shy	12
"I've Got the Blues . . ."	17
The Science of Mental Fitness	20
In Charge of Yourself—You!	24
Can People Be Remade?	29
What's Wrong with Daydreams?	32
Lonesome or Lonely?	34
Our Dreams: Nonsense?	38
The Well-Adjusted Person	42

. . . YOUR FAMILY   47

Are Parents Necessary?	49
Getting Together with Parents	52
Parental Ties	54
Why Do We Hurt People We Love?	56

CONTENTS

Dr. Jekyll and Mr. Hyde	60
I Want to Grow Up—Fast!	62
Should Sisters Have Brothers?	65
Divided Loyalties	69
Fathers and Sons	71
Can a Child Hate His Parents?	75
The Greater Loyalty	79
Can Youth and Age Be Friends?	82
"The Kind of Parent I Hope To Be"	85

... PEOPLE 93

Can We Learn To Be Popular?	95
How Can I Make People Like Me?	98
"It Is Not Wisdom . . ."	102
The Gentle Art of Making Enemies	105
Anger: Its Uses—and Abuses	109
The Feeling of "Being Different"	112
Ten Commandments for High-School Students	115

... THE OPPOSITE SEX 121

"Haven't We Met Before?"	123
Steady Company	125
More of "Going Steady"	128
The Wolf Who Goes Steady	131
Only a Passing Fancy	134
From "Brother" to Boyfriend	137

CONTENTS

"I'm in Love—"	140
"Love? Ah Yes, Indeed"	147
Love at First Sight	151
Happiness in Marriage	153
Boys Like Girls, and Girls Like Boys Who ...	157

... FRIENDS — 163

Outgrowing One's Friends	165
Unmatched Ages	167
When Friends Prove Untrue	170
"I Do Not Like Thee ..."	172
How to Lose a Friend ...	176

... YOUR CAREER — 181

I Haven't Any Idea What I Want to Be	183
On Choosing a Career	186
Detour or Main Highway?	188
Which Kind of I.Q. Have You?	192
Can I Be An Artist?	195
If We *Can't* Get What We Want ...	198
Are Women as Intelligent as Men?	201

... SCHOOL — 207

Overcoming Stage Fright	209
"I'm Just No Good in Math!"	212
"Aw, What's the Use of Studying!"	215

CONTENTS

Do You Know How to Study? 219
Are Teachers and Pupils Natural Enemies? 224

... SOCIETY 231

Are Young People Mature? 233
You're Young Only Once 235
War Jitters 238
Psychological Preparation for War 241
What Success in Life Means to Me 245

... THE UNIVERSE 251

What Can Young People Believe In? 253
"Oh, World, I Cannot ..." 256
How Can I Conquer Fear of Death? 259
The Art of Breaking Bad News 263
"How Kind She Was, How True ..." 267
What Is Man? 273
To Be Or Not To Be 275

YOUTH SPEAKS FOR ITSELF 279

WHAT DO BOYS AND GIRLS REALLY WORRY ABOUT? 281
YOUTH'S BILL OF RIGHTS 296
PHRASES TO WHICH YOUNG PEOPLE ARE ALLERGIC 299

Foreword: For Adults Only

George Bernard Shaw once said that it is a shame that youth is wasted on young people who don't know how to enjoy it. Presumably, it is to us oldsters learned in the ways of the world—the mathematics of pleasure and the chemistry of pain—that youth should be given. Actually, of course, we spend all our lives studying how to live, and then, when we think we finally have learned our lesson, we find few opportunities to recite.

Youth ought not to be wasted. It should be a thrilling, joyous period. The springtime of life is full of promise and bloom and hope. But this is all theoretical. That is the way it looks to us old fogies. In reality, youth is beset by problems, not necessarily grim and tragic ones, but serious difficulties, nevertheless.

Young people are suspended between two worlds, or, rather, between two lives: one not yet dead, the other not quite born. The young person is growing into life, that is, slowly taking on the habits and thoughts of adults, and saying a long, lingering good-bye to childhood. Good-byes to something we love are always hard and a little sad. We cannot quite drop hold of the hand and turn away.

There are countless adjustments boys and girls have to make as they meet new experiences of all kinds and gradually shed

FOREWORD: FOR ADULTS ONLY

the disguise of childhood they have been wearing so long. It is not easy to carry on the game of make-believe day after day, not easy for the young person, and certainly not easy for those to whose care they have been entrusted.

Indeed, it is difficult to be neither caterpillar nor butterfly. Grownups, it would seem, cannot decide what to ask of a young person. At one moment he is criticized for being a child —since that is the very moment when parents and teachers want him to be an adult. The next minute he is chided for trying to be a grownup, for that is precisely the time when they want him still to remain a child. He must not mind this too much, for young people have always been treated thus. We, the parents and teachers, were once young, far-off as that may seem to us now, and, like them, also used to grow confused at times in trying to fathom the caprices of those in charge. We, too, could not easily decide on the type of person we wanted to be nor the kind of life we wanted to lead. I hope any young person who happens to read this will be patient with us adults if we forget that we were once what the young person is now.

Every young person is trying to learn the lines of a new part he is soon to play. But he is not quite ready to step out on the stage. Restless as he may become with the child's role which he knows so well—too well, he exclaims—he himself is afraid to let go of it. The young boy or girl is puzzled and hesitant because he is not entirely sure what the world expects of him or what he should expect of himself. Life is a kind of picture puzzle he is trying to read aright.

Yet all this is only to say that young people are young. The adolescent is one who is growing into life. His mind and his habits are still in the process of formation. Everything he does is tentative and experimental. He advances, then retreats. One moment he is over-bold, the next over-cautious. Life to him

FOREWORD: FOR ADULTS ONLY

is perplexing and mysterious but always turbulent. He is eager yet half-afraid and more than half-confused in anticipating all sorts of adult experiences which he is soon to inherit as part of his birthright as a human being.

Youth is a period of sudden adjustments for which adolescents frequently are entirely unprepared. Moreover, they have not one load of adjustment to carry but two. That is why parents, and adults generally, should regard the struggles of young people sympathetically and their antics charitably. Young people must adjust themselves at one and the same time to the inner world of their own impulses and desires and to the outer world represented by society and its requirements. Dawning needs and desires stir a boy or girl violently and strangely at times. The adolescent craves for emotional experience almost as much as he does for food and drink, and he is in love long before he finds a person to love.

Adults may deem a young person at times lazy or moody or erratic. However, he merely may be trying to accustom himself to the newness of things. Grownups should remember that the young person is being pulled in different directions at the same time by conflicting emotions and desires. If he adopts a course of action, he does so only to drop it and go off on another tack. An apparently hostile world must be subdued if the young person is to grow up. But youth can't struggle against the world, because its energies are engaged in a civil war. It is a time when the emotions and feelings run riot. Sex and love and fear and thoughts of death and feelings of guilt and inferiority and intimations of greatness assail one all at once.

One moment the young person is sure he is a genius, and the next, he knows he is a fool. One moment he longs to make a grand gesture of self-sacrifice, and the next he is off on plans of self-exploitation. Now he will work for humanity, now he will work for himself. Now he sighs because life is not long enough for all he wants to do or to be; the next he is serene because he has decided nothing matters. From the ecstatic certainty that he has found a love that will endure forevermore, he plunges into the agonizing doubt of whether there be any such thing as love at all. He packs up ready to bid farewell to parents who do not understand him. A day or an hour later he is unpacking, preferring, it would seem, a distasteful family circle to a cold, harsh world. For the adolescent finds himself too late for childhood and too early for adulthood. If any grownup reading this cannot understand his son or daughter, let him try very hard and very honestly to recall his own youth.

Society demands action, demands that young people select a calling, that they get started on a career and prepare for full adult responsibilities. Yet how are they to know what they want, when they do not know who they are or what and how much the world contains? They find life so full of a number of things that they are dazzled. They hesitate to choose once and for all because the mere act of choosing immediately drops the shutters on the rest of the marvelous array of the world's goods on exhibit.

To grownups it appears that young people live in a half-dream world. But to young persons the world is not a half-dream world; it is too real. For some young people the reality of the world is an intolerable strain. The true twilight realm for young people is the adult's world, because adolescents often do not have more than a glimmering of what patterns of social behavior they are supposed to adopt as adults. Or, if they do have a full realization of what is expected, they find it very difficult, almost impossible, to fulfill these obligations. The call to exchange the child's dependency for the

FOREWORD: FOR ADULTS ONLY

adult's responsibility comes with too much suddenness and shock.

Young people, like all human beings, want three things: freedom, security, love. These are the most powerful hungers we have. The struggles of the adolescent are the attempt to satisfy these longings in a way which fits both the requirements of society and his own personality.

Boys and girls want freedom; they are fascinated by the novelty and privileges of the world outside their home. But they don't know what freedom is or what kind they want. They rebel, but they don't know just what it is they are rebelling against. They think it means rejecting school, routine, old friends, etc. And they don't want to remain sheltered and protected by their parents forever.

But they cannot accept freedom, because it has its dangers and responsibilities, and they come scurrying back home to its warmth and familiarity. You see, they also want security, and that means all the things they discarded in the chase after freedom.

The same is true of love. They are groping toward the love of the opposite sex. They are making the first tentative search for a mate, and obtaining an invaluable education here. But there is still the powerful tie to their parents, a love attachment of another kind that they are not willing to admit is still primary, no matter how beautiful and thrilling the other variety is.

They want freedom, love, security—it is true. But they are not yet ready for these in adult terms. This they do not realize and will not accept.

If they think back easily, perhaps they may recall two themes on which they had pondered every single day of their high-school life, though neither they nor their elders had been fully aware of them; the themes: "What do young people need in

FOREWORD: FOR ADULTS ONLY

order to be happy?" and, "What do I want of life and how am I going to get it?" Many of them eventually will answer these questions to their satisfaction; a few may never find a thoroughly adequate answer.

Every life period has its pleasures and joys, its responsibilities and problems. Young people should make the most of what youth offers them (I really don't believe that it is wasted on young people), and then let them become adults without any backward looks.

G. L.

How It All Started

Some years ago I was a teacher of English in Evander Childs High School, Bronx, New York. I also served as the school psychologist and director of its Bureau of Tests and Measurements. In 1943 I left the teaching profession and went into full-time private practice as a consulting psychologist.

Relatively early in my teaching career I had started to work on a research project dealing with self-put questions to which persons of all ages try and fail to find satisfactory answers. The section dealing with high-school students was published in the Journal of Experimental Education, *under the title "A Study of Questions Which Adolescents Find Unanswerable." This study caught the attention of Kenneth M. Gould, Editor-in-Chief of* Scholastic Magazine. *He thought it would be interesting to try to answer these questions that bother adolescents and offered space in the magazine for such a service. And that is what led to the articles which now go to make up this book.*

Where did the problems come from? The chief source was in the unsolicited letters of Scholastic readers and from the entries in the annual contest called "What Is Your Greatest Problem?" Another source was in the thousands of young people who, during the many years I was at Evander Childs, consulted me about every conceivable problem a young person might have—and some inconceivable ones.

HOW IT ALL STARTED

Let me tell you a little about how the answers were worked out. As a young person, I myself had listened to many all-wise adults who had formula answers for everything. When I started on this Scholastic project, I made up my mind that I would work out my answers, then present the problems to a group of young people, listen and take notes on their solutions, tell them mine, and finally decide whether my original answer could stand or how to change it.

Practically every letter and answer in this book was worked over that way with a group of young people, generally my English classes. I want to pay tribute here to the intelligence and wisdom of high-school boys and girls. When we grow up we are apt to underestimate how much young people see and feel, how much of our final understanding of life we already possess in our teens.

This book contains practically all the pieces I wrote for Scholastic, starting in 1939 and ending in 1946. A few pieces touching on war problems have been omitted as outdated, all have been carefully gone over, some have been extensively revised, some have been lengthened. Two new pieces have been especially prepared for this volume as indicated in footnotes. The handling of all the themes in this book represents my thinking as of today.

During the years when I was doing guidance and counseling with younger people, I saw parents in connection with the problems of their children, and I couldn't help but notice how often the adjustment difficulties of a young person were tied up with the problems faced by his parents and grandparents. This led me to broaden the scope of my professional interests to include men and women of the middle years and older. And that is how I have come to specialize in opposite ends of the age scale. However, they are not opposite if we consider what human beings want out of life. I find a great deal of similarity in the problems of the "growing into life" phase and in the "growing out of life" one, except that I should like to see young people equipped to grow into life at younger ages than they do today, and adults equipped to postpone the "growing out of life" stage until a much later time than at present.

I greatly enjoyed my association with Scholastic Magazine. Never once was there any attempt to interfere with the questions or answers. It is a splendid magazine, and I still read every issue from cover to cover for pleasure and instruction. I should like to take this means of thanking Kenneth M. Gould, Maurice R. Robinson, Jack K. Lippert, and Margaret Hauser for their co-operation and helpfulness.

This material would have slumbered on in my files except for the keen eye, the imagination, and the literary perceptiveness of my assistant, Helen Winner. It was she who saw the possibilities in these pieces as a book for young people. It was she who undertook to handle the publishing details, scrutinized each letter and answer, arranged and rearranged them, nursed them skillfully through the trying editorial chores of revision and rewriting, until they emerged as a book.

I won't feel these acknowledgments are complete without saying something about the great aid in writing the original pieces which I received from my late wife, Stell. She had a profound knowledge of human nature and great literary taste. It was she who made a preliminary screening in the "What Is Your Greatest Problem?" contest. After that, we would spend hours going over her choices and mine, deciding which entries best stated the most typical problems and which presented special problems we ought to consider.

Whatever merits or demerits this book has, at least I hope the young people among my readers will agree that I have done an honest job. I have tried not to talk down to them.

HOW IT ALL STARTED

I hope I haven't preached at them. I have not said things I didn't mean. I have tried to view young people in all their aspects. Young people are interested in everything, not merely sex and manners, but parents, friends, moods, love, death, and so on. And so this book is a sampling of practically all the problems of both boys and girls as they themselves present them. And now I want to give you their book and yours: **HOW TO BE HAPPY THOUGH YOUNG.**

G. L.

Yourself

Can We Manage Our Moods?

Dear Dr. Lawton:

What are moods and why do we have them? Some days I get up feeling on top of the world. Everything seems wonderful, and I feel like running instead of walking and like singing instead of talking. I even find myself smiling in a silly sort of way at everyone I meet. Then, for no reason at all, I feel wretched and depressed. I can hardly drag myself around, and everything anyone says I find irritating. I've tried to find reasons for these changes of mood, but they seem to come and go in a mysterious way, for just no reason at all. I'd like to be a calm, even-tempered person, but how do you become one? This moodiness worries me.

Mary L.

Possible But Not Easy

Dear Mary:

If human beings were machines, they would simply function, and act in the most direct manner. A machine does not analyze or try to learn from its mistakes; it has no feelings or imagination, it never wants what it cannot have or regrets what it has or has not done. A machine has no moods. While admittedly the most efficient way to handle a problem is to work out a plan and then act upon it, sometimes we have no plan or we are afraid to act for fear of the consequences. That is when it is easier to have a "mood" in which we can feel bitter, drench ourselves in self-pity, blame everyone else, have gorgeous daydreams of becoming great and famous, and of getting even with our enemies. But when our emotional spree is over, we find ourselves just where we were before it started. Whatever had to be done and decided still awaits us. The mood, you see, was an escape from the real world. It was a substitute for a constructive plan or a definite program of action.

Of course, we all need such little rests from time to time, and moods and daydreams not only make life endurable at critical moments but may also yield the germ of a plan which can be developed later on. Some days we are carefree, perhaps because things are going smoothly. At other times, without our being aware of what has happened—a snatch of conversation, a glance, last night's dream, the most trivial thing, in fact—may seem to threaten the loss of possessions important to us. We become a little frightened and anxious: we have a mood. But to change in this way from gaiety to sadness (and back again) is our human heritage. People who never have unhappy moments can never have really joyous ones, for it means their imagination and emotions are undeveloped.

In the course of becoming grownups, high-school boys and girls encounter many new experiences and responsibilities and many unfamiliar emotions. How can one expect them to be always ready to act with wisdom and dispatch if they are still in the process of learning what they can and cannot do, still learning what people and the world are like? Since young people will often be at a loss as to the proper action to take in a given situation, it is plain that they will often take refuge in moods. Moreover, it is natural for young people to overestimate the true meaning of their successes and their failures, because they can see themselves only in terms of day-to-day existence, and not as personalities whose complete life stories will take many years to unfold. As we grow older, our moods are likely to become less changeable, because we will know ourselves better and have learned to translate what we want of life into terms of what we can hope to obtain.

Moods are like a barometer. If it always reads "Stormy Weather"—that is, if you are always hopelessly miserable—or, if the barometer keeps shooting up and down, and you follow a regular pattern of riding on top of the world one day and sinking to the lowest depths the next, your first step should be to consult your family physician. Next, ask yourself what problem are you evading, what situation is too much for you to handle. Remember that extreme gaiety may be just as much an attempt at escape as extreme dejection.

Let's suppose you've made a hard, honest search to learn what makes you feel unsuccessful. And this search either reveals nothing or else you find the cause but can't mend it and still are going back and forth all the time between being "up" and being "down." In that case, seek out someone in the school or community who has specialized in the treatment of emotional difficulties. If you do this when you're young you'll save yourself many mistakes and much floundering about later on.

Memories That Are Too Real

Dear Dr. Lawton:

Why is it that some of the things that happened to us in the past seem more real than the things of the present? Only the other day I was walking down the street and through an open window I heard a radio going. Someone was playing the

"Moonlight Sonata," and at once I seemed to be transported back years ago when we lived in another city. A girl in the house across the street had practiced this beautiful music day in and day out, and I used to think of it as "our" piece, although I never knew the girl—she was years older. It used to make me feel very sad and yet happy at the same time. When I heard it on the radio, my present surroundings seemed to disappear, and I actually *felt* that I was the *me* of long ago. The same thing happens when a particular occurrence reminds me of some painfully embarrassing episode when I was a little kid. I begin to flush all over, and I actually experience the humiliation of that time all over again. Can't we ever forget anything that happened to us—must these memories always intrude into our present life?

Felix Z.

Are Constant Sources of Pain and Pleasure

Dear Felix:

Human beings really deserve to have two drugs they can take: one to help them remember what they want to remember, and the other to help them forget what they want to forget. We all experience occasionally the same sensations you do. During recent months I have received and gathered together several letters that touch on the same subject, and your letter has just given me the idea that perhaps I can comment on them all here. For example, the first letter I picked up in my folder is from a girl who writes as follows:

It was on a dreary night four years ago that I first saw the friend of whom my brother had spoken so much. When he came I was doing my homework, but after he left I couldn't think of or see anything but him. He was so handsome. Yes, he was tall and dark too. I really never had bothered looking at boys before . . . I was only thirteen.

After that night, I was always on the lookout for him. Sometimes when I knew he was in front of his house across the street I would go up on the roof and watch him. I would stay there as long as he was out. Sometimes I would imagine he was holding me in his arms and whispering things to me. As the years went by, and I became older and more attractive, I noticed that every time I passed his house and said hello to him, his eyes would light up and they would follow me until I reached the door of my home.

No words can express how overjoyed I was during those little moments. I say "I was," because those moments no longer occur. You see, I've moved far away and only in my most secret and beloved dreams can I see him.

A boy tells us the same thing, but in another way:

Girls are my problem! You see, I live in a seashore resort, and for two months of the year our small town plays host to a huge crowd of visitors.

Each July, without fail, I meet some beautiful siren who steals my heart. Until September, my life is an idyllic adventure.

How can a fellow settle down to the boring routine of school, homework, eating and sleeping, when only a short time before he was a carefree Romeo?

The other day I was sitting in my English class listening to a rather dull discussion of prose fiction. Soon I was deep in a reverie about some girl who had left with the birds. Suddenly a voice rasped, "Young man, what are you thinking of?" Dreamily I answered, "Ruthie." The professor is a pretty decent fellow, and he gave me the period off to think about my "Ruthie." My classmates, however, never have let me forget this degrading episode.

This condition of mental suspended animation lasts until about December, and by that time I'm just a rambling wreck. Summer has just ended. Dear Dr. Lawton, please rush me first aid, so there won't be trouble in class again. How can I forget Ruthie?

Here is another girl troubled by the merging of present and past:

My father died when I was a little girl of about two, and my mother died when I was twelve.

There is a teacher in school who reminds me very much of Mother. The subject is most difficult for me, and trying to concentrate is impossible, for my mind just wanders back. "She" told me that if I am to pass I would have to make the tests up. I came in one day after school, but shortly after I got started, I gave up and asked to leave the room because I felt very funny inside. The teacher wanted to know what was wrong. I didn't know what to say, but I began to cry and ran out.

She asked me to come in after school this term for a little help, but I just can't make myself. I still feel the same. How can I stop seeing Mother in this teacher?

What, then, shall we do with our past, or, rather, the memories of our past?

Life is not so much a series of peaks and valleys, great joys or great sorrows, as a road with bumps and detours. Whenever the present is without challenge and interest, we think back to those few unusual moments, whether those moments be jeweled or sombre.

Of course, it is best for human beings to live mostly in the present and future. If we do think of the past, it should be about our exceptionally joyful moments, so that these can act as a stimulus or inspiration to us, making us desire more of them and giving us something to live for.

When it comes to thoughts of the painful past, that man is lucky who is grateful even for his moments of unhappiness, who finds that these have added a certain wisdom to his life. To think of the past and fill ourselves with reproach and pity for what never can be again, for all "the sadness and tears of things," is an attempt to run away from the present, which always chases after, crying "Escape me never."

What shall we do about our memories? We can enjoy the beautiful ones, treasure them, take them out and count them once in a while. As for the painful memories, it is good to realize that life is not a continuous story but something that is meant to end and meant to begin again. And if we are so built as to remember one kind of experience, we also are built to remember the other kind. "One drug to make us forget and another to make us remember?" Lovely, but impossible.

Fears: Their Causes

Dear Dr. Lawton:

Do childhood fears last throughout life? Ever since I can remember, I have been afraid of many things: of staying alone, of water, dogs, lightning. Instead of outgrowing these fears as I get older, I seem only to add new ones to the list. Now I am afraid of examinations, meeting strangers, being in a moving vehicle. I don't dare tell anyone, because it seems so silly to be afraid of such things, and of so many, too. What makes one person afraid of something and another one not? Is there anything that can be done about these fears?

Marion L. S.

and Their Management

Dear Marion:

Infants show fear of but two things: a loud sound and the sudden loss of support. For all practical purposes, it may be said that we are not *born* afraid, but are *made* afraid, most often as the result of contact with those who show fright. Some youngsters catch fears as easily as they do colds. In one family, the fear of toads was transmitted from mother to daughter over several generations, almost as if it were an heirloom.

Many fears are the result of unpleasant experiences. A child bitten by one dog may be afraid of all others. Some fears are implanted through a threat made in haste or anger and then forgotten by the person making it, although not by the one to whom it was directed. Similarly, a grownup in a mood of make-believe may say or do something to frighten a child. Though the adult offers reassurance at once, a genuine fear may be instilled.

The emotion of fear is so powerful, it is no wonder that it is played upon by all those who desire instant and unquestioning obedience. How often is a child told if he does not behave in a certain way, this or that unhappy fate awaits him.

We often attempt to cure a person of fear by forcing him to meet it, especially when he is least prepared. But pitching a lad into the lake when his back is turned will not reduce his fear of the water. Ridicule is another everyday method of treating fears. However, even though a person is afraid of such odd things as cap-pistols, contact with a dry sponge, or an invasion from Mars—if he is afraid, he is in genuine distress.

Poking fun at him merely prolongs his fear and makes him feel even more unlike other people than he did before. And all of us with a given fear feel different enough as it is, at least until we have found several others with the same fear.

We are afraid of something as long as we think it can hurt us. Once we are convinced there is no danger, our fear will go. Hence a person afraid of dogs might get one as a pet or have friends accompany him during a planned-for encounter with a dog. Directing a joke at the fear-producing object often works well. Getting angry at it may also help, on the principle that fear suggests flight, but anger means holding our ground. A good example of how humor and anger can be used to dispel fear was offered by the attitude of Londoners during the blitz.

Without fear in its milder forms—caution, foresight, etc.—we could not long survive. Every life has its moments of danger, but the best procedure at such times is to analyze the risks involved and then to decide on how they can be cut to a minimum. Dwelling on lurid details either causes alarm or increases the fascination which danger can sometimes possess. Often the fear of a particular experience can do more harm than the experience itself. The parents of a boy who had been ill as a child had him lead a sheltered life thereafter, though medically this was not necessary. As a man, his countless fears did him more damage than could have been caused by any activity.

Some older people may not be very hopeful about the prospect awaiting boys and girls in general, or they may think a particular individual lacking in some quality essential to success. However, for a young person to hear constantly that failure is just around the corner often implants in him a great fear of the future. He may hesitate to attempt anything, a condition often in error called laziness. Fear is probably the chief factor which prevents boys and girls from making the most of their intelligence. A typical case is the student who knows the right answer but is afraid to recite.

Behind every fear is a story, and behind the story is a person. Some fears are cleared up when we recall the incident which caused them. That is why it is so important to discuss our fears with a sympathetic listener.

Yet sometimes a fear persists, despite everything one can do. We then must accept it as another fact about ourselves, in the same class as our height, age, etc. To fear one's fear is only doubling trouble. A brave man is not one without fear, but one who faces his fear when that is the thing to do. A high-school girl afraid of snakes handled and killed one last summer in order to rescue a little child. Note: She is still afraid of snakes, but hopes to improve with practice!

Fears are most damaging when they shape an entire pattern of living, when, in order to shut out pain and trouble, a person tries to shut out the world as well. One should go out to welcome all the factors in a changing experience, even those which bring suffering, since it is chiefly from this that we keep on developing emotionally.

Fear is the chief reason for the difficulties which crop up in the relationships of individuals and of nations. It is the main cause of human unhappiness. A country could set itself no higher goal than to discover and eliminate those aspects of its social and economic life which breed fear in its citizens.

So You Are Shy

Dear Dr. Lawton:

I want to make friends and be liked by people, but I dread social contacts. When I have to get up and say something with people around, I begin to stammer and tremble and feel all jittery inside. The result is I make a fool of myself and wish I could run away and be alone in my room at home. The funny thing is that once I do get home, I become a totally different person. I'm "terrific" then. I go over the scene and think of all the brilliant things I could have said and done. But that's when I'm alone in solitary grandeur. What keeps me from behaving this way when I'm with people? I hate being this "shy" type. Is there some way to overcome such a handicap?

Tom K.

A Common Problem in Growing Up

Dear Tom:

The world is filled with people who are quiet and retiring but who don't feel they have any problem. They make up the millions of people who sit in the audience and who watch and applaud the talented people who talk, sing, declaim, and, in general, "do big things." These spectators don't feel they are inferior to the "actors" or that they are being different by remaining quiet and part of the crowd. They like it that way and have a swell time just watching.

Then there is the small group of people who can get up and talk at any time about anything in front of anybody, without a qualm or a fear. They just love the limelight, the attention, and the flowers. A sea of rapt faces; a roomful of enthusiastic silence —that's what an "actor" (regardless of his exact name) thrives on. The only problem such a person has is absence of opportunity to "stand up and shine."

In between these two groups, there is Tom K.—you (and countless other boys and girls). What I'm going to say here will strike you as being downright silly. You are quiet and retiring, but you don't want to be that way because you want to be the actor, yet you are afraid you can't make the grade. A person who considers himself shy is often a repressed actor, an ambitious, creative person, with a great need for affection and admiration, who (1) has not yet found the proper outlet for his ability, or (2) having found it, is afraid to submit his ability to appraisal.

Shy people really have an exaggerated view of their importance in the scheme of things, and an exaggerated view of the seriousness of any test of their ability. They are extremely self-centered and imagine that the way they dance on the dance floor or talk in front of a class or deal with an examination will be front-page news the next day and will affect the remainder of their lives, and perhaps the destiny of mankind.

You believe that you are better than the next fellow, but you are also afraid that if you tried to prove this you would be slapped down. You are afraid to let yourself go, because you feel that if you do you will only reap disapproval. An extra-conceited person who also is sure he will be a flop if he attempts the very thing about which he is conceited—there, Tom, is the shy person.

You weren't born shy, you know, Tom, you were *made* shy. I don't know your life story, of course, but I'm fairly sure it went something like this: As a tot, your family overlooked your shortcomings because you were young and very dear to them. It was pleasant never to be judged by any strict standard of achievement. You therefore clung to your timidity and didn't want to grow up. When you began going to school, you dreaded every test of your ability, since you were not accustomed to being appraised impartially. And so you began to feel that life expected more of you than you could ever hope to achieve.

Others may have urged you to try harder and warned you of the dangers of failure, but this only made you feel more unsure of yourself. You felt safer when quiet and withdrawn, both at home and at school. Without being aware of it, you acted on the belief that this strategy would save you from harsh criticism. Shyness, you see, has its advantages, too.

If you were alone on an island you would not be shy. Nor are you that way when you work by yourself. You "break out" with the "signs" of shyness when your achievement is to be compared with others your own age, as in an examination, at a party, or on the athletic field. It is natural for you to feel more at ease with older people than with those of your own age. Older people are not your competitors.

You have had a long history, not so much of failure but of expecting failure. I know how hard it is for you to break this pattern. By being shy you avoid the struggle and striving common to the lives of other young people. You don't have to face real problems in a real world, but in your day-dreams you can achieve success at bargain rates. Another complication is that you, not knowingly, want to fail, since you believe you have certain serious faults and handicaps for which you merit punishment.

Since you learned your shyness, you can unlearn it. Your fears and your feelings of not being up to the mark or as good as others can be educated out of you, assuming that the part of you which doesn't want to be shy is stronger than the part that does. But the education will have to come gradually.

After you have done everything to make your appearance presentable, you should make a great effort to accept as many examinations, contests, or parties as you possibly can. Tell yourself that you will do your best. And you should believe and hope that this best will represent successes. The shy person cannot accept failure; that is what makes him shy. The first step in curing shyness is getting strong enough to accept failure if it comes.

Joining clubs is probably very difficult for you. Perhaps it will be a little less difficult if you start with those that make little demand of you, like a hiking club; then go on to one on current events. Volunteer for membership on a committee, then run for office in a club. If a uniform or insignia and some authority goes with membership in the club you choose, so much the better. You will then be judged not as an individual but as a group representative. As such you will be given respect and privileges that will make you feel more secure. Many a policeman is shy in plain clothes.

If you ever got good enough for a dramatic society, that would represent the final stage in your escape from shyness. Taking private lessons in dancing, singing, public speaking, would be a good idea, for you know it is a teacher's job to help young people develop skill. A good teacher does not scold or scorn; nor does he compete with his pupil. His job is to help.

You should ask some wise older friend or relative to help you make a list of your superior qualities and of your resources for enjoyment. That's to help bolster you up in case you fail at something. For it is important that you develop every talent or ability so that wherever possible you can have a real success and acquire a sense of strength. Moreover, you need to forget, if possible, your own so-called deficiencies.

Develop strong interests. Then you will be concerned with *what* you are doing, not *how* you are doing it. You can also forget yourself through helping other weak people. Take to gatherings someone even shyer than yourself. Or befriend a greater wallflower than you are. It would do you a world of good to find a person who needs the knowledge that you possess and to become his teacher. At first, you should reveal the "real" you and try out new ways of expressing yourself only in the company of close friends. In that way, you will prepare a cushion for possible failures.

In fact, when you have gone beyond the preliminary lessons,

you might stop trying for perfection, and if you make mistakes, use them as a chance to laugh at your shortcomings. You will realize you exaggerated the importance of success and failure because you were thinking of *who* you were rather than of *what* you were doing. You will also reconcile yourself to the absence of special treatment. Did it ever occur to you, Tom, that other people have as many faults and problems as you, but they don't tell you about them? Have you ever thought that people may like you more if they discover that you are just as imperfect as they?

Ask questions of people whenever this seems in order. This will get your attention away from yourself for a little while— maybe. Try it first in personal contacts, then in a group. If you ever feel that someone is seriously damaging your self-respect, any attempt to stand up for your rights which meets with success is all to the good.

Shyness cannot be cured, as such. As you develop in ability, in emotional maturity, are able to admire and love and be admired and loved in turn, you are "actor" easily and calmly when you have to be, and "audience" easily and calmly when you have to be. You know what you can do and what you can't do. Develop your vocational skills and become also a successful human being and, when the time arrives, a successful husband. When that happens you'll tell your children: "I used to be so shy. Why, when I was your age, I was so shy I once had to write to a Dr. Lawton . . ."

"I've Got the Blues..."

Dear Dr. Lawton:

I've got "the blues" and I've got them bad. One minute I feel swell. Then all of a sudden everything goes blooey. Or I wake up feeling like the last rose of summer. But that same night I'm cutting a rug into shreds. I can't figure it out. Are "the blues" like the weather—unpredictable and uncontrollable?

Dot E.

". . . And I've Got Them Bad!"

Dear Dot:

The blues are as common as colds. Even animals have them. The person who is never depressed is the one who should worry. Either he never longs for anything, or something is wrong with his capacity for emotional response. All of us want things we don't get and get things we don't want. No life is free of problems. Whenever there is something we want to do or achieve, and we are getting nowhere fast, there is likely to be conflict.

Let's suppose you think your older sister hasn't treated you just right. You want to tell her off. But you're afraid of three things: the way your sister yells; the loss of her affection; and your own ability to prove that she is wrong. Result: You cry, "Oh, what's the use? Who am I to do anything?" Then you swallow your angry words. But they continue inside you. The attack is now against you yourself. Thus you become your own worst enemy.

Or suppose it's Saturday night and everyone but you has a date. You have always doubted your social popularity, which means your ability to interest boys. Dateless Saturday nights may be rare for you. But, when they do occur, you tell yourself: "Dot, you've always been a drip and always will be a drip." One night alone makes you decide you are a lifetime failure as a woman.

Your blues are worse in the morning because each day offers a new chance for accomplishment. But you are never sure just what you want, or whether, if you knew what you wanted, you could get it. At night you can relax and have fun because there is nothing more you can do that day. You can say, "Tomorrow I'll *positively* . . ." and you feel better. But this is a temporary remedy.

The only way to cure the "blues" is to *solve the problem* which causes the glum mood. Some problems arise from an immediate situation—like choosing a college. These aren't too hard to handle. Other problems cannot be understood until one knows a person's entire life story, his relationships with parents, brothers and sisters, friends, and teachers. And learning this is no easy matter, I can assure you. It often requires many technical procedures and a great deal of patient listening. We don't always know what is back of our current reaction. We can't find the right words for the wrong music!

Friends may tell you to "cheer up," and "forget it." This doesn't help. You need to learn *what* has made you feel that you haven't quite made the grade. And while solving your problems, you can seek temporary relief. You should talk about what is bothering you (if you know) to any attentive and discreet listener. Even crying may help ease the tension. (As long as you don't overwork any one shoulder. Or come to rely on *sympathy* instead of *solution*.) The important thing for you is to get your trouble out in the open where you can fight it, instead of keeping it pent up inside you.

You should fight for a cause or an idea, grab every opportunity to assume responsibility and take the initiative. You should speak up good and loud whenever in your opinion anyone is treating you unfairly. If you get smacked down for talking out of turn, that isn't bad. For then you'll be angry with someone besides yourself.

To maintain a balanced outlook, you should be sure your

body is in tip-top condition, that you get plenty of rest and good food. But, oddly enough, fatigue is usually the *result* of the blues, not the *cause*. Even more than you need rest, you need some strenuous activity every day: a brisk walk, a good swim, a fast game of tennis, a dance or two, a stretch of strenuous housecleaning, or work at some art or craft or service to some person.

The real answer to your blues will come only when you achieve a balance between what you want and what you can get. That means you have to exert yourself. You can't just look wistfully at your goal. This is a case where you can be your own best doctor.

The Science of Mental Fitness

Dear Dr. Lawton:

Everybody talks about psychology these days, and about psychologists. But when you ask anybody what does a psychologist really *do*, nobody seems to know. Then, too, there is the psychiatrist, and the psychoanalyst—how are they all different? It seems to me and my friends that this whole field is very important, but it is also very confusing. Since we know you are a psychologist, would you take the trouble to explain this subject to us?

Donald K.

and Its Practitioners

Dear Donald:

I'll try my best. Psychology is the science which studies the way human beings behave and think and feel. The psychologist mainly is interested in the difficulties that people face, whether they are five, fifteen, or sixty-five, and how they can be helped to adjust themselves to these difficulties.

There is nothing mysterious about our work. Anyone who studies people in a scientific manner eventually discovers why some human beings behave normally (you, I, and our friends) and others (neighbors, relatives, etc.) sometimes behave differently.

The troubles we have are due mainly to conflicts. Sometimes the struggle is in ourselves: between us and our sense of right and wrong, or between us and some painful memory, intense longing, or earlier frightening experience. At other times the conflict is between us and another person, or between us and our surroundings.

All through life we have to choose between doing one thing and doing another. It is very human to want good times without having to think of consequences, and to want achievement without hard work or suffering. We all finally learn to take the thing we want most and let the rest go. Or we accept what we can't avoid, and save for our daydreams the "what might have been." We call this growing up.

But when the two sides to our conflict are very strong and equally matched, our machinery for choosing and letting go may become jammed. At heart we really know the kind of person we want to be and the kind of work we want to do, but we've gotten a little mixed up about it. The psychologist holds up a clear mirror so we can see ourselves as we really are. He helps us face our problem, *but not by telling us what to do.* Instead, he removes the things blocking our ability to make up our minds: the fears, false ideas, impossible wishes. As we learn about our strong and weak points, about ways in which we can utilize to the fullest our mental abilities, personality, and emotional equipment, we are able to make our own choices.

Talking to parents, friends, and teachers is often very helpful. There are times, however, when the untrained person can't aid us, chiefly because we are not able to put into words what is bothering us. That's why we need somebody who can lead us along gradually and give us a language so we can explain what's inside of ourselves.

It takes the psychologist years of study and experience to learn, for example, how to make it easy for people to talk, how to help a person put himself together again after he has taken himself apart. The way a psychologist looks to a client is described very well in something a high-school girl wrote while sitting outside in the waiting room:

"I've been thinking about what coming here has meant to me. You are a balance wheel, you're not a person. It's almost as if I were talking to myself, but with someone listening in and trying to think about it. . . . What you do is to let a person talk and put in comments that keep it going instead of stewing in a circle. That's why I say you're a balance wheel. . . . When I first came here, you were a person. I disliked you because you were touching sore spots. Now I know you'll be a person when I need you to be. Other times you're someone to blow off steam to and to talk to so I can make up my mind."

Now for the ways in which a psychologist, a psychiatrist, and a psychoanalyst differ.

The psychiatrist is a medical man who has specialized in the diagnosis and treatment of serious mental and emotional problems. Psychiatrists treat patients through medicines and drugs, occupational therapy ("work" cure), and psychotherapy (or "mental" cure)—sympathetic discussions with the patient of his life experiences. Recently medicine has achieved remarkable cures of certain mental diseases. Patients who are young or whose illness has been of short duration stand an excellent chance of being cured today.

Certain psychiatrists employ psychoanalysis instead of medicines and drugs. This is a method developed by Sigmund Freud which allows a patient to talk himself out day after day over a period of several years. This method relies on a method of free association (saying whatever comes into your mind) and also on dream interpretation.

As for the psychologist, he takes the educational road which leads to the Ph.D. (or Doctor of Philosophy) degree and not the M.D. He, therefore, requires a "go ahead" signal from the family physician before undertaking a case. While much of the time the psychologist talks back and forth, he also makes considerable use of tests and questionnaires in studying a person.

The clients of a psychologist are normal people whose difficulties of adjustment in school, on the job, in the family circle have gotten the better of them for the time being. Often they merely want to find out something about themselves, their mental abilities and special aptitudes and whether they are likely to meet the requirements of a particular job or career.

Psychologists played a very important part in classifying men, both in the army and on defense jobs during World War II. Perhaps if Hitler as a child had received psychological treatment, that war might not have occurred at all, but I'll leave that for the historians to decide.

People sometimes wonder if reading articles and books on this subject is good or bad for us. For one thing, reading about other people's problems shows us we're not alone in our difficulties. Perhaps, too, we can pick up a useful suggestion, or maybe the article will lead to valuable discussions at home or at school. Most important of all, such articles show that just as we have a science of bodily health so we have one of mental fitness. If we are in great trouble we can obtain help—unless we'd rather suffer, and some of us would rather. But persistent and intense unhappiness, like constant headaches or fever, needs treatment.

It cannot be corrected by reading books or articles, regardless of who writes them, I or anyone else.

Each one of us is an individual with his own experience. What happened to us, and what we may or may not be able to do in the way of altering ourselves—that is something which can be found out only if we personally are studied. Changing ourselves in a thoroughgoing fashion often requires a trained person to guide the whole process, someone in the flesh to whom we can talk.

Every boy and girl has problems, but that doesn't mean that everybody who *has* a problem *is* a problem. Most people manage to go through their lives without ever having any contact at all with a professional person in this field, and they don't ever really need to cross his doorstep. They can figure things out for themselves, sometimes with the aid of a good friend, or a wise relative or teacher. However, I am glad that you wrote me, because it gives me a chance to describe the different practitioners in the mental-hygiene field. I do believe that this kind of information should be part of the equipment of every modern young person. I don't imagine you will ever need to know any of this for your own sake, but I would not be surprised if some day someone among your friends or relatives should need professional help, and I hope you will find this information useful then.

In Charge of Yourself—You!

Dear Dr. Lawton:

I am going to confess something I've never told a living soul before. I am a coward. No one ever saw me do anything cowardly, but deep down inside I know it. There are many things I am afraid of: how I would act under fire in a war, or in a bombing raid, or if I were stricken with a terrible illness, or if there were a fire in our house. I'm even afraid to go out alone at night. I don't mean I don't do it, but all the time I have a prickly sensation down my spine, as if someone were going to spring out at me from every dark doorway. Most of the fellows I know don't seem to feel this way. It scares me to think that in an emergency I would go to pieces. What do you suggest for me to do about this?

Victor W.

You: Your Best Friend or Worst Enemy!

Dear Victor:

I'm not going to answer you directly, but rather I'd like to tell you of an experience of my own when I wasn't much more than a high-school boy myself. Please realize that I don't claim I was a professional hero or that I knew ahead of time what would happen.

We all think we know what it is to be afraid. I used to think I did, but that was before I started out to climb Mount Marcy one summer day, many years ago. This is the highest peak of the Adirondack chain in upper New York State.

I had been up twice before, and had had a grand time on both climbs. After a long stretch of rainy weather, this day dawned beautifully cool and clear. I was as happy and eager about the whole business as a fellow could be.

I wasn't very lucky about hitches, and so I had to walk about fifteen miles before I reached the base of the mountain. I planned to reach the top of the peak at seven in the evening. Then I would go halfway down the other side, spending the night at a lodge. I had gone along the trail for about an hour when I decided it was time for lunch, partly because I was tired, and partly because of the delicious meat sandwiches and half a lemon meringue pie that lay inside my knapsack. I also told myself I ought to lighten my load.

It was now about three-thirty and I began to meet people on the way down. During our chats I'd casually mention my schedule, and they would look at me in a very peculiar way. Then I would laugh reassuringly: "This isn't the first time I have done it. I can go pretty fast when I want to." They would say something about the "mud," but that didn't make sense, as I couldn't see any.

Every once in a while I would rest, finish off another sandwich, and read some more in a magazine I had brought along. Of course, I also arranged to drink from every stream and enjoy every view of distant country.

At six o'clock, I realized I had not met anybody coming down for a long time. By now, the trail had grown steep and difficult, and I had run into the mud. I sought to forget my exhaustion and climb fast and efficiently, but try to move upward rapidly in a sea of brown goo!

It took me two endless cruel hours to realize how stupidly I had planned and carried out my hike. At eight o'clock, I stood at the top, dog-tired and worried. Then came the mad race with darkness.

I originally had allowed myself from seven to nine-thirty to reach the lodge from the peak. Now I had to make it in an hour and a half, or else—. I had no flashlight, no food, and only a half-dozen matches and a skimpy sweater in addition to the one I was wearing. I was going at *my* top speed, but I kept saying, "You've got to go faster-faster-faster!" I slid and fell and lunged along. I shouted, but the echo frightened me more. I never could whistle, and now I was hopeless.

The trail went alongside a gorge, and five steps in the wrong direction would mean a drop of fifty or one hundred feet. Five steps in another wrong direction would mean my getting lost in the forest. As I clambered over rocks and fallen trees, I was grim and worried.

In the darkness, I came to a stream and had to go across from rock to rock on my hands, knees, and belly. When I stood up, I was terrified at what I saw, or rather at what I didn't see. Ahead was a black wall. There was a similar wall to my right, to my left, and back of me. I thought I had gone blind. Then I lit one of my six matches and made out this sign on a tree: "2 miles to Johns Brook Lodge." Never did I feel such despair.

Two miles! My watch said nine-forty-five. I crawled up an incline a few inches at a time. Then I heard the roar of the falls, and I stopped dead in my tracks, sinking dejectedly to the ground.

For the next hour or so, I lay there, not a human being, but an animal—helpless and panic-stricken. I kept hearing footsteps, calls, and whistles. Venus, the evening star, not only twinkled, it moved, it fell. The other stars also began to circle around, go zigzag, and drop. I knew it was cold. But my heart pounded so, I panted and dripped perspiration. How sweet and secure and very far away home seemed then. I wondered how it all was going to end for me, and I prayed.

Suddenly I thought of people who were in a real fix. Here I was on land and safe, except for animals and a drop down the gorge. Suppose I were adrift for days in a lifeboat, or were a prisoner of war who had escaped and was hiding at night in a strange countryside. One could be more alone and more in danger than I was. What bothered me most was my lack of a plan. At home, if anything goes wrong, you call a doctor, a wrecking crew, a policeman, the fire department.

Then I spoke aloud. "You can't call anyone. You have to help yourself. You are alone, alone with yourself. If you want to get hysterical, if you want to see and hear things that don't exist, go ahead, frighten yourself to death—see if I care! You're in charge of yourself. Nobody can start or stop George Lawton except George Lawton. He is either his own worst enemy or his best friend." Now, using my most friendly and man-to-man manner, I said, "Listen, George, you want to be a leader of boys and help them. Now, suppose you had to give them advice on what to do if they got lost in the woods at night." You see, I began to think of myself as somebody else with a problem. And this speech, funny as it sounds now, changed the tide.

I grew completely calm, but this only brought an awareness of the cold. (The water in the forest ranger's fire buckets froze that night.) I simply had to build a fire, despite the darkness and the rain which had begun to fall. It took two hours to start that fire, what with a few matches and the only paper, my maps. And the struggle to keep it going lasted all night. Fire meant security and warmth, something to look at, and something to do. As long as I had a blaze, I had a friend. I wasn't alone, and I felt normal. The stars behaved. I didn't mind the "steps" or "cries."

That night was not one night. It was a whole lifetime. In a way, I felt it was the history of man in reverse: from city boy back to the jungle. Never had I been so alone with myself.

I never knew when dawn came. But I was sorry that I had to leave the scene of what had been the most important experience of my life. The fire was going well. I had plenty of wood.

Then as I left, I noticed a sign: "100 feet to a lean-to." Had I seen this nine hours earlier, I could have spent the night like a king reposing on a bed of pine needles and protected against the cold and rain. Still, I wouldn't have had it otherwise, for I had become a free man. I had learned the strength I had inside of me. Starved, sleepy, and wet, I struggled down to the mountain lodge for breakfast, quietly happy that I had finally gotten myself in hand—that after the first mistakes I had done as well as I could. I had conquered my environment, my problem, my fear. As I ambled along, I kept murmuring cheerfully to myself: "Come on, life, do your worst. I can take it."

Can People Be Remade?

Dear Dr. Lawton:

Can human nature be changed? If a person has faults or weaknesses, can he get rid of them? For example, I would like to know how to attain a feeling of security about myself. So many people are said to possess this "feeling" and therefore go through life with few worries. I would like to know the true meaning of security and whether it would ever be possible for me to attain it.

Pearl F.

It Has Been Done

Dear Pearl:

All of us have certain basic desires: we want love, stability, a chance to express our thoughts and feelings, to use our special talents and pursue our ideas of happiness. But many things can interfere with the complete satisfaction of our desires. Life pushes us into some experiences before we are ready for them and denies us others for which we are actually prepared. We all grow up with some fears, feelings of regret, unsatisfied curiosities, thwarted ambitions. Hence all persons have difficulties of adjustment, or "problems." The person with the "normal" amount of security is merely one who, *most of the time*, feels equal to the challenges he receives and finds that the satisfactions which life offers counterbalance the dissatisfactions.

But some persons scarcely ever have their desires satisfied. These persons are convinced that they have not received a fair deal. As a result they feel they are not equal to the hazards of life. They may try to escape their difficulties through moods, worries, or daydreams. Or, as adults, they may struggle to wrest from life what they did not obtain as children, but their attempts fail if they use the same devices they did then: tantrums, bullying, boasting, threats of self-destruction, wheedling, etc.

Every young person has his own devices, however faulty, for trying to obtain what he wants. And he has his own way of reacting to victory or defeat. He also has his own particular equipment for grappling with life experiences: compromise techniques (shutting his ears to someone who scolds): consolation systems ("I haven't any friends, but then I am an honor student"); excuses ("How can I be a success with the kind of family I have?"); outlets (kicking the cat).

As long as all this machinery works fairly well, we do not worry nor change our habits. But when it begins to jam, we may become sorry indeed for ourselves and make the bravest plans for altering our way of doing things. What we want, nearly always, is to change, not ourselves, but the situation. We wish to escape from the present discomfort and restore to ourselves once more the old familiar patterns of obtaining pleasure and avoiding pain. Most of us will do anything to *be* different, except *become* different. But sometimes we really do undertake a radical overhauling of ourselves, as did Jane R.

Jane's envy of her girl friends' social successes kept her from getting along with them. And she spoiled every friendship with boys because of sensitiveness and excessive demands. But Jane began to suspect that much of her behavior was the result of not being sure of herself. She decided to go in for the difficult job of self-discipline and tried hard to refrain from words or acts that would lose friends. In time, Jane was liked and sought after, and, as she developed more confidence in her own powers, she had less desire to appear "important" in a manner which others had found objectionable.

Jane had to take the hard way, which is the way for most of us. But an occasional person may have it easier. Dick S. was a shy and moody young man who devoted all his spare time to photography at home. Since he had talent, his services were soon in demand. The contact with people and the approval his work received brought out in Dick certain likeable traits previously concealed, and he became almost popular. Dick's feeling of insecurity is not yet gone, but it seldom shows itself on the surface any more.

There still remains the young person who cannot straighten himself out as did Jane, or count on the world rescuing him from himself, as happened with Dick. Such an individual might consider the advisability of some day seeking out professional assistance. The chief specialists in the field of emotional and personality disturbances are the psychologists, the psychiatrists, and the psychoanalysts. Though their methods vary, they all provide a situation in which the person with difficulties can relive and reinterpret his experiences, past and present. All these handicapping "fears, feelings of regret, unsatisfied curiosities, thwarted ambitions," are tracked back to their source. When the treatment is thoroughly carried out by a competent practitioner, the sufferer from insecurity generally stops spending all his time and energy in a battle with himself and starts tackling real problems in a real world.

What's Wrong with Daydreams?

Dear Dr. Lawton:

What are daydreams, and what do they mean? My younger brother seems to be always daydreaming. Friends of his who have been in his class in school say they often see him just sit looking out of a window as if he didn't know what was going on, and that he does this, too, when they are out together. He used to be a pretty good student, but his work has become worse and worse in the last year. Is his habit a bad sign? I'd like to see him change and would like to find out if anything can be done about it.

Frank N. F

Nothing, If You Control Them

Dear Frank:

All of us wish we could have pleasure without responsibility and achievement without struggle. Since real life generally denies us this wish, we have to satisfy it in the daydream, a form of imaginative play worked up into a continuous story. Whenever things become dull, or action is impossible or unsuitable, or we are thwarted and unhappy, we ring the curtain down on the outside world and raise up another in the little theater inside our skulls. Here it is easy to make the play go any way we like, since we are playwright, producer, and star— all in one. In our daydreams, we live out events which may or may not occur and relive what is gone but not forgotten. Daydreams give us what life is not ready to give, or perhaps never can. They usually have a chief character, nearly always the dreamer himself. Sometimes he is a conquering hero (or heroine), sometimes a suffering one, but usually the main theme of a daydream is that the merit of the daydreamer is unrecognized at first but later recognized in a grand finale. Occasionally in a sad, self-pitying daydream, recognition never comes, or comes too late.

We seldom tell our daydreams to other people, for that would mean revealing the method by means of which we solve our problems so satisfactorily. Yet daydreams offer a direct path to the secret chambers of the mind, and young people might learn a great deal about themselves if they kept a record of these reveries. This should be done for a short period of time, since constant thinking about one's self is not wholesome.

The daydream reveals our basic preference as to the kind of mate, vocation, life we desire. It is perfectly true that if we could press a magic button and make any particular daydream come true, we might not always choose to press the button. But it is also true that unless our real life satisfies to some extent the needs we reveal in our daydreams, we will satisfy these needs more and more in the domain of the imagination.

Daydreams may have a constructive value, especially for young people. We all need temporary escapes from everyday life in order to relax in a world closer to our heart's desire. Take the humor daydream, illustrated in the girl sitting by herself who suddenly breaks into a laugh. When you question her, she replies that she was thinking how funny it would be if, et cetera, et cetera. She is very fond of a good laugh and, not having anything laughable at hand, proceeds to invent it. Daydreams may also serve as a rehearsal for events to come and in this way stimulate imagination and ambition. For a little success, obtained even in a reverie, often furnishes a powerful incentive to go on. Daydreams, finally, may encourage creative work. The planning and problem-solving we do in our imagination can lead to many ideas of genuine value which we later apply to real-life situations.

The average person knows a daydream can be great fun, but he indulges himself only in his free time, and unless he is prepared actually to make the dream come true, he promptly forgets any reverie he has had. He puts himself on a daydream budget: so many hours of living, working, struggling in the real world for so many minutes of daydreaming.

But the individual who is lacking in self-confidence and initiative, especially in his relationships with other people, may take refuge in his daydreams as a substitute for real action. Instead of hustling about for the money he needs, or making a definite attempt at achievement in the athletic field or in the classroom, he has a grand time imagining all the great things he will do. Rather than go out and woo the lady of his choice, he shyly worships her from afar and merely dreams of winning her, sometimes doing this for months or years without ever even speaking to the girl.

As for your brother, in time he may find things to do which offer him genuine satisfactions, as a result of which his daydreaming is likely to diminish. But should there be no lessening or should his daydreaming increase, the wisest course is to consult someone in the school or community who has specialized in the treatment of personality maladjustments. It would be best if your brother himself sought assistance, but if this is not possible it will have to be done by some member of the family.

Lonesome or Lonely?

Dear Dr. Lawton:

I have a strange sense of being different from other people and apart from them. When I'm in a crowd I feel this difference most keenly—it's as if there were an unseen wall between me and the rest of humanity. The larger the crowd, the worse I feel. I have a family and friends, and I keep myself busy all day, and yet that feeling persists. I sometimes think I'm the lonesomest person in the world.

Max K.

Missing SOMEONE vs. Feeling All Alone

Dear Max:

When you call yourself lonesome, Max, you really mean lonely. There is a great and vital difference, and I cannot answer you unless that difference is made clear. The best way I can think of is to tell you about two people I know—one is *lonesome* and the other is *lonely*.

Bob, Alice's boy friend, has just gone off to his freshman year at an agricultural college, thousands of miles away. To Alice, an occasional letter isn't much of a substitute for the countless hours spent with him during the previous years. What shall she do with all this suddenly released time? School, a part-time job, and sleep still leave a vacant space in every twenty-four hours. But that's not the only problem. There's the fact that Bob isn't there when she stretches out her hand.

Did you ever mash your thumb? Remember how the world was all "thumbness" for the next few minutes—but how things eventually got themselves straightened out? In the same way, after Bob left, Alice's mind was one word—"Gone!" During the next few days, she showed the characteristic shock reaction which nearly always follows separation and for which there is no remedy in any first-aid kit.

In a few weeks, Alice recovered from her "separation shock." Since Bob is not available in the flesh, Alice tries to reach out and in some way overcome interferences with their "togetherness." She writes a letter, sends a telegram, makes a long-distance call. She has tried going out on occasional dates to see if that would help. But so far she has only felt worse. She is debating whether to postpone good times until mind-filler and time-occupier No. 1 gets through with his education and comes back for good.

And so Alice patiently waits for Bob's permanent return, gazing at his picture, reliving his last visit or letter, or dreaming over the details of the next one. Alice's ailment is "lonesomeness," a common occupational disease of separated lovers everywhere.

The pain of missing someone specific, of longing to look at him and talk to him, for most persons doesn't last forever. It has an end which steals upon us unawares, just as it does in the case of a mashed thumb. Life and time cure us sooner or later by what they have to offer, once the intense ache stops.

But now let me tell you about Phil. Phil has two brothers and a sister, and works on a paper route after school. He insists his days are filled and that he can't get enough privacy. But that's only talk. At heart Phil is an extremely lonely boy. He wants to be a regular fellow and liked by the "gang," but his clowning and biting sense of humor often are only annoying and make him the more unpopular.

In his earliest years, Phil had been sickly, and as he was also the youngest, he was always mother's favorite. Until Phil was eight, his mother dressed him; thereafter, she never let him make his own decisions, and in every way tried to put herself between him and reality. It was natural that Phil should be Phil's first love, but we hope it is not to be his only romance.

Phil's mother, however, could not always shelter him, or give him what he wanted just when he wanted it. These sudden losses of affection and attention would make Phil feel weepy, anxious, "lonely." But he discovered that yelling and kicking would sooner or later restore Mother's love and care, and he would be all-powerful and all-important again. Phil, of course, doesn't realize how much he wishes it were possible to return to babyhood, that wonderful but tragically brief period when life consisted entirely of being loved and admired.

Loneliness is not so much a quesion of having people around us or not, as it is one of whether we feel ourselves an important and self-sufficient part of the universe. Many a person who lives and works alone, say a lighthouse keeper, is not lonely. It is because he does not feel thwarted or unworthy.

Self-love, loneliness, and anger are all related. Phil is so much in love with himself that he is incapable of loving anyone or anything else fully. Since the world is a mirror reflecting our interest in it, if we have no love to give to people and to things because it is all directed inward toward ourselves, we will see the world around us as a blank.

Phil's "stunts" and general disagreeableness really represent disappointment and anger at being unloved. When he meets anyone, these are his unconscious thoughts: "I want you to love me, but you won't be able to, because I'm not worthy of your love or that of anyone else, and so I hate you and all the world." If Phil can't get affection and attention by being just what he is, he will try to get it by force. Friendliness is preferable, but he will accept fear and awe as substitutes. Other people may see Phil as a boastful youth, but he sees himself as a brooding person filled with self-contempt.

Let us imagine that Phil in his childhood had broken a leg and that it had been badly put together. In that case, he might go through a long life, handicapped but functioning, except when he needed to have perfect legs. However, if he wants a permanently satisfactory healing, the fracture must be reopened and the bones set again. In the same way, Phil may be able to escape temporarily his emotional crippling ("loneliness") by trying the popular remedies. The lonely person, we have heard, should assume that everyone is his friend, should be receptive to friendship, not resistant. Phil will be advised to take up a hobby in which he can find congenial friends among girls, or he will be told to help others, especially those even lonelier than he. Finally it will be suggested that he try to make life so interesting for himself that he can do without people, and that this very self-sufficiency will in time attract others to him.

This advice is all very good, but it has one slight drawback. If Phil could follow it he would have done so already. Even though he should later receive much affection and fame, any major disappointment will bring back the same lost feeling he had years ago when Mother was unavailable, and Phil will tell himself, "No matter how busy I am, I really have nothing important to do. All my success still leaves me alone. Where can I find someone who will really love me for myself, who will understand me?"

Most cases of severe loneliness can be thoroughly cleared up only by intensive psychological treatment. Only when you know how you got "that way," why you distrust people, why you have a desperate hunger for reassurance that you are okay—only after this self-understanding can we have a strong Phil who will no longer be afraid to share himself. When this happens, his spells of thwarted self-love ("loneliness") will decrease greatly.

Our Dreams: Nonsense?

Dear Dr. Lawton:
Can we stop ourselves from dreaming? I have tried to, but I seem to dream all the time. Night after night lately I have had

two queer dreams. In one I always wear shoes made of solid gold. In the other I see a small sea lion resting on a table. In front of him are some plates containing chicken and mashed potatoes. The sea lion eats up the chicken, the potatoes, then the plates, and finally the table and cloth. Now, what do such strange dreams mean?

Marie A. G.

or Clues to Personality?

Dear Marie:

Many people find it hard to believe that dreams can have any serious meaning. Dreams are often disconnected in form. Should a dream tell a straight story, it often makes no sense to the dreamer or impresses him as ridiculous. The most violent transitions, the most impossible sequence of events occur in dreams. All the laws of time and space are set aside. And as for the hues and tints of some dreams—no technicolor film can compete with them.

In our dreams, consistency is thrown to the winds and scenes shift in the middle of a speech. A character who starts out as one person will merge suddenly into someone else. The dreamer himself in turn may be different persons: now he is an actor, now, spectator. Just as we believed when we were younger the most outlandish claims made in fairy tales or comics, so while we dream we accept without question unheard-of combinations and rearrangements of facts and events. Indeed, dreams seem very real while they last—too real, occasionally, for our comfort. We sometimes awaken from one and ask ourselves: which is the true reality, the world our dreams created or the actual work-a-day world which now faces us?

Dreams are forgotten very speedily. Hence we think them insignificant. For the same reason, many of us claim that we rarely, if ever, dream. Nearly everyone has had the experience of awakening from a vivid dream which fades away almost instantly. It is this airy and fantastic nothingness which explains Shakespeare's words: "Such stuff as dreams are made of." Sometimes we remember a dream until we are about to tell it to another person and we discover we can recall only fragments.

Generally the dreamer recalls best the dream which is repeated many times or one that has left an imprint on the memory because it has been unusually painful or pleasant and tied up with an important happening in his life. Experiments show that when we make an effort to record our dreams, we remember many more than at other times. Such experiments also show that in our dream we can relive incidents that happened many years ago but which we have completely forgotten. Frequently, these can be recalled only after proof has been given by outsiders.

Many dreams are merely recollections of some recent intense experience. We see a movie and dream about it, perhaps adding a role for ourselves. In this manner, we may become co-hero or co-heroine, or even co-victim. Some young people are happiest in such parts.

Another common dream is caused by physical disturbance: an uncomfortable bed, a noisy room, an over-rich meal. For example: We dream we are in an air battle, leap out in a parachute, and, after falling millions of miles through space, hit the ground with a terrific crash. We wake up, discover we have fallen out of bed, that a car is backfiring outside, or the shade has suddenly snapped up.

A particular fear may be responsible for many dreams. We all know the wild yet senseless cries we can make in this kind of dream, especially when we are falling helplessly. It sometimes happens that in real life we pass safely through a grave danger during which we showed great bravery and self-control. Yet for a long time afterward the experience returns in a painful dream of one kind or another, showing how severely we were affected by what happened.

The longing to be strong and masterful leads to an exciting kind of dream, illustrated by those in which "we fly through the air with the greatest of ease." It gives us a sense of power to be able to glide gracefully up a flight of stairs or to step lightly from the street onto the roof of even the tallest house.

Many dreams are so interesting we hate to have them broken up by awakening. The wish-satisfying dreams are a good example of this. We dream of finding money: first, a nickel in the dust; then a quarter close by; then more and more coins—until the alarm clock goes off and spoils all the fun.

If life ran on an even keel, with few hurts or disappointments, we would dream little or not at all. However, we all need a chance to continue working on the problems unsolved in our waking hours. That is why dreams were once defined as "the life of the mind while asleep."

Some dreams tell an obvious story. Other dreams have a double meaning, like a fable or political cartoon. In such cases it is not what the dream actually says that is important but what it wants to say.

Take this simple dream: Hannah R. needed a fancy coat for a special occasion. A search of the stores by her mother proved in vain. The next day Hannah reports: "Last night I dreamed I had a new coat, I had two new coats!"

This dream did two very necessary things for Hannah. It gave her a coat and a night's peaceful sleep despite the disappointing news of the evening before. A dream, instead of interfering with sleep, is often its guardian. Whenever we are upset by our dreams, especially by one that is repeated, it may mean that there is some disturbance in our life which should be corrected, if such dreams are to cease.

Modern psychological science finds that dreams are worthy of the most careful study, often giving us more knowledge about a person than we can obtain by any other means. But a dream has significance only in relationship to a particular dreamer. It is he who decides what his dreams mean, not a dreambook with its standardized and codelike explanations. The basic theme of a dream is best discovered when the dreamer under expert guidance takes each element in his dream and relates it to experiences which he has had in the real world, to events of the day before, to expected happenings of the future, and to any other real thoughts and feelings that may seem to have only the slightest possible connection with the dream.

People work off their feelings in many different ways. Some do so through creating a poem, a song, a picture. Others find conversations with an intimate friend helpful. But the universal creative outlet, the safety valve of all humanity, is the dream. As a quaint Chinese proverb has it: "What is pent up in the deepest recesses of the heart sneezes itself out in the dream."

The Well-Adjusted Person

Dear Dr. Lawton:

The other day someone said that a friend of mine was not well adjusted. This friend isn't perfect, I admit—he certainly has some faults—but I can't see that there is anything seriously wrong with him. I've been puzzled ever since as to how it is possible to tell whether one person is well adjusted and another is not. I've asked many people, but each one has a different opinion, and I don't know where to look for the right answer. How do we act when we are well adjusted? How can I tell if I am, or how could anyone else tell?

Jeanne L.

Is There Any Such Animal?

Dear Jeanne:

Nowadays when we wish to show approval of someone's personality we are apt to say he is "well adjusted," rather than "honorable," "generous," "ambitious," etc., as we did years ago. For what are all the virtues worth, we feel, if a person does not know how to get along with himself, his friends, the members of his family, and his community.

Perhaps this change of styles in the way of judging people is all to the good. To think of the individual solely in terms of himself, examining him as a kind of machine whose performance is smooth and efficient or irregular and wasteful, does yield a more intimate and truthful picture. At any rate, the ideal of our age and a primary aim of all our education is the development of a personality that works without lost motion or hesitation, knowing exactly what it wants and heading straight toward its goal.

Of course, it is easy enough to attach a label to someone, but when we try to describe what is behind the label we run into difficulties, and that is why you received so many different answers. One is really hard put to draw up a list of standards of adjustment.

Though volumes have been written on this subject, and especially on the factors in a person's life that help or hinder a good adjustment, the following list attempts to set up certain simple standards. They apply to everyone regardless of age, sex, intelligence, or education, and are drawn from actual observation of the behavior of well-adjusted and poorly adjusted individuals.

Lest you become concerned at the thought that you must measure up to the entire twenty standards before you can qualify for the honors, it should be pointed out that the list, *taken as a whole,* describes an ideal person who doesn't exist. Most of us are doing very well if we can live up to a majority of the items.

1. The well-adjusted person is able and willing to assume the *responsibilities* appropriate to each age or period of life as he reaches it.

2. He participates with pleasure in the experiences that belong to each successive age level, neither anticipating those of a later period nor holding on to those of an earlier stage.

3. Though he may object to a particular role or position in life, as long as he must fill it, he is willing to accept the responsibilities and the experiences that pertain to this role or position.

4. He attacks problems that require solution instead of finding means to evade them.

5. He enjoys meeting and destroying obstacles to his development and happiness, once he has decided that they are real and not imaginary obstacles.

6. He can make important decisions with a minimum of worry, conflict, advice-seeking, and other types of running-away behavior.

7. After making a choice, he abides by it, until new factors of crucial importance enter the picture.

8. He accepts the authority of reality; that is, he finds the major satisfactions of life in accomplishments and experiences that take place in the real world and not in the realm of daydreams and make-believe.

9. His thinking is a blueprint for action, not a device for delaying or escaping it.

10. He draws lessons from his defeats instead of finding excuses for them.

11. He does not magnify his successes or extend their application from the field in which they originally occurred.

12. He knows how to work while working, and play while playing.

13. He is able to say "No" to situations that may provide temporary satisfaction but that, over a longer period, run counter to his best interests.

14. He is able to say "Yes" to situations that are momentarily unpleasant but that ultimately will aid him.

15. He is able to show his anger directly when injured and to act in defense of his rights, with both indignation and action appropriate in kind and amount to the injury.

16. He is able to show his affection directly and to give evidence of it in acts that are fitting in amount and kind to its extent.

17. He can endure pain, especially emotional pain or frustration, whenever it is not in his power to alter the cause.

18. He has his habits and mental attitudes so well organized that he can quickly make the essential compromises called for by the difficulties he meets.

19. He is able to bring his energies together and concentrate them effectively on a single goal, once he has determined to achieve it.

20. He would not change, even if he could, the fact that life is an endless struggle in which human purposes are hurled against external resisting forces, human and natural. He knows, and makes use of the knowledge, that in this struggle the person who fights himself least will have the most strength and the best judgment left for the outside battle.

Your Family

Are Parents Necessary?

Dear Dr. Lawton:

Whenever I tell my mother I want to go to work, she throws a fit. She begins telling me about all the sacrifices she's made to prepare me for college and become something in the future, and how she has had more experience and knows better than I what I should do. It's the same with my sister Adele, who's fifteen. Mother treats her like a baby; every time Adele stops after school for a coke, my mother calls up the principal to find out if anything happened. If the phone rings it's "Who is it, Adele, what's he saying?" If she goes to a party, when she comes home there are all the usual questions: "Did you dance? What games did you play? Did he take you home?" And on and on. Sometimes I really wonder if parents are necessary after you grow up. They seem to want to treat you like babies forever.

Ned H.

Indispensable When Well-Adjusted

Dear Ned:

We all are born needing care until we are able to go it alone. However, the good parent gives a child love, approval, physical care; equips him with ideals and a basis for judging people;

tries to make him a "self-starter." And then, the good parent lets go.

Your mother, I am sure, sincerely wants you and Adele to be self-reliant. Yet she has a real tussle with herself and that eternal mothering impulse.

You are each fighting in defense of what you think your rights: mother to rule the roost, the children to work out their own destiny. Such a tug of war occurs in most households and in mild form is normal. As quarreling alternates with discussion, parents and children begin to see something of each other's point of view. Once in a while, this getting together may be hastened by calling in a relative, friend, or teacher to act as go-between or referee, as the case may be.

In some families, however, the feuding gets beyond control. When this happens, some children leave home, if not in body then in mind—this is bad. Others give in completely—this is worse.

You and Adele are leaning on your mother more than you suspect. Unsure about yourselves and the future, you flare up easily and overdo your struggle for independence. It isn't *mother* who is pushing you around so much as the difficulties coming up in *your* daily life. With increasing security, you will feel closer to mother, develop more open-mindedness toward her suggestions, and find it easier eventually "to let go" yourselves.

Being a parent gives a person an authority and an outlet for his creative impulses that he probably finds nowhere else. Moreover, as your mother got older she may have grown disappointed with her lot, and you children offered her a second chance at life. Since you two will be the fathers and mothers of tomorrow, you should now realize that the more genuine interests you will have in life, the less likely are you to depend on your children as the only source of mental and emotional satisfaction.

When your mother thinks of your going to work, her mind stops talking and her emotions take over. To her, a person in a trade simply doesn't rate. Your arguments may silence her, but they cannot convince.

She needs to be freed from the attitudes and fears carried over from her own childhood. It will be easier then for her to go out into the world and develop new interests and contacts. And it will be easier for her to let you go your own way. Is there some family friend or some relative who can explain your needs and point of view to her? And who can interpret your mother to *you!*

Are parents necessary? Well, you and Adele and even your mother often have your doubts. But if anyone can think of a satisfactory substitute, will he please speak up soon? Until then, let us ponder this poem by Kahlil Gibran:*

> Your children are not your children,
> They are the sons and daughters of Life's longing
>   for itself.
> They come through you but not from you,
> And though they are with you yet they belong not
>   to you.
> You may give them your love but not your thoughts,
> For they have their own thoughts.
> You may house their bodies but not their souls,
> For their souls dwell in the house of tomorrow, which
> You cannot visit, not even in your dreams.
> You may strive to be like them, but seek not to make
>   them like you.
> For life goes not backward nor tarries with yesterday.

* Reprinted from *The Prophet* by Kahlil Gibran by permission of Alfred A. Knopf, Inc. Copyright 1923 by Kahlil Gibran.

Getting Together with Parents

Dear Dr. Lawton:

My mother was brought up in a home where children and parents worked and played together. But in Father's family, the husband was lord and master, the wife was second in command, and the children were vassals to carry out the father's wishes transmitted by the mother. Father and Mother both have ideas on how I should act, but they won't voice these ideas or tell me if I've violated one of their sacred laws. Father discusses me with Mother, she tells sister, and sister tells me. If we could talk it out among ourselves, we could alleviate many headaches, but we are so distant that this seems improbable.

Joan M.

or Reconciling Yesterday and Today

Dear Joan:

Every parent has been brought up according to one way of living in a family and one system of child-rearing. He finds it hard to let go of the familiar and try something new. That's the way the "dictator" father generally acquires his role. Sometimes, however, you find a father who just has a natural affinity for the part.

Now, the system where father is autocrat of the dinner table may be better or worse than the one where he is "one of the gang." We won't argue that. The fact is that most Americans tend toward the partnership type of marriage in which the husband and wife are "loving friends," equals in rank, but with different tasks and responsibilities. Parents make decisions on matters concerning the whole family, set standards of behavior, but allow the children to make up their own minds about things that will affect their lives (choice of a career, mate, etc.). Children are junior members of the firm: "adults in training." In rank the children are subordinate, but, as people, they are just as important as their parents.

The family exists to make each unit stronger than it would be alone. Every member in the household has duties and obligations, but also he is entitled to certain rights, rewards, and pleasures. It is natural under such circumstances for Mom, Dad, Bud, Sis, and Grandma (if she makes her home with them) to sit down and present their views straight from the shoulder.

Your father probably works hard and does everything for the family's welfare according to his lights. I am sure he believes his method of directing you by "remote control" is best. Moreover, a father doesn't relish coming home after a day on the job, with all its headaches, and then having to deal with problems that might disturb him. He may use the "relay" system, not from a love of power, but because he doesn't want to be bothered. It often takes time and hard thinking to work out the details of a plan for you to follow or to give concrete reasons for some regulation. Also, there are men who can't express themselves easily in words and who are shy of situations where they may have to show emotion and sentiment. So, he "passes the buck" to mother and she passes it to your sister.

Since young people generally are more flexible than adults and have less position to lose, you should take the first step and speak to your father. He may be unaware that his "discipline by long-distance" is making you unhappy and lessening family morale. Once you speak up, he may change.

I recently had the case of a parent and child who were like two blindfolded people trying to reach each other. When the daughter made the first move, she was amazed to discover that the "problem" parent (in this case her mother) was only too glad to go more than halfway. Behind a parent's mask of remoteness there is a person of warm feelings and good intentions, but sometimes a little confused as to what to do or how to begin. Being a *good parent,* as you will discover one fine day, is the toughest assignment in the world, and some children—to be fair—don't make the job any easier.

If you aren't able to speak to your father or if he doesn't prove receptive, you should ask for a family meeting. Beforehand, you should ask your mother and sister not to let their services be utilized in the relay system any longer. You have every right to ask for direct "communiqué-tion."

But should the family fail to budge father, then a respected and liked outsider: teacher, friend of the family, relative, etc., could be your spokesman.

Big oaks from little acorns grow. The way to have democracy in the nation is to practice it in every household, classroom, and factory.

Parental Ties

Dear Dr. Lawton:

My mother is always telling me that she lives only for me and that I don't appreciate all the sacrifices she has made to bring me up. She says I should always stay with her and take up the work she wants me to. I have my own ideas about the future. I don't want to hurt my mother, but haven't I a right to my own life?

Sidney P.

Melt Them or Use an Axe?

Dear Sidney:

Successful parents always have been aware that a child does not exist chiefly for their own benefit or pleasure, that they are trustees, not owners, and that when a child is born he is granted rights, not privileges. They also know that the only reward of parenthood is the knowledge that one has contributed to the making of a free, self-reliant human being who is able to meet whatever problems life may present and to lead an existence useful to himself and others.

Parents like these give their child love, understanding, and guidance; they try to achieve emotional maturity for themselves and to analyze their own behavior, especially the extent to which *they* are influencing their child to act in ways they deem undesirable. How hard this task is, particularly that of attaining a proper balance between tenderness and discipline in rearing a child, no young person realizes until he himself has become a parent.

A child is a very important additional experience in the lives of grownups; but he cannot take the place of other satisfactions nor act as a solution to some problem in the adult's own life. There are parents, however, who because they are unhappy in their relationships with the world, try to escape from it and obtain from a child emotional rewards they cannot find elsewhere. Such a mother (or father), by agreeing to live only for a child, hopes to persuade the child to live only for her, thereby doing herself, her husband, and her son or daughter a great injustice.

Furthermore, parents are the patterns of adulthood which the child knows best. If they seem to find adult life so barren, the son or daughter will not enjoy growing up. Parents must be brave in keeping to themselves any sense of defeat in their own lives that they may feel, if they want their children to make better adjustments than they have. While parents and children should love, respect, and assist each other, neither generation can evade the responsibility for working out its own problems and obtaining its major experiences and joys from those of its own age level.

Behind adolescent bravado is a hunger for advice from their elders who can teach them a great deal. But they will learn only if they feel the adult has a genuine desire to be of service to them and is trying to understand them better than they understand themselves. Parents should set up ideals, certainly, and the child may accept them, but he must feel that he has made the final decision as to the kind of person he wants to become and the kind of life he wishes to lead. Whenever parents seek to dictate the older adolescent's choices in crucial matters like those of a career and marriage, and refuse to consider his own individual needs, the normal youngster will resist.

However, rebellion is the easiest, but not the only, answer. I suggest that you plan for an evening of calm discussion, having present a sympathetic relative or adult friend, perhaps a teacher. Only through such "get-togethers" can both sides be given their due. Parents must realize that every young person wants to become emotionally independent of them and make a success of life as an adult on his own. If he feels that they stand ready to help him in this struggle, he will be only too glad to call upon them for the guidance he so urgently needs.

Why Do We Hurt People We Love?

Dear Dr. Lawton:

I'm writing to you to see if you can explain me to myself. This is the point. I always seem to do such stupid things. For instance, the other night I asked Dad to take me to the movies. He was tired and was reading and didn't want to go. But I kept on insisting and insisting and finally he went, but he looked miserable all through the picture. Then there's Dick, whom I hope to marry some day. He took me out to dinner. I wanted to be my sweetest self, but before I knew it I was calling him "stingy," and he got angry and hasn't been around for a week. Another example is my best friend, Joan. She's a very pretty girl. She gets a new dress, which I like, and I say, "That's a lovely dress—but not for you." I didn't mean to add that, but still it comes out. If I keep on that way, I'll have to be quarantined. Why do I hurt the very people I love and on whom my own happiness depends?

Ruth L.

Because We Have Been Hurt by Others

Dear Ruth:

Just as we reveal our personalities, our inner thoughts and feelings by the way we act with friends, in school, on the job, so our behavior when in love is a reflection of what we are as people. Love does something to *us*, and *we* do even more to it. We can turn it into something which adds strength and beauty to two lives, or we can make it a device for exploiting and inflicting pain on the loved one and thereby bringing on ourselves an inevitable defeat.

Love is popular and necessary for many reasons, one being that it gives us a sense of importance we can't get any other way. The girl in whom self-love is overstrong looks upon a boy's affection as a kind of mirror.

True, we all start out loving ourselves more than anything or anyone else, and as children we care only about our own needs and satisfactions. By the time we've grown up, most of us learn to work in a team. Some men and women, however, remain to the end the most important thing in their lives, never really giving themselves to any cause or any other person. Dick, no doubt, has many fine and endearing qualities, and you love him for these, but what you admire most, perhaps, is his good judgment in selecting *you*. What you love in him is his love for you.

When Dick does something which brings you down a peg or two, like not showing up at a date, or neglecting you at a dance, then you hate him, because he has been mean to *you*, a person you love even more than you love him.

Some people, who inwardly feel small, shrink even more when they are criticized or neglected, and that's why they fly into a rage. In fact, it is only the well-balanced person who can stand being criticized by someone he loves without turning against him and wanting to hate and get even with him.

Ruth, you unconsciously hurt your father because other things in your life have gone wrong and you want to get a sense of power and success somewhere. By bossing your father, you imagine for a moment that you also are boss over many other situations and people as well. And so, Ruth, when your spirits are low you launch an attack on dear old Dad.

You called Dick stingy in order to pull him down. When he goes down, you go up. Being able to inflict pain gives a weak person a sense of strength. You don't want to be happy, you want to make other people as unhappy as you are. Hence, that catty remark to Joan. You can't pick on strangers or acquaintances, and you therefore select those persons who can't escape because of geography and their own love for you.

When we love someone, we lose a certain amount of independence. We can't come and go as we wish any longer, nor can we think only of our own selves. It's not "I" now, it's "We." A self-centered individual will be annoyed with the person he loves merely because this love forces him to consider the needs and wishes of someone not himself.

When we love someone, we give ourselves over to him for safekeeping. Someone once said, "The happiness of a woman depends on the kind of man who loves her." If he is fine, this is one thing; if not. . . . Though men are not quite that dependent on women, since their careers come first, to some extent this observation also applies to them. Without realizing it, we may quarrel with a loved one only to get a rise out of him. If we can make him protest both his affection for us and our importance, this will prove we haven't made a mistake in turning ourselves over to him.

All of us, therefore, rebel at times because another person, through our need for him, should have such a great power over us. Some fights arise out of our desire to prove to ourselves that we can wriggle loose from the "chains" of a love which we ourselves have created. You are attached to your father and still need him. When you quarrel with him or flaunt your unconcern, it means you are rebelling at your own weakness, your inability to stand on your own.

It won't do any good, Ruth, to tell you "Count ten before you utter the harsh word." We've first got to make you a person aware of the needs and rights of others. We also must get you to really understand why you act as you do.

A wise man once said that you can't forgive others until you've forgiven yourself. The people who find the most fault with the world are the most dissatisfied with themselves. Until you have learned to accept yourself, Ruth, you won't accept other people.

Dr. Jekyll and Mr. Hyde

Dear Dr. Lawton:

Why is it that I can be kind and easygoing with my friends, but when I'm home with the family I get so cranky and irritable? When I enter the bus or trolley and see a friend, I'll go over and make every attempt to be pleasant, but at home I don't want to talk, but would rather read the paper or listen to the radio.

Martin S.

Which of Our Many Selves Is the True One?

Dear Martin:

We all know the person who is the prince of good fellows away from home but who turns grouch or bully the moment he crosses the doorstep. That we should behave one way with our friends and another way with our kin is due partly to the difference between relationships with friends and family and partly to problems in our own make-up.

Friendship is the free companionship of equals. A friend accepts and likes us for what we are, or else he would not have become our friend. We do not have to explain to him, unless we want to, just where we've been or what we've done. Faced with the challenge of earning the liking and esteem of a new acquaintance, most of us try to show him our best side, and we see him only at those times when we can do so. He, on his part, will attempt to heighten our sense of importance, or at any rate will keep his knowledge of our shortcomings to himself, since this is the way to become more necessary to us. A friendship must be equally pleasant to both persons, because once it ceases to give each friend what he needs, all further obligation ends.

Among members of the family circle, however, greater responsibility and deeper emotions are involved, not only because of mutual affection and interest but also because it is felt that what one member does reflects on all the others. Since our close relations cannot be chosen or replaced as friends are, we are likely to think that their affection and good-will is as unchanging as their presence. Sure of their love, we are not concerned much whether they like us or not, and consequently we don't think it essential to be agreeable and helpful or to refrain from harsh speech and petty behavior.

While anger and rebellion are normal and healthy reactions in certain situations, to be always in a fighting mood at home or to shut ourselves in our room is a sign that we are unhappy in our relationships. The cause may lie in the attitude of our parents and brothers and sisters. Perhaps they have always treated us coldly and denied us a chance to feel important or to share in the family activity and management according to our ability. Any favor done for them may have been taken for granted with not even a "thank you" in return. There may also have been little respect for our privacy and for the ways in which we have a perfect right to be what we are and not somebody else that might suit them better. Or because of the arrival of a new brother or sister or some other altered circumstance, our parents may have withdrawn the great attention we once received.

But often the family is not the immediate cause of our irritability at all. Having failed at something in the outside world, we do not stop to consider just what factors have been responsible or wherein we have been at fault. Instead, we want to punish somebody who is not likely to strike back and whose good opinion and affection cannot be easily lost. This generally means that some innocent member of the family will be the target, since he fills the bill most conveniently.

Tom R. has an older sister who is brilliant and attractive and has loads of admiring friends, while he himself is just an average boy. With his own companions he is good-natured enough. His parents have been dazzled by their daughter's success and popularity and have unwittingly let her become the center of things. Though Tom means to behave well, a deep resentment and hostility always gets the better of him when he reaches home, and he retreats into a sulky silence or else has a streak of fussing and fuming. Lately his school work has gone to pieces. His family first met Tom's anger with their own, then they denied him all privileges, and finally they tried the method of scornful silence, but matters have only become worse.

Yet Tom has a perfectly natural craving for love and recognition. His behavior is merely a kind of blackmail with which he is unknowingly seeking attention as a way of escaping his hurt feelings. He can be helped only if the family attitude changes and if he himself learns to work for approval through constructive means.

I Want to Grow Up—Fast!

Dear Dr. Lawton:

I'm sixteen years old, and I know what is wrong with me. The trouble is that I have been pampered by my parents all my life. They cater to all my whims, and all they seem to want is that I accept forever what they have always given so generously. But I know that this is bad for me. I don't seem to have the self-reliance and independence of the fellows I see around me. Everything has always been too easy. How can I stop this? Shall I scold them each time they hold out their crutch, upon which I have become so dependent? Who is to change a little Fauntleroy into some kind of maturity? Where do I begin?

Bert F.

Have You a Magic Drink?

Dear Bert:

The answer, of course, is with *you yourself*. It is paradoxical that at the very moment you most desire to be considered mature, you are still dependent on others. If you are to learn how to stand on your own two feet, the zero hour is *now*. The difference between your dependence on others and on me is that I am impersonal and intent on getting you to dispense with me or any other crutch as soon as possible. The job of parents is to make themselves unnecessary. Mine even more so.

You claim your parents have made you a mollycoddle. Perhaps they have tried to overprotect you and dominate you through generosity. Such an attitude may have been fostered by insecurity or poor psychology in their own upbringing. Regardless of the cause, there is no reason for you to keep "passing the buck." Aren't you going to have to manage your own life soon? When you have a family of your own, when you establish yourself in the working world, aren't you going to have to take the responsibility for your actions?

What makes you weak is not the "crutch" your parents offer, but your acceptance of it. You have a right to reject their help, if you do so good-naturedly. Young people sometimes think it proves emotional independence to stop showing respect or to run away from home. Actually such "treat 'em rough" methods only prove childishness.

How should you assume the responsibility for establishing your maturity? First, you had better evaluate yourself, your interests, your abilities. It would be excellent if you could find yourself a job, at least part-time. If this is not possible, you should live on a budgeted allowance. You should select your own recreations, reading, clothes, and see to the planning and furnishing of your own room. This control over your private affairs would establish the confidence you need to tackle the more ticklish problem of social adjustment. You should plan your own parties and be your own host, take a camping trip with companions of your age or make a long visit out of town. At the outset it will often be easier to relapse into your passive attitude of letting your parents arrange plans and solve difficulties; however, if you really want to grow up, you had better jack yourself up and harness all the potential energy that might turn your daydreams of independence into reality.

After establishing your personal independence, your second step will be to extend your newly acquired capability into a group situation. At home, you should take on regularly such tasks as running errands and cleaning your room. The third proof of your independence will be evident in your ability to adapt yourself to a group outside your immediate family. It would pay you at the same time you are taking the initiative at home to widen your horizons by meeting people of different customs, religions, and political beliefs.

To make decisions intelligently and to evaluate things in an adult manner, you must have a broad perspective. Too, you should acquire a familiarity with those skills young people value—dancing, dating, popular songs, current games and sports. You should cultivate your own opinions and individuality, remembering in the process that individuality, when it is extreme and inclined to be overbearing, is no aid to fostering group cooperation.

In the initial stages of acquiring the independence, the adaptability, the broad-mindedness that will characterize the mature you, you should remember not to be *too* cocky or arrogant. You should not disregard completely the judgment of your parents. They, after all, have the benefit of broad experience, whether you recognize it or not. There is the almost classic story of the ex-soldier who remarked, "When I went away, Pop didn't know anything, but by the time I got back, the old man had managed to learn an awful lot!" Your parents can help you a great deal, and asking for advice is not the same as asking them to make your decisions.

You have your "homework" cut out, Bert. A very wise psychologist, Lillien J. Martin, once said that it is the duty of society to evolve adults fit for children to live with. Let's hope you make it.

Should Sisters Have Brothers?

Dear Dr. Lawton:

Why is it that my brother and I cannot get along? We quarrel constantly if we are together. He never wants to do anything I suggest. For instance, I will ask him to go to a show or a friend's house, but he always has some excuse. When my mother asks him to go any place with her, he always says he would rather stay at home. If he is around his friends and I approach, he will insult me or he will tell me I embarrass him, but his friends all seem friendly. It seems to me that he is just spoiled.

Emily P.

and Vice-Versa?

Dear Emily:

Children in the same family may differ from one another in many ways: in size, looks, intelligence, ambition, sociability, etc. Sometimes brothers and sisters are attracted to each other by these differences, sometimes they are repelled. Again, one child may be like a particular parent, and another may be very unlike. This leads to additional complications all around. For example, there may be a deep sympathy between a lively, sociable girl and a mother of the same type, while both may consider a quiet, retiring brother quite a puzzle.

However, it is a gain to the world rather than a loss that we are not all alike. For it is through our differences that we educate each other and become more adaptable and understanding human beings.

Brothers and sisters quarrel, not merely because they have differences but because they are unwilling to admit that these differences have a right to exist. They quarrel also because they do not know how to adjust their differences and practice that give-and-take which alone makes for satisfactory relationships between people.

Even where the domestic scene is generally happy, flare-ups are to be expected. But an occasional quarrel, properly handled, can aid in the development of a family group. In the "useful" quarrel, the participants treat each other as equals who are justified in talking up when they feel they have a legitimate grievance. They do not resort to name-calling, bitter accusations, or any tactic that will split a family and estrange one member from another.

In situations where there is a conflict of demands among the children, each one should gain a point at times but yield it at others. Yet in some homes, one sister or brother will always walk off with the victory. Perhaps it is because he is the chief breadwinner or has the most wilful and obstinate disposition. Or it may be that he shouts the loudest or knows how to grow faint at the crucial moment. In the same family there may be someone else who always does whatever sacrificing is required. This person, instead of fighting on to achieve a reasonable compromise, abandons his demands.

Temporary peace may be achieved this way, but the final

price paid for it by everyone in the home is too great. The victor's selfishness and love of power will grow, making life harder for others and finally for himself. The loser will be more and more consumed by jealousy and resentment, though he may seem meek and resigned on the surface. Differences within a family should never be settled so that one member thinks he did not get justice.

Brothers and sisters who feel they have nothing else in common may find it possible to agree on loyalty to the family as a whole. The more members of a family can work and play together, and the more they are willing to share with each other whatever power, privileges, opportunities, or sacrifices life brings them, the more will the spirit of loyalty grow. We find this feeling strongest in those homes where parents stress the ways in which the child can co-operate with them and with the other children. Such parents think of themselves as leaders, who play no favorites and whose position rests, not upon force or authority but upon the feeling of loyalty they can arouse.

A stand-offish brother may be hard to figure out until we know something of what is happening inside him. Between twelve and twenty, everyone must change from a child to a grownup, free of his parents emotionally, if not financially. A boy may be worried about his ability to make a success of his future and to break this close tie to his family. He may realize the need of outside interests and contacts, but, to a person afraid that failure awaits him in the world, there is indeed "no place like home."

This boy may put on a show of being strong and self-sufficient. He may act tough to his "womenfolk" and violently spurn their "kind" invitations and suggestions. While it seems as if such a brother is not proud of his sister, actually he is not proud of himself. Moreover, a young man can be sensitive about his masculinity. Perhaps he has had a mother who was over-careful and possessive with him, and now has to deal with a sister whose own development leads her in a "maternal" and bossy direction.

A brother and sister get along better if they respect each other's desire for independence. No matter how concerned one may be about the other, they are still two persons. A sister cannot live a brother's life for him.

If a brother asks for our assistance, we should do everything we can to help him. But if he does not ask, our job is to stand on the sidelines and let him struggle on alone. We can help from afar, by showing that we believe in his importance as a person, that we think his work and ideas grand. We can also make it clear that we love him for what he is and not for what he might become if he accepted our pet system of self-improvement.

As for this matter of being "spoiled," the "spoiled brat," instead of having had too much love or approval, in reality often has had too little of the right kind, where tender affection and encouragement is offered without its going to the extreme of smothering overprotection. The "spoiled brat" endlessly craves and battles to obtain not his own way but some sign of wholesome interest and reassurance from those around him.

The story is told of a youngster who was once brought to a physician, wise not only in the ways of the body but in those of the mind. After examining the child, the doctor told the mother that the problem would be cleared up with the filling of his prescription. But when the mother handed the blank to the druggist, the latter only shook his head and returned the slip. For the doctor had written: "Love, three times a day," which, incidentally, might be a good motto for every household to hang under its "Home, Sweet Home" sign.

Divided Loyalties

Dear Dr. Lawton:

I'm in a terrible predicament. My mother and father have just gotten divorced. I tried hard to stop them, to bring them together, but I didn't succeed. Now there is a new problem. Shall I go with Dad or Mom? Both want me, both need me, both are fighting to get me. How can I decide which one to go with when I love them both so much? One minute I decide to go with Dad, because he understands me and why I want to be what I want to be: a physical-training teacher. Mom has been against this, but Dad agrees with me. He also tells me just how to go about things and explains phases of life that Mom won't even talk about. But then I think about Mom and decide to stay with her. I can have heart-to-heart talks with Mom and tell her things I never could say to Dad. Mom understands me almost as well as Dad and encourages me to become a social success. If only there were some rule to follow. It's ironic, I think, that I used to run to Dad and Mom with all my troubles, and now the greatest one in my whole life I must solve myself. Can you help me make this terrible decision?

Jane

Those Who Need Us vs. Those We Need

Dear Jane:

Let's go over it all again, Jane. If you stay with Mother, your health and grooming will receive more care and you'll have a closer and more constant friend. Also, you're apt to have your mother to yourself longer, since she is less likely to remarry than your father. Now, let's look at life with Father. That would mean seeing less of him than of Mother, and also less supervision of your health and general behavior. For a little while you might enjoy this loosening of discipline. Later you would realize the absence of the care which every girl needs. You are apt to have a stepmother sooner than a stepfather, and she, like all mothers, will make herself felt more than a father would.

If you go with your father, you'll be given a good deal of authority in the house. There'll be some disadvantages attached to this. You may have to cook and clean and hang around till he comes home and can be served dinner. You also *may* learn to depend on him for male companionship more than you should and become overattached to him. That may make it harder for you to get married.

Divorce is a heartbreaking thing. It should not happen. But it has happened, and you'll have to face the fact. You want to grow up and enjoy all the experiences of a normal young girl. Some day you will want to make a better job of your marriage than your parents did.

There are some mistakes you must guard against. In regard to your parents, don't say, "I'll go to the one who needs me most." It is not your job to compensate either your father or mother for the present or future unhappiness and emptiness of their lives. They are grownups who have had their chance and muffed it. It is up to them to learn to do better next time. You alone can never be all-in-all to either your father or your mother. If you attempt it, you will only add your own dissatisfaction to theirs. Be generous and loving to them, but think mostly of your own future home, your own husband and children-to-be.

What has happened should not make you become a man-hater. Only a very wise person could decide who failed in this marriage. Even so, that doesn't mean that you need to fail in yours. Don't make up your mind to suffer so as to atone for what Mother did to Father, and certainly don't try to punish men for what your Dad did to your Mom.

As for your own life, you should go out with many boys and have many friendships. Be careful not to go overboard about the first boy who notices you because you are starved for affection, or are overcome by the lonesomeness of a household without both your parents.

Young people all want to be like the rest of the crowd and have what their friends have. And most of your friends will be fully equipped with two parents right there for you to see and to hear. Comparing that complete family setup with your own limited one certainly will hurt. Nor will it be easy for you to explain about your parents when others ask questions or when the gang drops around to your house.

Some day every high school and college will have courses on the requirements for success in marriage and on how to choose a partner wisely. Some day, too, every town will have its marriage consultation bureau, where husbands and wives about to make a forced landing might find out what's wrong and so keep flying.

If you're a smart girl, you'll use your present experience in a way which will help you. Let it teach you about people and about what men and women need in order to be happy, especially when married. Resolve to avoid the mistakes of your parents, if you can, and to be careful in the choice of a mate when the time comes for you.

Fathers and Sons

Dear Dr. Lawton:

How can I stop my father from drinking? This causes us a great deal of trouble at home. He comes home, starts to cut up and say disagreeable things. Sometimes he makes my mother so angry she seems ready to do something desperate to stop him. This often keeps me from going out because I feel I'm needed to control things.

Don't think I'm blaming my father. He is a good man, and I'm really proud of him. It is just that he has developed a liking for drinking and now can't go without it. Dad was retired two years ago, after working hard all his life. What I am looking for is a way to get him to stop, but without letting him, or even my mother, know what I am trying to do. Why do people drink? Is it because they are bored or want to forget their troubles? Yet my father hasn't any real troubles that I can see.

Joe D.

and When They Need Each Other Most

Dear Joe:
What is behind a term like "boredom," or a similar one, "laziness?" The human animal when unconfined, and physically and mentally healthy, is active and interested; just being alive is exciting. If we are *always* bored or *always* lazy, it means that we don't believe ourselves equal to the tasks facing us. We shrink from them because a voice inside warns: "What's the use of exerting yourself! You will only fail, or else the degree of success won't be worth the effort and won't change your life in any way. You just weren't meant to be happy or successful." That inner voice is often merely an echo of what everybody outside is saying. Also, some people get a kick out of being miserable. They think suffering and failure are the inevitable punishment for their worthlessness, as well as a method of atonement.

Many things happen in a man's life that he doesn't desire, and many other things that he seeks are never attained. Your father may be troubled by much of which you, and perhaps your mother, are ignorant; much that even he couldn't put his finger on. No child realizes all that has happened to its parents. Will your own son know everything about you? Will you yourself remember in 1980 what you are going through now?

Your Dad also may be one of those men for whom retirement is a bad thing. As long as he worked, he felt he counted for something, and the daily routine of a job kept his mind off inner and outer dissatisfactions. But now he feels useless and rejected. What your father needs is another job. It is a great waste for a man who is able to work to stay retired.

Life in the country is another plan that might be tried. The chores of a farm, for example, would help distract your father's mind. Then, too, people are happiest when their current activities and achievements bring them closer each day to some desirable goal. A farm, with growing and developing things, with such challenges as building one's house, etc., will give your father something to plan for.

There are other devices you might try. Ask your father to take you on fishing and camping trips, or on a bicycle tour. Ask him also to play games of skill with you: chess, checkers, etc., or put to him difficult questions about politics or world affairs. You might start a boys' club, soliciting your father's advice first on methods. Arrange, if you can, to have him made honorary president and invite him to come around occasionally and talk to the boys, or act as a judge of contests.

In order to be mentally healthy, people need to be creative, to have some outlet for expressing what *they* feel is important within themselves, to stamp their own point of view or particular talent on the world about them. If one can't do this on his job, then he must utilize hobbies. Ask your mother and your grandparents about your father's interests when he was younger. Then take up these hobbies yourself and have him teach them to you. In that way, he may return to them himself.

You haven't said much about your mother, the other children and life at home generally. However, I don't believe that the experiences of married life or of adulthood as a whole are the *chief* causes of your father's difficulty or that changes in the family's attitude would effect a *complete* cure. But I will say that the more companionable and "sharing" you people are at home, the jollier, more interesting and more social family life is, the more he will be helped.

Your mother and you have good reason for feeling that your father has treated you unjustly. But if you want to help yourself and your mother, you won't do it by harping on how he is squandering money, disgracing his family, and so on. He already feels his unworthiness, already is convinced that he is isolated from your mother and you and that the only way to escape from his loneliness is through drinking and the artificial social life that goes with it. Scoldings, lectures, direct suggestions won't work. Beware especially of pity and acting as if the family were straining itself to the utmost at an impossible job of salvaging human wreckage. These methods will only make him feel more of a failure and scoundrel, more alone.

Your enemy, then, is not the act of drinking, but your father's feeling of failure. What you are competing with is a dream of a richer and more exciting life, a dream that takes the place of real achievement in the real world. You must therefore make your father feel that his opinions, his advice, his companionship are important to everyone, but particularly to you, that people retire *to,* not *from.* Think of him not as a father but as a person, and one who is having little real satisfaction or fun now. You yourself must first draw up a list of this person's good points and convince yourself that he is worth working over. Next, you should subtly let others know how you feel. Eventually it may get back to your father that he is not yet scheduled for the scrap heap.

In a way, Joe, you'll have to be a kind of artist. In your mind, you have an idea of the man you want your father to be, and your task is to make a reality of that idea. Of course, your father isn't a bad man. Somehow in the shuffle of living he has lost hope, lost his image of the kind of man he wanted to be and the kind of life he wanted to lead, and now he must depend on synthetic sources of hope and fulfilment. You have to help him hunt for that lost image of himself, help him return to the natural sources of self-realization.

These methods I have indicated are simple and prosaic. But should they help your father become more sure of himself, the real world will turn pleasant and rewarding again for him. There will be much less need for drinking, his unkind remarks will decrease and your mother will find him less trying. Eventually, he may really become the man whose image you've been holding before him.

However, if the methods don't work, I know of nothing else to try except professional psychological assistance in the form of someone who helps older people with their problems of adjustment. Men and women, fathers and mothers, have special difficulties no matter what their age, and they need someone who has studied the problems of that age period and knows how to meet them most effectively.

Can a Child Hate His Parents?

Dear Dr. Lawton:

I have a father who hardly ever is home. Whenever the mood to see the world strikes him, he just goes. Sometimes he sends us money, and maybe instead we receive a flowery letter of apology. Once every few years he pays some attention to me, but then it is so exaggerated and sentimental that I prefer neglect. I can't remember a single occasion when my father acted like a father or when he made me happy or even tried to do so.

As for Mother, she works, and I don't see much of her either, so I can't say that we are any closer. Mother is charming and youthful, and she can be sweet and companionable—but always with other people.

We are always quarreling, because she criticizes everything I do, no matter what. She says the cruelest things: "What man could like a girl with a face like yours!" or, "A girl who dresses that way will never get a husband!" Our house is always disorganized. I have no father really; and Mother is out with friends almost every evening. I *hate* my parents!

Sue D.

Yes, But It Is an Almost Impossible Task!

Dear Sue:

If we are to take the word "hate" in its usual sense of wishing complete and permanent destruction of the object hated, it is almost impossible to succeed in hating your parents, much as a boy or girl may try.

The average child of average loving parents often has moments when he becomes intensely angry with them and may throw around freely the word "hate," but he means merely that he is greatly vexed. The teens is a period in which a human being stops being a child and starts becoming a grownup. In the process of discovering himself, working out his *own* standards, his *own* life choices and goals, the ex-child may rebel at parental attitudes and discipline. He will do this even if there actually is little to rebel against. That's the way he develops his emotional "muscles."

We often find that the more a young person feels life pushing him out of the nest and the more he fears to venture forth, the more he will insist that it is his parents who are the cause of his problems, and the obstacles to his happiness. He may even say, "I hate my mother (father)." But if he could find words for his deeper thoughts he would say, "I hate my weakness, my inability to stand on my own two feet; I hate the way I am influenced and bothered by my mother's (father's) advice and criticisms."

In the counseling work that I have done with young persons and with their parents, perhaps only once in a few hundred times have I come across a case where a parent deserved to be hated and actually was hated. Real hatred is rare, but it can be so fierce that the average person might refuse to believe that such tortured human relationships could ever exist.

You, Sue, I admit are certainly not an example of the everyday child's dissatisfaction with his parents. But neither are you the extreme case of real hatred. Overcome by bitterness, you feel that you haven't received from your father and mother something that you need and want more than anything else in the world.

But you have given your emotion a wrong name. You hate, not your parents but the unhappiness which is the result of their not loving you as you wish they would and as you need them to. When you say, "I hate (that is, want to destroy) my parents," you mean "I hate (that is, want to destroy) this situation in which I can't be sure of my parents' love and good will." The most important influence in your life and the thing you require most to help you face the world unafraid is your certainty that you have your parents' affection and approval.

Recently I saw a young refugee child who had been

separated from his parents and didn't remember much about them. The lad's intense curiosity about his Papa and Mama and the longing to see and be with them again is something one can never forget. Every boy and girl is tremendously interested in the details of parental lives. We all want to know about the people from whom we have come and whether that can help explain why we are what we are.

In the life of a man or woman who has had a complete experience the three major loves are those for his mate, his child, and his parents. This need to love and admire our fathers and mothers is so great that we are willing to forgive them again and again for some blunder on their part. The best dad and mother in the world have moments when they unjustly punish or cause pain. Young people want parents and teachers to overlook their occasional shortcomings and whoppers. Parents, too, are equally entitled to say, "Let's skip it. It was a mistake."

Fortunately, let the parent just give the slightest hint that he realizes it was a mistake in judgment which he regrets, and the average boy or girl is only too glad to explain it away as either unintentional or as a passing mood.

In a sense, parents are lucky, because their child, for its first ten or even more years, will let them start each day with a fresh slate. As times goes on, however, and if that child goes to sleep night after night feeling a stranger in his own home, a kind of psychological orphan, he may want to forgive, but no longer can he forget. A mixed attitude of deep hurt and anger develops from which he cannot shake himself loose, though as long as he lives he will seek to find some excuse for his parents. He generally concludes that "It must have been something in me, some fault or weakness of mine." This, by the way, is how a feeling of inadequacy, better known as the "inferiority complex," usually begins.

Probably the best solution for child-parent difficulties is for each one to know himself and then to know the other. But to understand either ourselves or another human being—especially one as close as a child or parent—is enormously difficult.

But there is a short story which may help a little if we all take it to heart. It is the story of the two bears: Bear and Forbear!

The Greater Loyalty?

Dear Dr. Lawton:

My father has gone to *prison*. I am well liked by all of my school friends. If they ever find out about it, I would not be able to face them. My oldest sister, seventeen, does not go to school; she works and has her own money. My older brother, sixteen, works and goes to school in another state. I have two other smaller sisters and one smaller brother.

What I want to know is whether or not I should live with my dear mother who is awfully sad or whether I should go live with my aunt far from here. I hate to leave my mother with the children. I hate to stay and live and face the boys and girls in school and outside. I don't know what to do.

"Puzzled Girl"

To Ourselves or To Our Family?

Dear "Puzzled Girl":

If we could always handle difficult situations in our lives through the use of logic, then this dilemma might be easier to solve. One would say that every person is responsible only for what he is in himself, that no one is to be judged by the deeds of others.

We don't think much of the individual who tries to shine by reflected light and who acts high and mighty because some relative is this or that. If secondhand glory means little, so does secondhand "disgrace." When a member of our family breaks some social code, we need not feel that we must share the guilt or punishment, or even the suffering. No one can disgrace a person except that person himself.

That is what we might say if we managed our emotions by rules of logic. Actually, however, anyone who wishes to remain untouched by the fate of others must uproot in himself the desire to love and be loved. We are bound by unbreakable ties of affection to other human beings. When they prosper, we are proud and happy; when they meet with reverses, we are cast down.

We often wish that parents and children could think of themselves merely as good friends, since in that case home life might run more smoothly. But relations within the family are much closer than friendship. For one of the characteristics of love is that we become a part of that which we love. In our close kin we see ourselves.

That is why we are so interested in family history, and why children and parents become so upset over each other's shortcomings. It is a serious blow for us to learn that someone we admire, and boast about, someone we want to resemble, has fallen into disrepute.

There is a second sense in which "man cannot live alone." Most of us feel stronger and happier when we are part of a group whose members feel and think as we do. Hence the importance to us of the team, the club, the "gang." There is no more thrilling moment in a person's life than when he stands up in meeting and hears from his comrades those sweet words: "We are proud of you and have gathered here to do you honor."

In the same way, the extreme of bitterness is felt when we think we have been rejected by our group, and see (or imagine we see) stony stares or averted faces. Great spirits in religion, philosophy, or science have been able to stand all alone in a crisis. With their backs to the wall, they have faced the displeasure, even scorn and hatred, of their group.

But we cannot expect everyone to reach such heroic heights. We all will sympathize with a young girl who thinks she will find it hard to make friends, obtain employment, or get married, after what some relation has done. We can understand why she might wish to go away and start afresh.

Could she, however, forgive herself for going, particularly if she felt she had walked out on someone who needed her? It may be that, once in a new town, such a young person could furnish her family with more financial aid. Perhaps for this or some other reason she might find a way of silencing her own conscience. Yet she still may be unhappy at the plight of her family. In addition, the truth may finally come out anyway, despite all the labor and strain of trying to conceal it.

On the other hand, suppose the girl stays with her family. There will be a period of humiliation plus pain. But in time she may be able to salvage more of her self-respect this way than if she left. There will be a feeling of relief that, instead of having to live a lie for the rest of her days, the worst is known; no past, no skeleton in the closet.

Moreover, the true friends of such a girl and the really fine people will want to help and protect her. The world may contain its quota of tongue-waggers and mean people, but it also contains those who will rise to an emergency when they see any individual, especially a young one, staying where she is needed and going about her business with her head held high, the very embodiment of a saying by Charles W. Eliot: "What do we live for, if not to make life less difficult for others?"

Sometimes it is a little easier to accept our own fate when we learn how much harder it may be for someone else. There is not only one child involved here but many; not one parent but two! What about your father: his thoughts and feelings, his realization of the trouble brought to others, his sense of lost years and wasted ambitions?

There was a parallel case a few years ago. In this instance it was a high-school boy, Mark S., who wanted to leave home. One of Mark's chums, Ned, seeking to help his friend make the wisest choice, hit upon a very risky plan.

Without explaining anything to Mark, Ned called a meeting of his schoolmates. To a large group Ned presented an imaginary situation, asking them what they would do and how they would feel if right in their midst sat a schoolmate whose father had gone to prison. Without suspecting whom Ned meant, since no details were given, one young person after another rose and said that such a fact would not interfere in the slightest with his attitude toward the unknown classmate, and that the boy or girl ought to remain at home.

But no outsider can make the decision here. Only the person concerned knows all the circumstances; only *he* knows what courage, what resourcefulness *he* can muster in support of any particular step that may have to be taken.

Can Youth and Age Be Friends?

Dear Dr. Lawton:

Since my mother died, I have been living with my father and *his* mother. I call her "Aunt May," not "Grandma." She is stricter with me than Mother ever was. She nags me and is disagreeable to my friends. She talks as if everything young people do is wrong. Are *all* old people that way?

Lately my father has been away working in another city. When he visits us, I try to explain why he should take me away with him. He says he can't. I don't want to run away from home, but what else am I to do?

Bob S.

Yes, If Each Has His Own Life

Dear Bob:

Running away from home never solved any problem. Certainly it can't solve this one. You should realize that with your father away you are the "man of the house." Because of that, you have certain responsibilities. You should try to understand your grandmother's loneliness. Rather than ignore her completely, you should lend a hand in making her life interesting. You might suggest things she would enjoy doing and make an effort to talk about things of interest to her. If "Aunt May" had a life of her own, and other interests besides you and your father, she would be absorbed by her own activities and plans. She would forget to worry about what her grandson was doing every minute of the day.

We think we can recommend a book that will appeal to "Aunt May." *Aging Successfully* * shows that an older person can learn new things if he wants to, and that life is always beginning for the person who is willing to change and grow.

If "Aunt May" were to spend an occasional afternoon with friends of her own age, if she participated in community activities or did something to earn a little money, she would feel less dependent on you. And she could talk to you about something besides your faults.

* Published by Columbia University Press.

You aren't happy with "Aunt May" because you want a real home with a mother and father. You resent being instructed and disciplined by anyone else. "Aunt May" feels a great responsibility in supervising you, since she is replacing both your father and your mother. By being stern and harsh she tries to get your attention and respect. What she really wants is your affection but she doesn't know how to go about gaining it.

You should realize that your grandmother doesn't mean to be unkind. She simply has another point of view. When you are a grandfather, you, too, will have a point of view different from your present one. You should not resent "Aunt May's" slant on things but should try to understand it. And help her to understand yours. Young and old *must* and *can* learn to work together. They certainly need each other. You need the wisdom and experience of "Aunt May." She needs your help, interest, and enthusiasm.

I have come across many older men and women who love fun, who know that the world of *tomorrow* belongs to young people, and are glad that this is so. One grandmother in particular has told me she believes her grandson has a right to make mistakes, provided he accepts the responsibility for them. When this grandson brings up problems, she outlines the probable results of a given action. But then she lets him make his own choice. When he does something worthwhile, she praises him. When he goes off the beam, she corrects him patiently and signs off with a humorous story about a similar experience in her own life. They can't help being friends.

Now, it may be that "Aunt May" can never be like this grandmother I just described. She may be so set in her ways that she cannot change. I'd like to suggest that first of all you try to talk the whole situation over with her. Not in a spirit of resentment, nor in anger, but quietly and calmly. See if she can understand your problems, and if she seems willing to take them into consideration in her treatment of you. Give her a chance. If this doesn't work, you might try talking it over again with your father, explaining the situation in the light of my answer to you. If none of this does any good, you will then have to adjust yourself to the situation until you grow up and can establish a life of your own.

By "adjust yourself," I don't mean that you must always give in to "Aunt May's" criticism and nagging. It is good and necessary for you to stand up in defense of your rights if you feel "Aunt May" is getting real rough with your sense of self-respect. Regardless of her motives and of her position, whenever she gets after you in a way you can't take and you believe is damaging to your integrity, you should fight back. If necessary, you may have to threaten to leave. But I hope you won't. It is best to stay put until you can make a success of life away from home. In the meantime, for your sake and "Aunt May's," I hope you can both learn to respect and understand each other.

"The Kind of Parent I Hope to Be"

"What is going to become of the younger generation!" If all the persons who ever have said this could only read the hundreds of letters submitted in the contest conducted by *Scholastic Magazine* on "The Kind of Parent I Hope to Be," they would no longer doubt that young people today have an intense desire to live up to their responsibilities as the parents of tomorrow's children. These letters eloquently proclaim that high-school boys and girls want to make a happy home for their future offspring, to give them all advantages: good schooling, love of books, training in music and art. Many specify that they wish to provide high ethical standards for their children, including religious education. If the young people live up to half these plans, their sons and daughters will surely be lucky.

But most of these future parents have no illusions about the difficulty of the task they have set themselves. For while they have ideals and dreams, they also are hard-headed realists. If they are conscious of their parents' limitations, they also know that they have their own too. They may not achieve their goal, but they are going to try as hard as they can. One can ask no more. At any rate, here is one person who will be standing on the sidelines rooting for them to win. I must confess that reading these letters was for me a deeply moving experience, and a very cheering and strengthening one, especially welcome today when the world's events offer so few opportunities for optimism.

Of approximately four hundred entries, girls outnumbered boys by three to one, but whatever other reasons there may have been for this, it is true that most girls, even in the early teens, have already given some thought to the possibility of marriage and children, with or without a career. High-school boys, however, are often so intent on the work they expect to do in the world that marriage and especially "papahood" rarely enter their minds. But ultimately boys become husbands, and husbands become fathers, as aware of their parental roles as the mothers. In fact, the boys who submitted letters nearly all said that rearing children is as much the father's job as it is the mother's, and that they hoped to play a very important part in the lives of their sons and daughters.

Most writers agreed that firmness is necessary with children, but they were against harshness and particularly against physical punishment. A parent guides his children, they felt, not through force or preachment but by offering an example and by earning the respect of his children for his superior wisdom and judgment. Love and obedience tendered from a sense of duty were worth little. Children were to seek the advice of parents as to the selection of friends, but the young person was to make the final choice.

Many writers felt that children as well as parents have responsibilities in the home, that households should be democratically run with weekly family councils, where budgets for each child, the division of family chores, the time for coming home at night, etc., should be considered. Any decision reached was to be strictly enforced. It was generally agreed that children should have an allowance from early childhood, the amount depending on family income. Some set a minimum of a dollar a week for high-school students; others favored larger sums, up to ten dollars, but the latter was to cover all expenses, including clothes. However, providing children with sufficient money is not enough, according to the contestants. Parents must also provide love (plenty of it), and understand the child's problems from the child's point of view, which means that adults must also understand themselves. Parents should be friends and comrades of their children, but they must realize when to retreat to the background and when to let go completely. Summing up these letters in one sentence, we might say that the contestants hope that as parents they will be fine human beings, experienced in the ways of the world, broadminded, sympathetic, with an unfaltering faith in themselves, their children, and humanity.

Most writers did not refer to their own parents at all, which may be taken to mean that neither approval nor disapproval was extreme enough to be mentioned. But about ten per cent said they had the finest parents any child could have, and they hoped for nothing better than to be like them. A few were sad and bitter at the unhappiness their parents caused them. A very few did not ever want to be parents. One girl, for example, said she loved little children and therefore was planning to become the head of an orphans' home, but she did not wish to have any youngsters of her own. Another girl headed her letter "To Be or Not To Be" and wrote: "Although I am sure I should desire a family of my own, yet I could not bear the thought of raising one in a universe of such turmoil and strife." A young man entitled his amusing entry: "One who wishes to be an Amiable Bachelor, a Foster Parent and not a Fond Papa" and explained how he hoped to assist the boys in his community, but these would never be his own.

Several writers said they were going to save copies of their letters and reread them some day when they were parents in order to check up on themselves. This seems like a good idea. Perhaps *Scholastic* will hold a contest twenty-five years hence on the subject: "How I Became the Kind of Parent I Once Had Hoped to Be." None of these future entries will be accepted unless it bears a statement signed by their children: "I have read Mother's (or Dad's) essay and hereby certify that it is all correct and true." But before we get completely lost in fancies about these sons and daughters still unborn, let us introduce the three presentday prize-winners, selected with the greatest of difficulty, since so many excellent contributions were received. They came from the following high schools:

> Altoona High School, Altoona, Pa.; Council Bluffs High School, Council Bluffs, Iowa; Evander Childs High School, New York City.

Parents As Mature People

I think the ideal parent is an intelligent, tolerant, very mature individual with a great capacity for loving, understanding and living with other people. I hope to be this sort of parent and thus provide for my children the type of home they deserve.

I shall try particularly hard to make the teen-age period of my children's life as happy and free from unnecessary emotional strain as possible. I shall try to make them realize that the success of our home and family life is as much their responsibility as their parents'. At this period of my children's life I think it absolutely necessary that we be the best of friends, with equal regard for one another's feelings and with complete mutual confidence. I do not mean a blind sort of trust, a feeling that my children can do no wrong, but rather a knowledge of their abilities and limitations and respect for them as people.

In regard to the problem of friends, I shall urge my children to have many friends and several close friends. I would not expect them to be very wise at first in choosing friends of the opposite sex. However, I would not tell them this and I would not interfere unless I knew the person to have a definitely bad effect. I shall try very hard to prevent the serious high-school "crush" because of the emotional stress involved. I shall urge my children to be tolerant in their friendships and not expect an overwhelming amount from their friends.

I think the best preparation parents can give their children for future marriage is to help them to be responsible, friendly, and appreciative individuals. I would see that they have a normally considerate and friendly attitude toward members of the opposite sex, and that they have a chance to associate with many of their own choosing.

Concerning the ever-present money problem, at the high-school age I would expect my children to keep a written record of how they spend their money, and how much they save. I would give them a sufficient weekly allowance to cover all necessary expenses, and also the miscellaneous ones which arise. I would discuss with them just what this amount should be, and come to an agreeable settlement.

At all times I would be firm but friendly in dealing with them, and I would try to be as fair as possible.

Parents as Patient Guides

When the time comes for me to add the title "Father" to my name, I hope to be able to steer clear of the four extreme methods frequently employed by well-meaning but misunderstanding parents. What I would classify as the four extremes are:

1. Close supervising and strict regulating of any moves the child might wish to make, giving him the feeling that he is not trusted, and the strict censoring of any actions or thoughts contrary to theories of parent.

2. Up-bringing by the process of neglect. Allowing child to do and think as he pleases and to form his own habits and opinions. Letting him lose such respect for his parent that he will not expect anything from him will almost undoubtedly ruin any child.

3. Coddling and shielding of the child from anything unpleasant. The getting of special privileges for child because of disagreeable tasks at school.

4. Constant nagging and unnecessary cruelty to child. Severe punishment for small disobediences, and the excess piling of duties and work on child.

Although my child's future will be mapped out for him years before his birth, I shall anticipate changes in my plans due to whatever type of personality my child may develop.

He'll be taught to think and plan for himself, but his independence shall have limits. He will be adequately disciplined and given definite tasks to perform. I shall make him understand that his golden opportunity won't come to him on a silver platter. No sacrifice that I can make will be too great, provided he is worthy of it. If he's not, it will be my fault.

Parents as Artists

Surely there is an art in parenthood, and, as such, it challenges the best that is in us. It is an art demanding as tools our intellectual capability, our emotional balance, and our very way of life. Thus, to be successful in our art, we must use these tools wisely. If I were a parent, I should want to give my children the best that is in me. I should teach them to desire more than I possess, to seek higher goals than those I sought, and courageously tell them that nothing is impossible. I should teach them what I know of life, but tell them that my theories aren't valid until they've lived to prove them. I should attempt to train their minds in the ways my parents have neglected to train mine. I should inculcate in them a love of learning and the arts, that these things may enrich their lives, if all else fails.

I should try to be honest with them, and not clothe the world with false illusions, that they may later suffer from reality. I should try to keep young enough in mind to understand their problems and be a willing listener to them. I want to be close to my children, but not close enough to destroy their personalities, and though there is nothing I desire more than their confidence, I shall teach them to meet circumstances without my counsel. I should practice self-control to foster their respect for it, thus making home peaceful, free from emotional outbursts.

These are the things which I should attempt to give my children, these, and all of the tolerance, wisdom, and understanding every human being needs. I should give them all this, and, doing so, neither subordinate my personality nor dominate theirs.

People

Can We Learn To Be Popular?

Dear Dr. Lawton:

You have been so helpful to many of us in our problems, that I have summoned up the courage to write to you myself. I am fairly attractive (or so they tell me), have quite a few friends, and get invited to gatherings pretty often. But once I find myself in a roomful of people, I seem to get lost in the shuffle, I can't make conversation easily, feel self-conscious when I do speak, and as a result feel pretty miserable. There's nothing I'd like more than to be popular, but if you can't make contact in a group in an easy, informal way, you get neglected, and gradually people prefer not to have you around. I have a lot of interests and get along fine when I talk to one person alone who cares about the same things, but chit-chat—that's where I get tongue-tied. Can one learn how to make the kind of light conversation that makes you a popular guest at a party?

Florence R.

Yes, By Acquiring Social Skills

Dear Florence:

There is no magic way for a boy or girl to pass from neglect to popularity overnight. But a young person can study a list of *don'ts;* he also can try to meet a great many different types of people. Then, if he is the kind who learns from his mistakes, he should gradually eliminate those social blunders that keep people from appreciating him for what he really is.

To get along with people, we must know how to talk to them. But the skillful conversationalist is rare. Shaw once described a person who "lacked the power of conversation, but not speech." Now, what would pass for "conversation" among boys and girls interested in bookish subjects would certainly be put down as "speech" by a group whose favorite topic is sports—and vice versa.

Though I realize I am sticking out my neck, here are a few simple rules to guide conversational traffic. I'm sure, Florence, that once you catch on, you can supply a dozen others.

It is grand to have an all-absorbing interest or hobby. But in ordinary social contacts, don't concentrate on it unless your companion is on his knees pleading for a lecture on that very theme. Otherwise, choose things to talk about and a vocabulary to suit the interests and educational background of the person with whom you are talking. Conversation is something that goes back and forth between two people, like a game of tennis. It isn't handball, with your companion the wall.

We all have strong likes and dislikes, but no matter how logical or interesting we may consider them, there is no call for us to use social gatherings as a place for converting others to our way of thinking. The same rule of reticence applies to any custom we do or do not follow. A young person who doesn't smoke, for example, has a perfect right to abstain. However, when he is offered a cigarette, he should not discuss the tobacco evil in its medical, moral, and parental aspects (I've heard just that!). Instead, he can say, "No, thank you."

Mild disagreements from time to time give tang to conversation. No one wants to be "uh-uhhed" to death. But never argue unless you feel that the subject is of major importance and that by keeping silent you will lose your self-respect. In general, arguing is useless unless you and your opponent have similar backgrounds and unless there is a possibility that his opinions may be influenced by argument.

When your companion is talking, listen without squirming and without interrupting. To most of us, listening is that time interval between our most recent brilliant remark and our next, the very one we now are patiently grooming for its take-off. But listening should be an active, sharing kind of response. Your companion, if he has any sense, won't be flattered if you pose in a kind of open-mouthed trance. You don't want the silence to be deafening!

When you yourself speak, make your remarks short and varied, especially your stories, and omit all the boring details which make an anecdote last forever—unless you are a born storyteller and can prove it. We all know the man who once learned three stories and who intends to keep repeating these three and no others until his end—which everybody hopes will come soon.

Friends are tied to us by affection, not by law. Unlike members of our family they can escape if they don't enjoy our company. That is why we should see them only when we feel fit and in good humor. One of the most important commandments for social success is to stay home: (1) when you are sick; (2) when you are tired. From time to time we all feel as if the end of the world has come for us. But you should confess that feeling only to a very close friend. Someone defined a bore as a person who, when you ask him how he feels, tells you. To bombard ordinary acquaintances with your woes may gain you pity, but not affection.

The need to gossip is strong in all of us. Yet gossip not lest you too be gossipped about, for tale-telling feeds upon itself.

To keep silent about people we know personally, unless we can speak well of them, requires a tremendous amount of self-discipline. Nevertheless, we should hold it as a law, never to reveal anything of an intimate or disagreeable nature until we have proof that it is generally known.

Every pair of human beings talking to each other have some common denominator, are essentially kin, if we only can locate the nature of that kinship. The good conversationalist is a person who has a keen sense of those thoughts and feelings that are shared by all men and women of all ages.

How Can I Make People Like Me?

Dear Dr. Lawton:

I want to be liked by other people—who doesn't? Yet I'm afraid I don't really get along very well with other people. I've studied myself very carefully to see what my faults are, where I fall short, and I've come to the conclusion that it's my frankness. Lots of people say they like a frank person, but in reality they hate one. I don't like hypocrites who always say sugary things to your face but criticize you behind your back. I prefer to do the criticizing in a straightforward way. But it seems the truth hurts. When I try to control my frankness, I find I can't, that I must be myself. Shall I just decide to be one of those solitary people and live alone like a hermit? I know that won't make me happy, either. How can I get people to like me?

Frances M.

Not By Being the Official Truth-Teller

Dear Frances:

Each one of us must decide what kind of person he wants to be. Perhaps we feel that it makes no difference what other people think of us, that social gatherings are trivial, insincere affairs. Well and good. Many worthwhile people have few friends. They live alone and like it.

But if you desire the affection and good-will of people, then you must also realize that you cannot act just as you please.

You say you must be frank, no matter how much it hurts . . . *you*. It is odd that the "truth," as you see it, is usually poison to someone else. Actually, though you may not be aware of it, you are not seeking to tell the truth or to help another person, but to make yourself feel good by pointing out another's faults. Filled with a painful sense of your own weaknesses, you unconsciously act on the theory that as long as you can be a critic—the official truth-teller in your group—you escape criticism yourself. Of course, you protest, "I can't help it. I must be myself."

Every human being is—to himself—the most important person in the world. That's why people label as a bore the villain who talks about himself when you want to talk about yourself. Certainly your adventures, achievements, friends, family, miseries—all are significant beyond compare. Common courtesy, however, forces us to pretend that the other fellow has troubles and joys interesting enough for our ears.

If we want to be liked, we also would be wise to pay the other person the compliment of remembering his name from one meeting to another. This is the first lesson a politician has to learn. It's not a crime to forget a name, or to invent a new one, but it still is true that we all remember what we most desperately want to remember.

If you are studying to be popular, don't act cheated if the person or the evening doesn't live up to your expectations. A thrilling time on a date—with fascinating conversation, a perfect dancing partner, etc. (especially the etc.)—this is the exception. Better start out with moderate hopes. Then, if the evening is a flop, you won't be too disappointed. If it turns out to be one of those five-star occasions, why, that's all to the good.

Social success is built on certain essential skills. Without them, a boy or girl can still be a first-rate friend, citizen, brother, or worker. But he will miss certain pleasures and experiences which are his birthright. At his peril, a young person scorns a knowledge of popular music, movie and radio personalities, sports stars, recent popular books. As important as any scholastic achievement is the ability to dance, play parlor games, and engage in the common sports and recreations of your group. He must know what to answer when someone says "How do you do?" He should be able to introduce two people without stumbling. It is also important to be a good sport; to be able to "take it" and to "dish it out"; to have a "wisecrack" ready when it is called for.

The art of "small talk," for example, is more essential to social success than "big talk." Anyone who can learn to talk about the weather with the proper balance between deep feeling and casualness need not fear any social hurdle.

Small talk really protects each partner to a conversation against his being bombarded by information he doesn't want. It also enables two people to make reconnaissance trips to the unknown territory of each other's personality and interests. After that, they can decide whether they really want to make a return visit. You may be wonderfully kind to dumb animals, or be a deep thinker, a peerless athlete, or a great artist on the piccolo, but let these facts "dawn" on your friend gradually.

In order to feel comfortable in a particular group, you must, to some extent, follow the crowd. If you don't see eye-to-eye with it, don't try to change yourself or the group. Just drop it and select another. Neither you nor your companions are to be praised or blamed because you have different tastes.

Popularity of a lasting sort is a person-to-person affair. It depends on what you are as a human being. Are you able to satisfy the mental and emotional needs of people you meet? The boy or girl who makes a hit *only* with the opposite sex, relying on cute tricks or he-man stuff, will not be really popular long, even with the opposite sex.

It is easier to describe a popular person than to tell how to become one. A brief character sketch may help. John S. is clean and neat, though not a killer-diller in dress. He is far from being a perfect physical specimen; yet he bounces with vitality. And he certainly has plenty of interests and activities.

John knows his faults. He is making slow progress correcting some of them. Others are likely to be with him for a long time. But he accepts himself as he is, and tries for improvement in the direction he has planned. Because he knows how difficult it is to be perfect, he doesn't demand too much of others. Hence he is easy to get along with.

John has an almost inexhaustible curiosity about people and places. He always manages to dig up at least one interesting fact about anybody he meets, and it is hard for anyone to spoil his good time.

John is a magnet because he is real and alive and makes you feel the same way when you are with him. He is himself, not an imitation of someone else. He is not a "Yes-Man" or a whiner. He talks up and against—when the situation calls for it. John is not liked by everyone—but what "self-starter" is? Yet the list of those who *do* like him puts him definitely in the "popular" class.

"It Is Not Wisdom . . ."

Dear Dr. Lawton:

I once spoke to a very successful person who said that many young people do not become well-established in life because they take an interest in the opposite sex at too early an age and this causes them to drift away from their studies. I know many boys and girls who used to be honor students, as I am, but as soon as they got interested in the opposite sex, they did not make high grades again.

As a child, I was sick and physically handicapped and I had no alternative but to take a maximum interest in my studies. But I still believe in devoting nearly all of my time to my school work and I give hardly any attention to social activities. In that way I can marry some day and make my wife happy by being able to support her comfortably. Regardless of how much a couple may love each other, if they do not receive the many good things in life, they never will be happy and gay, and the marriage may end in divorce. What do you think of this?

Vincent de T.

. . . To Be Only Wise" *

Dear Vincent:

It is important to know how to earn a living, but it is equally important to know how to live. Look about, and you will ob-

* This is a quotation from a poem by George Santayana.

serve that the happiness and unhappiness of most men and women comes from their relationships with other people. Very few of us can live alone and like it, though many make the attempt. And since we come in closest contact with our mate and children, unless we can be happy with them, the value of our vocational success is much lessened, to say nothing of our working efficiency.

Now while certain human experiences start and end during a particular age period, others begin almost at birth and last as long as we do. The chief example of the latter is the art of friendship. This is a phase of our educational development we must start as early as possible. It is during childhood that boys and girls can be most natural with each other, for then they are merely "people."

However, when we reach high-school age, many of these "people" have become the "opposite sex." Then it is that we must learn how to keep up with our studies and our friendships, without neglecting either. It is fine to give a satisfactory account of ourselves in the classroom, but it is equally fine to do the same at dates, parties, and dances.

Of course, scholastic and vocational success makes us feel good, but unless we have friends who are proud, we have won the world only to lose it.

Difficult as it may be in some instances, high-school students should divide their time so as to allow for studies, social living, and hobbies (this last to include time for getting acquainted with oneself). If a boy works after school, the problem is even more complex, but careful planning of one's daily program will solve it. For we must all learn how to become a member of the "gang" in good standing. That includes both sexes, which brings us to the main point . . .

Ever since the Garden of Eden, men have tried to find a way of dealing with Eve. There were always some who tried to solve the problem by taking flight. A good example of this at the teen age is the boy who regularly buries himself in a book on "date" night. But in the off-the-record history of science you will find many examples of a curious phenomenon: a pair of blue eyes has been known suddenly to peek out between the steps of a geometry theorem and a lock of hair has emerged from behind footnotes in a history text. The moral of which is simple: Passing a law not to think about girls is easy, but living up to it is another matter.

An important problem of our times is the way economic conditions delay the age at which young people can marry. Most girls, given the choice, would prefer to take a man when he was younger, and struggle with him, instead of remaining single until he had achieved a comfortable financial status.

Every marriage starts off with much glamor, intense emotion, and just plain "hoop-la." But while these factors should continue to play a part ever after, marriage does become in time more and more of a person-to-person relationship, a union of comrades and companions. When marriage fails, it is because one mate (or both) is poor in team-work, cannot accept difficulties, and is generally incapable of making use of those devices necessary to a smooth relationship between people. Suppose we think of our social life, not in the family circle but in the world at large. Our vocational success depends on two things: first, certain mental or physical skills, second, being able to convince others that we possess these skills.

We have only as much ability as our relationships with people permit us to use. Think of a doctor or a football player who could not get the trust and cooperation of others!

Anyone who had few playmates as a child has to fight the tendency later on to withdraw from friendships. The give-and-take involved in these imposes quite a strain, especially when the opposite sex is involved.

A boy may prefer to be alone because he does not like girls, and he may not like girls because he is afraid of them. It is not a theory which dictates his choice of a starvation social diet (that is, without vitamins G-1, G-2, G-3) but fear. Perhaps your successful friend doubted his ability to be interesting and attractive to girls or a "girl," and in order to avoid hearing or noticing an unfavorable reaction, he may have said "work first," postponing social engagements until he had become a "success."

But no subsequent financial or professional success can fully erase the effects of our inability *now* to feel comfortable with people, to get and give pleasure in our relationships with them. You can't live by yourself as a child or young person and then decide one fine morning when you are twenty-eight and a "success" that you are now ready for an active social life, ready to start making some "young thing" happy. A parallel example would be the man who expected to become a skilled craftsman overnight. "Success" in the sense of a satisfactory adjustment to our environment is something that is happening every single day of our lives. We must make good at the present stage of our development if we are to make good at the later ones.

The Gentle Art . . .

Dear Dr. Lawton:

I have an almost incurable habit of saying unkind things without the slightest intention of being unkind. Many people have received a very bad impression of me, when, after just having met them, I suddenly began to prick pins in their ego. Although later on they realize that I was not intentionally being mean, it takes time for the wounds to heal and causes me many uncomfortable moments.

It may be caused partially because I have grown up to be, like most of the youth of today, a know-it-all. However, this habit has reached an acute peak and I need help.

Irene D. V.

... of Making Enemies

Dear Irene:

While all of us want the approval and affection of others, we do not all know how to obtain these. One wrong way for achieving popularity is to use the "scare-'em and make-'em feel cheap" method. The follower of this system no sooner is introduced to someone than he pounces out of his corner leading with a right and then a left to the ego.

When the bell sounds and the hostess guides the killer-diller back to his seconds, he may still hope to land a knockout blow or he may be glad to accept a decision on points. But whether the verbal bout ends in victory or not, there are disagreeable consequences, so that the battler resolves to be a cooing angel with everyone thereafter. Yet the very next day often sees a repetition of the previous encounter, except that this time he thinks he has found a way to escape the unpleasant aftermath.

People who really want to give up a bad habit don't start out with a resolution. Making a complete break is the best way to start, but it is even better if this break is supported by some understanding of why we behave as we do.

It is natural for many boys and girls to feel that they are not as good as their companions and to torture themselves with the thought that they will be unable to make a go of things.

A young person worried about what life may do to him can react to this feeling in different ways. One boy will withdraw from social contacts. He hopes that by so doing he will avoid competition with other young people and escape situations where his equals and superiors may judge him and find him wanting.

As an example of a second type of behavior, take Fred R. The latter, instead of withdrawing from life, attacks people—principally with words. He thinks that if others can be led to appear weak and silly, he thereby has proved his own strength. Mustering whatever force he has, Fred tries to make other people feel as small, confused, unhappy, as he does.

While a normal boy or girl uses force only when he must protect his person and his self-respect, Fred launches an onslaught whenever his feeling of importance has run low. Fred believes that this is the way to gain the admiration of others and pep himself up, and he consoles himself with the thought, "If I can't make them like me, I can make them afraid of me!"

A good example of attacking behavior prompted by fear is the remark of Ruth S. "I hope you don't mind my frankness, but I simply must tell you how terrible you look in that get-up! Ransacking grandmother's trunk again?" If you show annoyance, Ruth defends herself with: "I can't help it if the truth hurts."

Of course, Ruth is not deliberately trying to be cruel, but she herself is so afraid of being hurt that when she is out in a group, she starts out with a critical remark lest her companions beat her to the first punch. Heaven forbid that she behave like an ordinary member of the gang instead of the chief critic and executioner, for then, people might think her a colorless nobody. Some Ruths like to play a childish game of hide and seek: "I'll conceal my true nature and pretend to be sarcastic and hard-boiled, but you must see through my disguise and discover how fine I really am!"

Anyone who feels within himself a genuine sense of power will not use his authority to show how important he is or to browbeat an opponent who cannot fight back on equal terms.

Find a man at the top who is sure he belongs there, and nearly always you will also discover someone who is simple, willing to listen to the troubles of others, and eager to help them. The individual who really believes in his own strength is glad to help create strength in others. Such a man or woman would never do anything that might result in a fellow human being losing faith in himself. Perhaps you will accept such a man as an instance of how to practice, as well as to preach, democracy.

Have you ever noticed that some of the most learned men of our time, the John Deweys, the Albert Einsteins, are very humble about what they know? That is because it takes a lifetime of study for us to realize how much there is to learn and how little one human being can acquire in his brief span of years. Perhaps the "know-it-all" attitude you refer to can be explained by the fact that it is found most often in young people who, however great their native gifts of intelligence, can hardly lay claim to encyclopedic knowledge and experience. The person who has become accustomed to the idea that he possesses real importance neither hides this fact nor tries to demonstrate it constantly.

How can our Ruths and Freds be helped? They must try to find out how they were once badly hurt and what secrets about themselves they are trying to hide the most. Next, they should attempt to reduce liabilities of personality and increase assets. Perhaps this will enable them to feel more at ease in their regular social group. If not, they might change groups until they have found one which does not demand more of them than they can actually give.

The town bully is a good illustration of someone working overtime in the attempt to convince himself that he is equal to the demands of life. Our tough friend can be cured, but first we must prove to him that he won't topple over as soon as he stops shouting and trying to bull-doze his fellow-citizens. He has to learn that a person's true strength and integrity is something inside of him. Only when the bully is sure that he can develop this kind of power will he dare give up the role of tough and dangerous man.

Anger: Its Uses—

Dear Dr. Lawton:

What causes a person to lose his temper? It seems that I have a very hard time controlling my temper when something goes wrong. I have been advised to count ten, or even more, but doing that does not seem to help me. I would like to improve myself and change. Will you please help me?

James K.

—and Abuses

Dear James:

For a human being never to know anger in some form is hardly possible and certainly not desirable. There are times when anger is necessary. The fact that a person is intelligent, liberal, and tolerant does not mean that he is a wishy-washy goody-goody, lacking sufficient opinions and energy to utter an unmistakable "No" or "Yes" when these are called for. Modern civilization would have been impossible unless our ideals were fortified by "righteous indignation." Every step upward from savagery has been due not only to the vision which some men have had of a better way of living or doing things but also to their fierce determination that this vision become a reality. Think of the men who have fought to conquer nature and eradicate disease, of such a fighter as Zola, whose angry, inflexible will it was that justice and truth prevail.

Some writers on popularity stress "amiability" and "compromise." These qualities are often very valuable and effective. But suppose our rights and self-respect are threatened? What then? A person of character has convictions, the courage to fight for them and take the consequences. The individual who is over-tactful, always retreating when the going gets rough, may or may not know his rights. But certainly he dare not exert himself in their behalf, because he is unsure of himself and of his ability to back up the stand he knows he should take. Moreover, he fears he will incur even more disapproval or punishment if he talks up. Such a person, instead of being outspoken in his anger and having it done and over with, will torture himself for years with silent protests and unworkable plans for setting things rights. Those who suffer from chronic cordiality must learn how to get angry, but before this they must discover why they are unsure of themselves.

Indignation, then, is sometimes desirable. But the same cannot be said of the common garden varieties of anger: rage and temper. Now, every emotion can be expressed in childish or adult forms. Rage is the first language infants acquire for indicating displeasure. Later on in childhood, rage is used as a way of attracting attention or as a blackmailing device. "Better give me what I want right now or else I'll make you sorry you didn't!" As we grow up, we learn that we cannot always get what we want through tantrums. They may work with members of the family who cannot escape or exile us. The outside world, however, does not have to put up with our nonsense and leaves us strictly alone after one taste of it. Thus we are forced to master another language, at least for strangers: we reason and persuade; we ask for things and work for them; we state our case with vigor.

There are some people who think a display of temper is a sign of power. This "temper-addict" enjoys whipping himself into a rage and noting the effect of this on the household. He is proud of the flashing eyes, the crimson (or deadly pale) cheeks, the mighty torrent of words, some quite fancy. When it is over, he feels as if he had had a workout on the football field, which is where it should have occurred in the first place. We all need ways of letting off steam, but we should use objects for this, not people.

Temper is really a weakness, a signal of defeat, and that is why it cannot be cured by displaying more temper or by counting. Our "addict" is seeking to make up for some satisfaction unattainable elsewhere. Things fared poorly for him at school or at the party and he therefore fusses at the table because he is served last. He cannot get what he wants or he doesn't want what he can get. Caught in a jam where he is unable to accept a situation or change it, he resorts to making faces accompanied by much sound and fury—all signifying nothing. The temperish individual seldom knows what he is actually angry about. This he proves by making a fuss of the same type and amount on almost a daily schedule.

The chief causes of chronic ill temper are fears, the sources of which we do not know, as well as a strong feeling that we have not received the approval and affection which is our due. Ill-health, insufficient rest, inadequate recreational outlets, over-excitement, worry about unemployment, war, family difficulties—all may be contributing factors. Study of a given individual is necessary if we are to learn how *he* got that way or how *he* can be helped. But this is clear: it is just as important to educate our emotions as our minds. Emotional education does not mean destroying anger or giving it free rein. Anger is an essential part of our lives. But it is most useful when it is most impersonal, that is, when its energy is harnessed to ideals and pursuits likely to prove beneficial to the individual and society.

The Feeling of "Being Different"

Dear Dr. Lawton:

When I was ten months old, I had an attack of infantile paralysis which left my right hand practically useless. My father took me to numerous doctors for treatment, but their answer was "the case cannot be remedied." My father then made up his own mind to cure it himself. He started giving me massages every day for two years, until I can use it to a great extent.

But from the time I entered grade school to the time I entered high school the disease left its mark. My arm is practically limp and is skinny. People notice my condition, and any time I walk down the hall they stare at me. My problem is this: How can I stop feeling miserable when people stare at me?

Ralph C.

and How It Can Be Met

Dear Ralph:

It is hard to stifle a certain resentment and sense of injustice when you know someone is staring at you merely because you possess some marked physical characteristic. Yet it is a universal human reaction for us to notice what differs in one way or another from the average. Fashion stylists rack their brains in order to create something which will make each member of the fair sex stand out from all her sisters. Little children find it hard to conceal their surprise: "Mama, that man has no hair *at all* on his head!" By the time we are grownups, we know how to take in everything from the corner of our eye. But at the in-between stage, some of us have not yet become sufficiently expert to peer without being caught in the act.

Yet we all stare. John, for example, who has some defect, may object now to anyone's prolonged glance, but a moment later John will be gazing intently at Bill because the latter in his own way differs from most people. Occasionally, one who stares may wish to convey sympathy and a desire to be helpful, not realizing that most persons with a disability want to be treated as if the disability did not exist.

Whenever anything happens which reduces our sense of importance to ourselves or to others, we must try to recapture it in other ways. If we can do this, staring will lose its sting.

Some people convert their very defects into assets. Demosthenes, once a stutterer, became a great orator. In our own day, there is Alec Templeton, the blind pianist, whose radio program is very popular. Perhaps you may have heard there was even once in professional baseball a one-armed outfielder.

A second method of dealing with a defect is to divert attention from it by offering something else more striking and admirable. Steve, a young athlete, permanently injured one of his legs and had to quit the team. But since he could also write, he eventually became sports editor of his high-school paper. Steve still dances, swims, and plays basketball—all after a fashion. But inasmuch as he is the first to smile at his own awkwardness, friends also treat his disability casually.

An illness left Mae with a very noticeable limp, but she developed her voice until its lovely quality became a magnet, drawing people to her.

Bert suffered a great deal from the remarks passed about his prominent ears. One day a schoolmate, continuing the tradition of teasing, told Bert that his protruding ears were a sign of musical ability, that is, designed to "catch sound." Bert, however, took this comment in earnest and went to a singing coach. Through one of those lucky coincidences, Bert found he had vocal ability. He subsequently became a professional radio singer.

Many boys and girls feel they are unlike other young people: that they are too tall or short, too stout or thin; that they don't have as many friends, as good a complexion, as much money or fun as others do. But no departure from the normal is a real obstacle unless the person in whom it has occurred considers it as such. Look at Helen Keller, at Steinmetz—extraordinary persons, of course. Yet an ordinary man can be successful in an ordinary way.

A person with a physical defect or lack might list in parallel columns those activities made impossible by his handicap and those still open to him despite it. Few disabilities bar an individual from the basic opportunities and pleasures of life. They don't keep him from making others happy, and many a so-called handicapped person has become a tower of strength to those physically normal. Frank N., for example, is a blind young psychologist who is planning to work with persons of normal vision. Everyone who knows Frank will wager that blindness cannot stop him from becoming very necessary to countless people.

G. K. Chesterton once wrote that there was nothing else you could say about a poor man except that he had no money. In the same way, a "skinny arm" is merely that and no more. All of us have met an individual with a physical characteristic on which our attention was riveted at first, but which we forgot about when we began to know him better. It is not the *outside* of a person that is important, but what he *means* to his family, his friends, and to society at large. The biographers of President Roosevelt all stress his contribution to the national life of his day and treat his infantile paralysis as only an incidental factor.

The true handicap is not the "skinny arm" but the feeling that it diminishes our value as a person and our chances of success in private life or in business.

We must meet real problems in a real world, whoever and whatever we are. It is tempting to pretend, to bury ourselves in soft daydreams, to drench ourselves in pity—either our own or another's. Yet a person with a disability should not use it as an excuse to withdraw from the world and from the struggle for approval and affection. We all at some time or other suffer a hurt or disappointment that makes us feel defeated and abandoned. Though this be a period of extreme wretchedness, it may also serve a useful purpose by forcing us to plumb our own possibilities and to realize how much human beings need each other. Everyone has within him a core of strength, an inner "something" which refuses to be downed by failure or misfortune. Suffering is worthwhile if it teaches us how to find and draw upon the deepest resources of our nature.

Ten Commandments for High-School Students

"If high-school students could describe, frankly and without fear of censor, the sort of behavior they expect of each other and of themselves, what ten commandments would they set down for their generation to follow?" That was the question posed to the readers of *Scholastic* in the form of a contest. High-school students in all parts of the country looked at their classmates and looked into an honest mirror, and then sat down to compile their list of Ten Commandments which would serve as guides for behavior in the particular situations that arise in school, on dates, at the prom, at the game, and around the family dinner table.

Hundreds of replies were received and analyzed, and a composite list was made of those Ten Behavior Commandments which were mentioned by the greatest number of students. Courtesy and thoughtfulness were the most popular of the virtues: students mentioned these two items twice as many times as they mentioned any of the others.

Composite List
(Items arranged in order of descending frequency)

1. Be polite and courteous.
2. Be thoughtful of others.
3. Be a good sport.
4. Don't be boisterous or conspicuous.
5. Be neat and clean.
6. Respect your superiors.
7. Be cheerful and friendly.
8. Always be yourself (that is, be genuine).
9. Don't show off.
10. Dress suitably to the occasion.
11. Don't criticize people.
12. Live up to the moral code.
13. Do all things the best you can.
14. Be careful of your language (that is, slang, profanity, etc.).
15. Be truthful.

The three prize-winning lists, and several other outstanding sets of Ten Behavior Commandments submitted to the contest are printed below. They came from students in the following schools:

>Madrid Central School, Madrid, New York
>Mansfield Senior High School, Mansfield, Ohio
>Marianna High School, Marianna, Florida
>West High School, Minneapolis, Minnesota
>Westbury High School, Westbury, New York

A Philosopher's List

1. Have reverence and respect for things and people deserving of them.
2. Learn to take suffering philosophically, remembering that no one really lives unless he suffers.
3. Keep your voice soft and take a deep breath when you are disturbed by anything.
4. Be sincere.
5. Recognize your faults and try to correct them.
6. Ask for and receive criticism with eagerness and gratitude.
7. Look for and expect only good things from people, remembering "the bad are half good and the good are half bad."
8. Sing often. "It's good for the soul."
9. Keep your promises or don't make them.
10. When you do a thing, do it because you want to, but if you are forced to do it, try to like it and you probably will.
11. If you are self-conscious or egotistical, it is because you think of yourself too much, therefore, get interested in other people.
12. Have your own code of morals and your own law of life and, if you listen to your conscience at all, they'll be all right, and serve you in every crisis.

An All-Purpose List

1. Respect your elders. Stand up. Stand back.
2. Don't talk so much. But don't be a sourpuss either.
3. Don't be a giggler.
4. Listen well.
5. You needn't be a gossip.

HOW TO BE HAPPY THOUGH YOUNG

6. Don't push.
7. You don't have to be a teacher's pet, but don't pick fights with her.
8. A little less lipstick. You have plenty of time.
9. When someone speaks to you give an answer that makes sense.
10. Don't put on airs. You'll get plenty of attention but not exactly the kind you want.

A Humorist's List

1. Remember: keep holy Monday through Friday.
2. Thou shall "park" thy gum before nine o'clock.
3. Honor thy teachers and thy principal.
4. If thou art a gentleman—or a lady—act as such.
5. Thou shall leave thy neighbor's lunch alone, **lest he go** hungry.
6. If thy neighbor sneezes, thou shall not laugh.
7. Thou shall not kill time.
8. Thou shall not be rocked in the "cradle" roll.
9. Thou shall not covet thy neighbor's papers.
10. Thou shall not covet thy neighbor's son—or daughter.

A Girl's List

1. Don't try to tell your parents how to rear the younger children. They reared you, didn't they?
2. Boys, please see to it that your date gets home at the time set beforehand.
3. Don't use the classroom or cafeteria as a powder room.
4. Don't always be patting yourself on the back.

5. Don't criticize other people just because you think it looks cute. It doesn't.
6. Boys, when you go out with a girl, don't see just how much damage you can do to her make-up and hair. And vice-versa.
7. Keep your off-color jokes at home, or somewhere besides at school.
8. Don't "hog" the conversation.
9. Don't keep interrupting or drawing attention to yourself in any way, when someone is speaking.
10. Don't chew gum in church and such public places if you can't chew it quietly.

A Boy's List

1. A good appearance makes a good impression.
2. An empty barrel makes the most noise—be quiet in such places as study halls, where your "loud mouth" is a nuisance.
3. When walking three abreast, break ranks when passing someone.
4. Don't litter your surroundings with paper wherever you go (—at camp, study halls, movies, football games. It lends bad taste to others' opinions of you and, of course, it is not sanitary).
5. Don't keep talking about what Aunt Minnie did this morning, what you think is wrong with Martha's lipstick, etc.; give a person a chance to speak on matters of his own.
6. "Don't say anything you wouldn't want your mother or best girl (or boy) friend to hear" is rather putting these two individuals "on the spot." You know what to do and say and what not to do and say. Act and speak accordingly.

7. We have a Mother's Day and a Father's Day. Why not a Teacher's Day—and make it every day.
8. Go to Sunday School, church, school, dates, and meetings on time. Many friendships have been ruined because of tardiness.
9. Driving an automobile is all right—but have consideration for the other fellow. Drive safely or not at all.
10. Make someone happy *today*.

The Opposite Sex

"Haven't We Met Before?"

Dear Dr. Lawton:

I was in the post office writing a card when a fellow walks over and pulls the old line: "You look very familiar. Haven't we met before?" I gave him a freezing look and stopped that mighty fast. But my friends tell me when I do that that I'm a prude. They say there's an art to saying "No" which every girl should learn, and that if you say "No" in the wrong way you might lose lots of nice fellows. I wonder? This one seemed awfully cute: blue eyes, tall, refined voice. Did I do the right thing?

Lucille L.

"Sir: How Dare You!"

Dear Lucille:

You seem to be sorry that you gave him such a brush-off. However, if that boy really wants to meet you, he'll manage it somehow. You know the saying, "Love will find a way." He could always sell you a raffle ticket even if he had to print it himself! I'm for introductions unless you're in the same class in school; then it's automatic. But how to be introduced is a problem when you don't have a mutual acquaintance.

Most girls are as eager for new contacts and as full of fun as boys are. At the high-school age, few want to go steady. Still, they don't want to do anything that would kill their chances of something serious ultimately developing.

Meeting people is always a gamble. Sometimes through an introduction you get to know a person who is swell, and you have good times together. And sometimes he turns out to be a dud. The same thing happens in the case of a "spontaneous friendship." It would be fine if young people always could meet naturally, at skating, tennis, and other games and sports that are popular with both sexes.

But suppose you are on a train or bus and see somebody who looks interesting. That is when you must know how to decide quickly if a person probably has the same interests and values as you have and if he is likely to repay further study. However, please don't think I am claiming any educational value for the introductionless date. But remember this: Girls don't have as many opportunities to meet the opposite sex as a boy does. Hence, every self-sponsored acquaintance she meets who turns out well is that much to the good.

How good it would be if when a boy wanted to meet a girl he would approach her in a straightforward way and say: "My name is so and so, what's yours?" or "I would like to know you, that is, if you don't mind." Every girl wants to be treated like a lady.

Of course, she is happy to know a boy is aware of her existence and approves of it, but she would rather have this enthusiasm kept a private matter. No yoo-hoo's and calls of the wild! A fellow should give the girl a chance either to accept or reject his self-introduction. If a girl talks to him, that merely means he has been put on probation, not that she is overwhelmed by his charms. But when she says "No" a half dozen times, he should take the hint and gracefully scram.

Every girl should learn how to deal out a rejection in a smiling "Not today, thank you" sort of way. Then it will be clear that she isn't a baby, a prude, or a sourpuss. Most girls have no idea of how some boys suffer as they are about to launch their sales campaign. Don't be misled by the "Hi, babe" approach. We all know the boy who acts dead as the girl passes by, but who gets brave and noisy when she is a block away, especially if he has his gang with him. He's a timid lad. It's because he is unsure of himself that he has to hunt in a pack or do long-distance yodelling.

Let me emphasize, however, that no girl should consider a "spontaneous friendship" in any situation which contains a possible threat to her safety and reputation. This means she must not enter the car of anyone she doesn't know, and she must not talk to a stranger in an out-of-the-way neighborhood.

And when you happen to make a new acquaintance—say at the beach or at the skating rink—it would be a good thing to find out something about your new friend and any people you both might know. Bring him up to the house and let the family meet him. Then you ought to make your first date a double one; but if it is single, arrange to have it at a time and place where you will feel secure. If you start him off right, you will keep him from getting ideas.

"Steady Company"

Dear Dr. Lawton:
A friend of mine in high school has been going steady with a boy for some time. She teases me because I do not like anyone special and no boy has ever become "that way" about me. This makes me feel I'm missing something or am different. Do you think girls going to high school should have regular "boy

friends" or boys have "girl friends"—I mean like going steady or keeping company with them?

Marjorie C.

Recommended Only for Mature Boys and Girls

Dear Marjorie:
There is only one way of deciding whether any particular experience of a given young person is desirable or not. It is simply to ask, "Will this help or hurt his chances of getting the most out of his life as a grownup?"

And so it is here. No definite age can be given for the time when one is ready to pass from the stage where he has many good friends of both sexes to the stage where he begins to form very intense and exclusive emotional attachments with some one individual of the opposite sex based on the understanding, spoken or not, that a lifelong partnership may follow.

It all depends on how near the young person is to attaining what *for him* is full mental and physical development, so that any important decision he makes represents not a passing whim but what he is likely to want as an adult. Such maturity, as a general rule, is reached by girls several years earlier than by boys, and hence girls begin forming serious attachments sooner and with more justification.

Jessie reached maturity earlier than most girls her age. Though she began to be friendly with boys when still very young, her interest in meeting people is limited and she has simple tastes and ambitions. Jessie has a very definite idea of the type of young man she prefers, especially where marriage is concerned. Since she knows herself pretty well, her views are not likely to change. Should she indeed marry the "boy friend" of high-school days, she is probably making a choice which will continue to be acceptable to her in later years.

Carl, however, has a complex personality, many needs, and conflicting tendencies. He also has a tremendous curiosity about the world and people. He is very ambitious but most uncertain about his future work. Carl therefore requires much experience, social, educational, and vocational, in order to iron out some of his conflicts and give his attitudes and plans a fair degree of permanence. Of course, all of us, young and old, make mistakes of judgment. But we are likely to make more if we try to reach serious decisions when our likes and dislikes of all kinds are still changing rapidly and when we as yet do not know just what we want of life, of people, or of ourselves. A boy like Carl frequently wants to go steady in his high-school days and often does, perhaps just because he needs to cling to something certain, but it is very unlikely that his present choices will be final ones.

True enough, the loss of the "boy friend" or "girl friend" of high-school days is regarded by few grownups as a major tragedy, whereas they often look back at it as having been one of their most valuable educational experiences. But it does involve a good deal of wear and tear on the emotions. To a young person of sensitive and deep feeling "calling things off" can be an extremely painful experience and may leave him with lifelong scars.

Romance may seem to be a very private matter affecting the feelings of two young people alone, and entirely independent of time and space. In reality, however, it often is largely dependent on social-economic conditions. Today most young people are faced by a high standard of living with great difficulty in achieving it, and hence there is generally a long delay before the romantic attachments of teen days can culminate in marriage. It is not easy to choose between a long engagement, with all its uncertainty and restlessness, and a complete break. Apart from exceptional instances, therefore, boys and girls (especially the former) make better use of their school days by enjoying many warm and comradely friendships with members of both sexes. To go steady may deny a high-school student a good deal of fun which comes from going out with his own sex or with a mixed group; it may mean a delay in one's career and enmesh one in responsibilities for which one is inadequately prepared.

Life, however, doesn't always fit into a neat little formula. Some young people, though they realize it is opposed to their own best interests, always insist on converting a perfectly satisfactory friendship into a most unsatisfactory "until-the-day-we-die" romance. Just why such a boy or girl should be led by some inner need to do this is a complex matter far beyond the scope of the answer to this particular question.

More of "Going Steady"

Dear Dr. Lawton:

I am seventeen and a junior in high school. What I want to know is whether it is wrong for a fellow my age to get serious about girls. My father and older brother lecture me all the time about it and say I have no right to be "in love." The whole love business, they claim, is the bunk anyway and only interferes with a man's life, but if I insist on falling for that sentimental stuff, I should at least wait ten or fifteen years. They tell me I should be thinking about how to earn a living instead of moping around the house and thinking about dates and girls.

Edward S. M.

Jobs VERSUS Girls or Jobs AND Girls

Dear Edward:

Your letter offers an opportunity to resume the discussion raised in "Steady Company."

Concerning the particular points you raise, it is important to realize that the chief task of a man is to work and his main joys come from successes in the field of practical accomplishment. It is a rare individual who can be happy unless he feels that society recognizes the value of what he is doing. One of the most painful emotional experiences is a man's realization that he is an economic failure, for it destroys his self-respect, disorganizes his personality, and ruins his sense of security in the world. Such an individual is going to find it difficult to be a satisfactory husband or father. Even if he is successful in his relationships with the opposite sex, this rarely compensates him for vocational failure.

But it is also true that young people develop "crushes," fall in and out of love, and, to some adults, seem to be wasting valuable time in thinking about each other and in going out together. However, this time is not really wasted. For not all of our education is acquired in school. The latter may equip us with academic skills and a store of facts. But a much more important type of education is social and emotional and is learned after school hours. We also learn from everyday living. We all have to serve an apprenticeship in friendship and love, just as we do in business and in the professions. So the love affairs of high-school days, whatever their drawbacks, may really serve a necessary purpose in our emotional growth.

Love, like the desire for money, attention, fame, power, and knowledge, is a powerful driving force in human life. But neither love nor any of the other forces are good or bad in themselves. They are good if used to make people more at peace with themselves, more courageous, more self-reliant, more useful to those about them. They are bad if they do the reverse. Those who deny that love is one of the great experiences of men and women are mistaken. But just as mistaken are those who think it is the *only* important experience in life. Many other experiences can be as deeply satisfying and exciting: a devoted friendship, success in a business deal, in making a scientific discovery, or in artistic creation.

In the earlier discussion, there was a reference to those young people who have a desperate need to be always in love. I did not go into it there, but I should like to offer an explanation now.

We all want to feel that we are necessary to someone and have a certain importance in the scheme of things. This is one reason why most of us seek to love and be loved in return. But we should be able to exercise some judgment and discrimination in our choices. And we should not behave as if being in love were a life-and-death matter to us.

However, the individual who doesn't feel sure of himself, who is lonely and bewildered, who sometimes finds "just living" a task almost beyond his powers, clings to love like a drowning man. He is not interested in making some particular girl happy but in what *she* can do to bolster him up. His affection is entirely selfish. Constant thinking about the current "only one" or association with her enables him to postpone coming to grips with his real problems, besides offering a pleasureable escape from the emptiness and pain which daily existence would bring if he faced it alone.

That is why some people go from one affair to another without rhyme or reason. Suppose a young person thought *only* about school work, a career, making money, or *only* about having a good time. We would say, "X lacks some emotional vitamin like self-confidence, affection, faith in people, and that is why he limits himself to a single aspect of life." In the same way a boy (or girl) for whom nothing else exists but the opposite sex is usually dissatisfied with life in general and will end up by being even more dissatisfied.

If we have received the proper kind of education in living, we have learned how to control and direct our feelings and experiences so that they help us in life rather than make us suffer; we have learned what we need out of life in order for us to be happy, how to get it—if we can—through methods which are approved by the more enlightened members of society, and how to accept disappointment, if we must.

We all have many sides to our personalities, and if we are to lead happy, normal lives, we cannot let any one impulse grow overstrong at the expense of all the others. Every one of us from time to time faces a situation where we should say "No" to a particular trait or activity of ours, no matter how much pleasure it may yield, because it has become a stumbling block in the path of something else that is far more important to us. Unless we are capable of making this decision without flinching or subsequent bitterness we never really grow up; we remain just children emotionally all our lives.

The Wolf Who Goes Steady

Dear Dr. Lawton:

Women are my greatest trouble. Usually, when I find a girl I like, she doesn't like me. But recently I met Joan. We liked each other right away. I thought Joan was my One and Only. Then, as soon as we began to "go steady," I suddenly noticed girls I never noticed before.

Once I saw an old flame. I asked her for a dance—while Joan was out, of course. Joan came in and caught me. So, just for spite, she danced with an old flame of hers. This happens all the time. We argue, make up, and I don't dare look at another girl—at least for a few days. I don't like the idea of "going steady" at seventeen. I guess I'm just a "wolf" at heart.

Max T.

That's Every Man's Dream of Himself!

Dear Max:

So you think you're a "wolf." It is much more likely that you are a sheep in wolf's clothing. Actually, Max, I bet you're just an average boy who finds he doesn't want to settle down to one girl yet. Instead of accepting the fact that this is perfectly natural, you make yourself out to be a "wolf" because that sounds dramatic and dangerous.

A well-adjusted boy of seventeen is ready for comradely and even romantic friendships with girls. His love may be *tremendous* and *beautiful*. But it is seldom *permanent*. He has much to learn about women and his own tastes. That's why it's hard for him to keep his attention focused on any particular girl.

As you grow up, you'll want a job offering a living wage and personal satisfaction. You'll also want the lasting love and companionship of a woman. But at this stage wanting to "go steady" is a sign of immaturity.

There are other signs. The boy who avoids girls altogether is equally immature. So is the one who always makes fun of them *except* in their presence. Then, he becomes lost and tongue-tied.

There is the lad who whistles and runs. He, too, is really afraid of girls. He starts whistling only when the object of his musical (?) attentions can't hear him. The whistler just puts on an act for the other members of the so-called wolf-pack in front of the Centerville Pharmacy.

There is the boy who constantly dreams of girls. Another type of "socially undeveloped" boy limits his relations with girls solely to petting sessions. Or he goes from one love affair to another. There is the boy who is popular only with girls. A really "regular fellow" gets along equally well with both sexes. He doesn't rely on his looks or charm. He depends upon loyalty, consideration, and the ability to work as a member of a team to get him places.

Among boys of your age, there are more examples of immaturity than maturity. At seventeen, it's hard to strike exactly the right balance in your concern for girls. You have seized upon the symbol of "going steady" before you are ready for the reality—"the ability to offer and receive a permanent love." To many young people "going steady" seems *the thing* to do at a certain age.

You want a girl to like you. But when she does, you can't take it. You dislike being dropped, but can't see why a girl should object when you do the neglecting. You both approve and disapprove of "going steady." You are uncertain what you want. At the same time, you are hungry for a dependable source of affection and approval. So you are willing to promise permanent loyalty even though you don't know what the words mean. It's as if you were afraid of being jobless, and agreed always to work for one firm if they agreed never to fire you.

When you are impressed on Tuesday with Margie's brown eyes, you might try to recall that on Monday it was Jane's merry laugh or Sally's auburn hair that "got" you. But at the same time, you should realize that your fickleness is not wrong or surprising. You're just not ready for the initiation into the circle of those who "go steady."

Both boys and girls like to shop around and enjoy the current styles in dates. As they know themselves better, they learn to go easy on their enthusiasms. They begin to realize that the big question, "Is this the *real thing*?" can't be answered right off the bat.

Only a Passing Fancy

Dear Dr. Lawton:

What do you think of girls fourteen or fifteen years old who fall in love, or fancy they do, with men from twenty-five to thirty-five years of age? I'll be frank to say I'm talking about myself. I am all gone over a man who is thirty years old. Of course, I'm careful to see that this older male I'm unduly interested in never suspects my feeling for him. Now, I know well enough that it is only a passing fancy, not the real thing. This has happened to me before. And in the past, given a little time, it wore off. It's not that I can't get interested in boys my own age. In fact, I enjoy them more. Knowing all this, however, doesn't seem to prevent me from falling hard for the aforementioned older type of male. I know it's foolish. Can you help me get rid of such silly emotions?

Jo P.

But I've Fallen Hard and Heavy

Dear Jo:

I once knew a wise old man who used to say: "Human beings are funny. When they are young, they don't want to be young, and when they are old, they don't want to be old."

THE OPPOSITE SEX

For both boys and girls, crushes on older people are part of the growing-up process. As infants, our chief interest is ourselves. Then we develop a love for our parents. Later, we begin forming friendships with those of our own sex and ignore completely the opposite one.

Sometime around ten, we start showing marked preference for those older persons of the opposite sex in our family. As a rule, boys get along better with their mothers, girls with their fathers. The next step is for our affection to spread out to relatives, friends of the family, teachers, movie stars.

Such older folks are a sort of bridge to our final goal: falling in love with members of the opposite sex who are near our own age, one of whom we marry.

Not all persons get across that bridge, and some marry persons much older than they. While the chances are against such December-May marriages turning out successfully, some do surprisingly well.

There's another thing to think about. All girls and boys have moments when they wonder about their ability to interest the opposite sex.

Perhaps no one ever has paid us any attention, or maybe we have such a craving for affection that we can never get enough to feel sure of ourselves. It often happens that a girl may find herself attractive to many men, but not to those she herself thinks most worth while, and this also may undermine her self-confidence.

This girl may look at an older man and feel challenged. The possibility that with her own tiny hatchet she might chop down his self-confidence and isolation gives her a thrill. Suppose he now shows this girl some attention. She'll be flattered and reassured, won't she?

Even if a girl is not personally interested in such a man, she is interested in his good opinion, and she'll hate to let that go. She feels that having an older friend makes her superior to other young girls who are still "babies." That's why she may make herself believe she really likes him.

Not being understood is a problem for many youngsters. Girls who go in for crushes on older men are generally unhappy in their daily routine of family life, especially in relation to their fathers.

A girl may, therefore, welcome the consolation offered by an older man, and make of him an ideal creature, though he has nothing that a young beau won't have in time. A shy girl sometimes turns to an older man because he knows how to make conversation and draw her out. Such a girl often mistakes sympathy for love.

Whatever the reason, she concentrates on older men *just because* she knows she will be unsuccessful. Without being aware of it, she seeks relationships that can never develop into anything, that must remain hopeless and unreal, enjoying melodramatic daydreams in which she suffers and is spurned.

In the capacity to feel deeply and to handle social relationships, girls grow up faster than boys. That's why you and your girl friends grow dissatisfied with boys your own age. An older man treats you with a courtesy you seldom receive from boys your own age. But this difference is the result of acquired skill in manners. The tribute of a young fellow, crude as it is, may be more genuine.

Women of all ages are attracted to men who are worldly and successful, men who are strong but gentle, aggressive yet respectful. While a woman expects to be treated as an equal by her man, at life's critical moments she wants to lean on him, his strength, and his judgment. She likes to feel he can be her leader and teacher.

Most girls see the possibilities for the development of these qualities in their young beaus, and that is enough for the time being. But there is the girl who simply can't wait to grow up. By having an older friend who has suffered much and really "lived life" she feels she has herself become an adult magically, as if she had handed him a glass and said, "Pour me some experience." But you can't acquire overnight the knowledge and judgment which only years of living can bring.

Being young may be lots of trouble, but then it has advantages. Youth can change its mind. Would you want to be tied down to this thirty-year-old forever, and never have another beau? Of course not! Well, let that be consolation for your not getting him. She who loves and turns away, lives to love another day, and another fellow.

There is nothing wrong with you, Jo, that the years won't cure. And in the meantime, I'm sure you are having a grand time.

From "Brother" to Boy Friend

Dear Dr. Lawton:

I wonder if there is anything wrong with me. I know several girls, but the same thing happens whenever I spend an evening with any of them. Sooner or later they'll say: "What I like about you, Bill, is that I can talk to you about so many different things. I can confide in you. Why, you're like a brother to me." Who wants a girl to treat you like a brother instead of a boyfriend? They go out with other boys and call me to the house only when they have a problem or something to discuss. When I'm alone with a girl I like how can I get her to give me the green light that means "Come on, big boy, let's hold hands!" How in the world can a fellow get to hold hands with a girl?

Bill

Not From Boy Friend to Brother!

Dear Bill:

I took the liberty of putting your question to a group of high-school girls, and one of them said: "Well, the trouble with Bill is that he doesn't think of himself as a dominant male. He shouldn't wait for the girl to ask him to her home. He should beat her to it and ask her out himself. After that, he shouldn't give her any chance at all to talk about herself or her difficulties with other boys, but he should center the conversation on different topics, preferably on himself.

"As for holding hands, tell Bill he must not ask permission—just let him get ready, set, and go. All he has to do is to stretch out, take her hand, and hang on."

That isn't a bad suggestion except that there is more to your problem than meets the eye. While you don't like what is happening to you, you are the one responsible for the way the girls treat you. You are in conflict with yourself about the kind of person you want to be. True, you may want to act the boy friend, but this brings with it certain risks. Without being aware of it, you therefore steer events so that you become the brother, a safer relationship, though also unsatisfactory.

Somewhere in the process of growing up you have gotten the idea that you can't be as successful with girls as other boys. In order to escape failure if you try to compete on the boy friend plane, you present yourself as the sympathetic listener, a role whose requirements you find it easier to fill.

Boys like you generally cannot dance, are poor at sports or uninterested in them, find it difficult to talk to strangers and introduce people to each other. In general, your type dreads failure in social situations. The chances are that you would not be able to get up and talk in front of a class or other group. Am I right?

The boy who has learned to share the interests and activities of young people and who can meet social situations with confidence has developed a certain initiative which helps him with the opposite sex. Girls are also people, and being successful with them is only one illustration of a young man's general social success.

Assuming you do want to shine in a romantic light, you must set the stage and pick out a time and place which will make this possible. If you just drop around occasionally, sit in the parlor, and ramble on, but never take your girl anywhere, she will look upon you as part of the household equipment or perhaps one of the domestic pets.

Your first aim should be to develop your initiative in human relations apart from the opposite sex, whether in the plural or singular. You must practice talking to a group. You should go out for sports, learn how to dance, take part in the games that young people play. You should work up a good vocabulary of chit-chat: the weather, the latest movie or swing record. We all need to become skillful at three kinds of talk: small, boy-girl, and deep.

You make the choice one of listening to confidences or holding hands, but there are many in-between situations where a fellow doesn't have to keep asking himself, "How am I doing?" A boy and girl can enjoy things together in a comradely way: taking a hike, playing tennis, going to the movies.

You and your girl ought to go out with a few other couples. One advantage here is that you won't have to start up a conversation. Another is that sooner or later the entire group will find themselves placed in a situation, say an evening boat ride, where holding hands will be something not hard to do, but hard to avoid doing.

One danger that the shy boy faces is that he may pass from being insufficiently bold to that of being over-aggressive just to prove to himself that he is not a coward or a stick-in-the-mud. In the attempt to make progress fast when he meets a new girl, he becomes a nuisance.

It is also true that shyness is not always a sign of social inexperience or fear. It may indicate a deep affection which two people have not yet acknowledged to each other. Many a boy has found that the more he has liked someone, the harder it was to engage in a normal conversation with her.

Of course, you aren't in a mood now to appreciate the observation that every boy ought to have some brother-sister friendships. In time, however, you may realize that it is a relief sometimes to let down your hair, be yourself, and escape from a heavy romantic role with its quick changes from ecstasy to tragic woe. We need friends in life almost as much as we need sweethearts. However, all you can hear now is the last word.

"I'm In Love—

Dear Dr. Lawton:

Last year when I was a junior in high school I used to see a lot of a boy whom I was crazy about. I thought this was the real thing and nothing could ever happen to change it. Now I am a senior and I seem to be falling in love with someone else. That first boy doesn't mean a thing to me any more. I hate to think that I am the fickle type, and that at any time I may meet a third boy and will have no use for the second one, either. How can you tell if you are *really* in love or just infatuated for the moment?

Eloise D.

—but Is It Real?"

Dear Eloise:

I'm afraid you are going to make me turn out an answer much longer than usual. For you've brought up one of the most important problems human beings face. That problem is whether, as the poet puts it, "love be truly love."

We all wish for a scientifically reliable method, like a blood test, to distinguish genuine and lasting affection from the pleasantly exciting disturbance in breathing which passes with the summer.

No mere psychologist can hope to utter the last word about such a complex emotional experience as love. However, analysis may help us see a little more clearly what *for us* is a "true" love as opposed to the many false varieties.

We can say that love between a man and woman is a compound made up of three principal elements or "needs." The first is simply the attraction of one sex for the other. This is a biochemical reality that has existed for millions of years. The attraction seems to follow some kind of law, because physically and even temperamentally contrasting types tend to be attracted to each other. Nature apparently tries to eliminate extremes and keep the race to an average in such things as height, weight, disposition, etc. Also, most females seem to prefer males who can protect them by virtue of superior physical strength and maturity, and most males seem to prefer females who need (or seem to need) such protection.

The second need which enters into the love relationship is that of the imagination. Every adult from childhood on carries around in his mind an image of particular qualities in the opposite sex which for him represent the utmost in desirability.

Our "style" in individuals of the opposite sex is most likely to have been set by a real person we knew in childhood. This may have been an uncle or aunt, a cousin, teacher, or the perennial boy or girl across the street—the one who never realizes we are alive, etc., until we've grown up and it's too late. Our "ideal picture" is most likely to contain elements derived from the appearance and manners of our parent of the opposite sex, or a brother or sister, all depending on how happy we were in our relationship to the particular person close to us.

As we grow into maturity, we are constantly comparing with our master model the boys or girls we meet, each time asking ourselves, "Is this he, is this she?" The odd thing about love is that nine-tenths of its cause and characteristics is in the one who loves, while only one-tenth is in the person loved. As Shaw says, love is merely an exaggeration of the difference between one person and another. To a certain extent, we are in love long before we find a person to love. A seventeen-year-old poet talks about how it feels "to wildly love and never to know the object wildly loved in vain." And a teen-age Chinese girl writes:

"I live alone and I am a young girl
I write long letters and I do not know anyone to send them to
Most tender things speak in my heart
And I can only say them to the bamboos in the garden
All day long I watch the shadows of people that pass."

If we find a person who seems to match our idealized portrait, something inside us clicks, we attach our mental identification tag to him, and cry, "I've found him! (or her!)" When this happens as eyes meet, we call it "love at first sight."

We all long to meet someone perfect and beautiful, someone who will bring a touch of poetry, adventure, and mystery into our lives. With that one at our side, we feel our existence will become satisfying and wonderful.

The male fancy is likely to dwell first on appearances, and next on "femininity"; a certain submissiveness, gentleness, and tenderness. As for a woman, her youthful imagination is stirred, not by looks as much as by certain qualities: physical strength and courage. When girls turn into women, qualities of mind and character, such as maturity, aggressiveness, and authority in men become especially attractive.

Bold and aggressive men are inevitably clothed with glamor for girls who find it difficult to distinguish between the qualities that make a man skillful and daring in business or athletics and those that will make him a suitable husband and father.

The last ingredient in the mixture "love" might be called "needs of the personality." Whether they are men or women, people want to feel they are important to someone in some way. They want to be understood, liked, and appreciated for what they really are, for their best and most interesting selves. This doesn't mean that both the man and the woman must have similar temperaments and interests. Similarity of strengths and of weaknesses are equally undesirable. Each mate should be strong where the other is weak, and should at least respect an interest or attitude of the other, if it isn't shared.

The best route to love is via a comradely friendship. The longer it takes to build up an emotion and sentiment, the more time is required to break it down. Even if friendship doesn't become love, the young person who never has had a chum of the opposite sex has missed a precious experience. For a boy and girl to help each other with homework, to share their enthusiasms and prejudices, ambitions and disappointments, to have discussions of platonic love—this may not send them soaring in the stratosphere, but just because their emotions are safe and comfortable they can be themselves and not actors in a life-and-death drama.

We can look upon these three needs as showing that we are in part animal (the biological needs), human (our personality needs), and divine (our imagination and idealism). In "real" love, all these needs in both persons are at least moderately satisfied, and this continues to be true, despite the physical and mental changes which the years bring to a married pair.

Infatuation, unlike love, is an experience in which only one, or at most, two of the three needs are satisfied, though originally we may believe they all are fully involved.

Infatuations are a perfectly normal and inevitable part of the business of growing up, and as the individual learns more about himself and the opposite sex, they become less frequent. Throughout youth, our desire for new experience is greater than our capacity to absorb it completely. As a result, we have to live out a great deal of our feeling and enjoyment in daydreams rather than in the only partially satisfactory real world. A boy who sees a pretty girl mainly through the workings of his over-zealous imagination may learn with disillusioning anguish that she will not do as a companion.

It is a natural thing for some young people to feel that unless they are in love they haven't made the grade and must be leading dull and empty lives. Impatient to be in love and enjoy its so-called thrills, they seldom make the effort necessary to test their feelings for genuineness or permanence.

One-sided loves, the "silent devotion from afar" sort of thing, are actually infatuations. The famous examples in literature of unrequited love—Dante's love for Beatrice, etc.—are really self-centered daydreams. It has been said, for example, that mature love is a fusing of two lives, a sharing of inner selves and common interests. If you define love this way, you can't be said to be really in love unless your feelings are reciprocated. How can a man, for example, satisfy a woman's personality needs, unless he gives of himself, and take her into the private world of his interests and ambitions?

Occasionally our personality needs are satisfied, but our imagination is not. The boy who is a most sympathetic and understanding friend may fizzle out in a romantic role.

In some instances, the satisfaction of a need does not last. Take the case of John Rivers. John had received little affection or approval from his parents. Criticized by his brothers and sisters, given little attention in school, he never knew what it meant to be accepted for his own sake until he met Edna. To be loved (not only liked), to be thought good-looking, to find his every word meant something—to John this was a wonderful experience. It satisfied his sense of importance and gave him an emotional security he had never enjoyed before and didn't know how to obtain in any other way.

In John Rivers, the hunger to belong to someone was so strong that the first member of the opposite sex to show him affection and admiration was bound to become "the girl." His "love" was due not to tremendous attraction for Edna herself, but for Edna as a symbol of uncritical affection and recognition of him as a person. And, as might be expected, when John developed inner strength and became more successful socially, he discarded Edna as no longer necessary.

To some people, sentimental illusions become a habit. The shorter the dream, the more often it needs to be repeated. There is an English one-act play called *The Constant Lover,* so-named because the hero was *always* in love. One life-long partner was not for him. It was the process in which he was interested, not the goal. The over-romantic young person longs to utter beautiful and moving lines—original, so he believes—just as if he were a character in *Wuthering Heights,* done in technicolor. Love to him is a kind of mutual admiration society, to which quarrels add variety and suspense. It is thrilling to write letters every week which end "Farewell forever," or to spend Saturday evening engaged in a tearful "Finis" and devote Sunday to an even more weepy reconciliation.

In youth, the biological and imaginative needs sway us most. With maturity, personality needs take the lead, and it is these which determine the success or failure of a marriage. Two people cannot make a go of living together in close intimacy over a long period, and of sharing their responsibilities, thoughts, and moods, unless they have in addition to masculine charm and feminine allure, certain simple virtues as people.

The familiarities, frustrations, and daily routine of living under one roof are neither dramatic nor heroic. That is why they are such a good test of whether we are well-adjusted or not. In fact, some couples recently celebrating their golden weddings gave cooking, co-operation, and children, as the basis for their success in marriage.

If our personality needs are so important and yet mature so slowly, how can we avoid mistakes? Only by trying to learn in advance, as far as possible, whether a given person is likely to meet our needs according to the best understanding we have of them today. Secluded nooks are fine, but it is also useful for boys and girls to see each other among their friends, and to know whether each gets along well or not with his parents and his brothers and sisters. Has the girl a sense of humor about herself? What about her behavior in a quarrel, in an emergency? How does she act and talk when the boy friend isn't around? Does she have several devoted girl friends? Does she *like* as well as *love* her father?

As for the boy, let us see if he enjoys responsibility. Are his ambitions realistic, even though high? What is his philosophy about women, about family life? Do little children take to him?

Is he fair toward those he doesn't like? How does he accept disappointment? What does he want out of life? Is he fond of his mother, but not over-dependent on her?

Particularly watch out for having to make a decision in an emergency situation, when a boy is about to take a job in another part of the country or world. I don't mean young people to be over-harsh in judging their infatuations. They are practice exercises, counterfeit loves. From them one learns to distinguish between a difficulty in breathing and a deep affection, between "It is wonderful" and "She (He) is wonderful." As Emerson said, "When the half-gods go, the gods arrive."

Love?

Dear Dr. Lawton:

I am very much interested in your opinions on "Puppy Love." I would like to know just how seriously you take it.

Do you believe a girl of fifteen and a boy the same age can really be in love? If they are, what would you say would be the cure for it?

I would appreciate it if you would consider this letter and voice your opinion on it. I am sure many other young people would, too.

Dorothy R.

Ah Yes, Indeed!

Dear Dorothy:

Millions upon millions of words have been lavished on "love" —words serious, gay, profound—but I often feel that Alfred

Kreymborg has just about summed up the wisdom of the ages in his poem "Vista": *

> The snow,
> ah yes, ah yes indeed,
> is white and beautiful, white and beautiful
> verily beautiful—
> from my window.
>
> The sea,
> ah yes, ah yes indeed,
> is green and alluring, green and alluring,
> verily alluring—
> from the shore.
>
> Love,
> ah yes, ah yes, ah yes indeed,
> verily yes, ah yes indeed!

Since psychologists often enter where angels (poets) fear to tread, may I put myself on record as taking love seriously? And so do most grownups. When you tell an adult that you are in love and then observe a curiously indulgent expression on his face, don't interpret this as disbelief or mockery or even sympathy. He is not thinking about you or your admission at all but of himself a long time ago.

Can a boy (or girl) of fifteen be in love? Of course he can if it is reciprocated. But since our tastes are changing so fast at this age, we are apt to fall in and out of love fast. "Puppy love" refers to this period in our life, not to the intensity of the experience. For such a love *may* be *one* of the most tender, most poignantly beautiful experiences of an entire

---

* Reprinted from *The Selected Poems 1912-1944* of Alfred Kreymborg by permission of E. P. Dutton & Co., Inc. Copyright 1945 by Afred Kreymborg.

lifetime. Anyone, young or old, who doubts this should read the long short story "First Love" by Ivan Turgenev, a Russian author of the last century. Read also the chapter called "A Diversion on a Penny Whistle" in *The Ordeal of Richard Feverel*, a novel by George Meredith.

All "first" experiences—first dance, first formal affair, first pay envelope—are big events partly because they are new and partly because they signify another milestone in our journey toward maturity. First love, therefore, *can* be real and important, strange and wonderful. But as a matter of cold statistics, "first" experiences are seldom "last" or greatest experiences. How can they be? At fifteen most of us have not yet reached our full growth, mentally or physically. And the peak of emotional growth, the capacity for joy and suffering, is as a rule much farther off. Our tastes in sports, clothes, books, ideas of good times—all change during the teen years. In the same way, our friends and crushes are likely to represent stages in our development. The very same boy who embodies for us, at fifteen, all that is perfect and thrilling in masculinity *may* be, when we are twenty, all that is dull and tame.

When you ask about a cure for love, I am inclined to be either flippant and inquire, "Why should you wish a cure?" or with pretended gravity shake my head and state, "Alas, when one is bitten by the love-bug, it is too late for science." There is, of course, the exceptional boy or girl who is completely bowled over by love and for whom little else ever exists. But here we are considering the average young person. With respect to him, then, it is safe to say that he makes a complete recovery without the help of surgery or medication. And there are no aftereffects, except a golden, slightly faded page in his memory book and a wistful smile at the far-off, dreamlike picture he sees therein: the person he was an eternity ago.

Granted that a boy and girl of fifteen are in love. What

then? Let them accept the disturbing moments along with the pleasant ones. Let them keep up with their work and studies, their other friendships and other good times. The love will either last or it won't. They need not fear lest the mere passage of time kill love. Time is like the wind which fans a large blaze and puts out a small one. And should the affections of young people change, let them remember that this is the price they must pay for something that is even more important than love: the gradual maturing of the personality. Such a boy and girl might try to answer this question honestly: Suppose they had Aladdin's lamp and could wish that their love at fifteen would last forever, would they make that wish?

Though I appear an old fogey or a disbeliever in a great American tradition, I must own up to the belief that most of our novels and moving pictures exaggerate the importance of love. Love is one of the great human experiences. But in the lives of adult men and women there are other experiences just as important. Falling in love doesn't solve all our problems, though we often believe it will. If love is overimportant to young people, however, we can hardly blame them, since this attitude is part of the social environment of us all.

Few of us know that we have brought the unreal and highly romanticized version of love upon ourselves. It was "created" only eight or nine hundred years ago in Western and Southern Europe and still is most prevalent there and in those nations with similar cultures, like America. According to John Dewey, our leading philosopher:

"Romantic love, as it exists today, with all the varying perturbations it occasions, is as definitely a sign of specific historic conditions as are big battleships with turbines, internal combustion engines, and electrically driven machines."

The next century will witness, I am convinced, **a** transformation of the *excessively* idealized love relationship of presentday men and women into something superior and more durable. But here I am becoming "deep" and "analytical," which will never do. Love? Ah yes, indeed!

Love At First Sight

Dear Dr. Lawton:

About a year ago I became close friends with a girl in school whose older brother was away working in another city. Jack came home on a visit, and the minute we met we knew we were made for each other. He's everything I've ever dreamed about, and he tells me the same about myself. He stayed only a few days, but we write to each other, and if anything we seem more in love than before. Now, Dr. Lawton, I'm only seventeen years old, and Jack is twenty-two. I'm a junior in high school. But school seems very unimportant to me as compared to how I feel about Jack, and I want to marry him. Naturally, my parents say I'm too young and that I don't know my own mind, and so on, and everybody says that love at first sight is impossible. Is it? Jack and I don't think so because we've *experienced* it.

Toni S.

Possible, but Not Probable

Dear Toni:

All of us, at some time, live in a world of fantasy. As children we have imaginary playmates. We build castles in the air about being baseball players and movie actresses. As we grow older, we dream about the places we'll visit, exciting people we'll know, and the kind of persons we'll become. Later, we devote a good share of our imagining to the kind of person we hope to marry.

This is all quite natural. But as a young person becomes an adult, he learns to distinguish the *real* world from this world of fantasy. How many boys who were *sure* at ten that they wanted to be baseball stars end up as baseball stars? By the time they are twenty, many realize that they really prefer to be doctors, engineers, or mechanics. We learn the hard way what we can and cannot do, what we like and dislike. In dealing with people, we find out slowly which ones we can trust.

You have probably dreamed a great deal about "this thing called love." So you can hardly wait to attach your "dream picture" to the first man who falls in love with you. Your desire to be loved is very strong. Getting married would mean adulthood, freedom from school, and from home discipline. While Jack is partly a real person to you, he is mostly an ideal and symbol. You have fitted him into your need.

Imagination is an important part of love. But imagination can play tricks on you. Marriage is the union, not of symbols but of people; of facts, not of wishes. One can't learn much about a person from a few meetings and letters. What do you two know of each other's characters and backgrounds? You don't know how Jack behaves under criticism and disappointment. How will he get along with other people? What does he expect of life and of his partner in marriage? Human relations are always a gamble. But you don't invest a large sum of money or hire an employee for a responsible position without a thorough survey of the situation. Can you do *less* when choosing a life partner?

It is possible that you are in love with *love*. First-sight lovers are apt to lean too strongly upon the old hocus-pocus about "soul-mates." They think that each male and female gets a number at birth, and that whenever one meets a member of the opposite sex with the same number, he yells, "Bingo!"

Actually, although I'm sure you won't believe me, you could fall in love with any one of a number of well-adjusted and attractive men and be equally happy. Jack is one combination of attractive qualities; there are many other attractive combinations.

On rare occasions people do fall in love when introduced. But only if they are emotionally mature persons who like and have met many people, and have had close friendships with both sexes. They are good judges of human nature, including their own. Previous experience has taught them that it is not love merely to have a "what-hit-me-where-am-I" feeling. You two may be safe in your love. But time is the test.

Some young people find the preliminary stages of friendship dull. They can't wait until they are in the thrilling, close-up clinch of "An Overpowering Romance." This is especially true if they have been denied their share of affection and praise at home and at school. They may have a deficiency of "emotional vitamins." *But* hasty decisions may result only in a bad case of indigestion.

Happiness in Marriage

Dear Dr. Lawton:

I am seventeen years of age and a senior in high school. My ambition is to become a good housewife, but it is against my mother's wishes for me to get married while I am so young.

Of course, I know that many young marriages end up with

a divorce, but I can't convince my mother that mine wouldn't.

This young man and I are so alike in some respects and so different in others that I am rather puzzled about the happiness of our marriage. As the old saying goes, "Love is blind." Perhaps I can't see through this problem as well as I should. How can one be sure of happiness after marriage?

Louise W.

Speaking the "Same Language"

Dear Louise:

Someone once said, half in jest, half in earnest, that men who cried in the movies made good husbands. However, one should not place too much faith in this "movie" test. Actually, there is no certain way of telling ahead of time whether any given marriage is going to fail or to succeed. All sorts of unexpected situations may arise to bring out equally surprising qualities of mind and character. Marriage is like a magnifying glass which reveals all our faults and virtues on a grand scale.

One way to estimate the probable chances of a person's making a satisfactory partner after marriage is to find out what he has been like before. Consider John R. He always has been fairly happy and has met his problems with some degree of success. John *now* lives up to whatever responsibilities he is given, *now* is a good sport about disappointments, *now* seeks fun out of life but accepts trouble and hard work when it comes. It would seem likely, therefore, that John will take every new hurdle in his stride.

But when we turn to Alice, we find that her record is one of continual unhappiness and poor adjustments. Alice might become a different kind of person, if she had a great desire to do so and willingly accepted whatever would make possible a change in her. But under average circumstances the odds are against average people's being transformed merely by the fact of marriage.

We are more likely to be permanently satisfied with our choice of a mate, the better we understand ourselves and the greater our skill in judging the true character of people, especially those of the opposite sex. Jane, for example, wants a boy who will be boss of the household. On the other hand, Mary is looking for a partner who will let her call all the signals. Richard seeks in a wife a pretty dancing companion whom he can use for display purposes. But Martin wants a homemaker. Jane and Martin, even in their teens, may know just what they are searching for and where to find it. But Mary and Richard, even at forty or fifty, will probably still be knocking at the wrong doors.

Some of us have a genius for marrying the wrong person. We marry only what we think or wish the husband or wife to be.

The best prelude to marriage is the slow-ripening, comradely friendship. It is only in such cases that we have any chance of applying "tests" or "rules."

Of course, if a girl is wise, she won't ask her boy friend to stay home and fill out a questionnaire covering every detail of his past and every hope he has for the future, though this plan might appeal to her parents and greatly simplify life for them. However, there are a few things we might do during the brief interval when we are still capable of thinking clearly. We might see our friend with his family and our family, his friends and our friends, since marriage is the most severe test of our ability to share and to live in a group.

Love is one kind of language by means of which a man and woman can communicate with each other. But in order to be entirely happy, a couple must master a second language: that of understanding the preferences which they have simply as people. Think of all the likes and dislikes human beings can have.

Despite these endless ways in which we can differ from another person, we may still agree on certain things of major importance to him and to us. Similarity of outlook comes from resemblance in age and experience of life, social and economic level, education, nationality and religious affiliation. Yet, unusual people who love each other may have had very different environments and still speak the same language, as did Miss R., an American woman in her late thirties, who married a European of different religious faith. In view of the great success of her marriage, she was asked to comment on this problem.

"My test," said Miss R., "of whether a couple dare bind themselves permanently is very simple. They must:

1. Be good friends as well as good sweethearts.
2. Like the same people or the same types of people.
3. Laugh at the same things.
4. Have the same tastes in music, art, books, etc., or else must tolerate each other's tastes.
5. Enjoy listening to each other.
6. Be willing to try to help the other.
7. Have friends of their own.
8. Be liked and admired by each other's good friends.

They must not:

9. Expect too much of each other.
10. Try to reform each other.

"Even though I believe in these ten rules, I am sure there are many other standards for a happy marriage. Perhaps if the couple have common sense, well-balanced emotions, and an interest in each other—no more is necessary."

Life is a series of adventures, the greatest of which probably is marriage. Ponder and scheme as we may, every step we take involves a certain measure of risk and uncertainty. This fact may discourage the fainthearted, but to the brave it is the very unpredictable and challenging quality of experience that makes life so exciting.

Boys Like Girls, and Girls Like Boys Who . . .

The most fascinating subject for boys is girls and vice-versa. This was certainly brought out in the avalanche of letters that came as a result of a *Scholastic* contest (1) "The Kind of Boy That Girls Like" and (2) "The Kind of Girl That Boys Like." We reprint here the letters of the first two prize-winners in each of these contests.

It is a tribute to the intelligence and maturity of the young people who entered this contest that so many of them are able to see that even though one does not regard every date as a matrimonial prospect, any permanent and satisfying relationship between a man and a woman (or a boy and a girl) has to be built on the qualities that wear well. Some of these qualities are: sincerity, loyalty, common interests, mutual understanding and helpfulness, enjoyment of each other's company. The romantic hero and the glamour girl were none too highly prized by our contestants. The boys thought more of girls who are naturally, not artificially, pretty. And the girls thought more of boys who have ambition, good habits, and self-reliance rather than the traits of a "great lover."

HOW TO BE HAPPY THOUGH YOUNG

The prize-winning letters came from students in the following high-schools:

Ashland High School, Ashland, Pennsylvania
North Central High School, Spokane, Washington
Senior High School, Springfield, Missouri.

The Kind of Girl That Boys Like

Eureka! My Girl!

I've found her! The kind of girl every fellow likes. For less fortunate boys who, as yet, haven't found a "dream girl," or are uncertain as to what traits they are really looking for, I would like to tell about my girl.

She is about five feet two, weighs between one hundred ten to one hundred and twenty pounds, and has a nice figure. She has the skin you love to touch and extremely white, even teeth. As for the color of her hair and eyes, it really doesn't matter when she has such a pleasing personality as my girl. She doesn't force any witticisms on her listeners, but carries her part of the conversation wittily enough, yet intelligently. She never impedes the conversation with talk about another boy or dates she has had.

That brings up the subject of dates. She never is late, she never stands me up, she likes to get home at a decent hour, and she knows there is a limit to expenses.

She doesn't go *too far* in sports, that is, she never loses that feminine touch. She doesn't act tom-boyish. She adopts neither an expert nor a disinterested attitude toward subjects that interest me.

She accepts with grace all the little courtesies which a boy so much enjoys showing. It's the little things like opening a door or helping her in and out of a car that give a boy that protective feeling.

Her wardrobe doesn't include enough clothes to stock a frock shop, but what she has, outside of sports clothes, are always neat, clean, and dainty.

Portrait of a Swell Girl

It is the ambition of every fellow to have a girl that he can honestly call *swell*. Not every girl that comes along deserves such a rating.

The most important thing about a girl is how much you enjoy her company. If she is agreeable and a lot of fun, even when you are forced by financial deficits to walk her through the park instead of taking her to the movies, she is O.K. If you enjoy the time that you spend with her, then she is worthy of being placed on your "swell girl" list. If she is a "circus" girl who likes to go out with you to make an impression on others, you would best pass her up. That kind of girl only drains your pocketbook, and you do not have a bit of real enjoyment out of it.

Second ingredient in the making of a swell girl friend is a little gray matter. If she shows a little common sense and takes a genuine interest in you and your interests, she can easily make your approved list. If she is too flighty or doesn't act herself at all times, she will never make a good girl friend.

Last, but far from least, she should be attractive. But she need not be the Hedy Lamar type.

If your girl meets all these requirements, but she does not want to go steady with you, she can still be a *swell* girl friend even if she is not your one and only.

The Kind of Boy That Girls Like

A Boy Who is "Somebody"

This is the chance we have been waiting for—a chance to pass a few friendly hints to our biggest worries, the boys! We're not sleuthing for one that is perfect, but just one unanimously called the "swell kid."

We admire a fellow who has an individual personality: that is, one who has plenty of backbone and a readiness to express his ideas without too consciously trying to be the life of the party. It is he who has a worthwhile hobby modestly lending him the air of "somebody," with whom we can thoroughly enjoy talking. We hate "show-offs."

His personality shows itself also in being well groomed without using a magnet on father's pocketbook. There is no excuse for sloppy, untidy clothes. We also like a boy who somehow earns the majority of his spending money, even if we have to be satisfied with a balcony seat and an ice cream soda instead of loge seats and double banana splits—at father's expense!

The fellow who willingly takes part in school clubs and athletics is most popular with us. We admire one who can get good grades and still have time for outside amusements. Naturally we like an all-around good fellow, who, even though he does not do well what the crowd suggests, is a good sport and willing to try.

Last, but certainly not least, is the delicate subject of "Boy Dates Girl." We don't care to be fed a "line"—we like it straight from the shoulder. We're sick of listening to the old Romeo technique. Why doesn't he just say he likes our company, and let it go at that?

Surely this is nothing that any boy can't be. Are we expecting too much?

I Like Boys—All of Them

This is the kind of boy that *I* like. I like the tall, blond, athletic type. And then I like little dark, dashing boys, too, and short stocky ones with red hair and freckles. I like a boy with shining shoes and that washed-behind-the-ears look, and a *boyish* boy with tousled hair and maybe a little hole in the elbow of his sweater sleeve. I like witty boys who keep me in a gale of laughter and the quiet kind who broadcast only when they have something to say; gallant boys who leap to help me with my 'cello and shy boys who do not.

In short, the boys I like are as varied in looks and personality as the girls I like; however they do all have certain characteristics in common. They have good dispositions and the naturally nice manners that are the result of being reared in homes of refinement. They are clean of speech and mind. They are considerate of my feelings and those of others, including their teachers. They are ambitious for the future, even though the ambitions of boys my age are likely to be fantastic. They have intelligence, and at least enough common sense to know that they are not the center of the universe, and to realize that there are interesting things to observe and talk about besides themselves.

Those are their major virtues, but they have many minor ones, such as liking to visit in my home, not being afraid of my mother. They do not think of dates in terms of money and can think of jolly things to do after their allowance is exhausted. They have a sense of humor, not necessarily the wisecracking variety, and they do not—oh, they *do not* call me "Toots" or "Babe."

Since it isn't possible to offer an adequate selection of the letters themselves, some preferred qualities in boys and girls are listed in the order of those most often mentioned by the opposite sex.

PREFERRED QUALITIES

What Girls Like in Boys

Courtesy and consideration
Good conversationalist (pleasant company)
Neatness and cleanliness (well-groomed)
Knowledge of proper etiquette
Pleasing personality
Respectfulness
No bad habits
Ambition

What Boys Like in Girls

Attractive appearance
Pleasant company (good conversationalist)
Cheerfulness (sense of humor)
Make-up used with discretion
Pleasing personality
Good appearance (well-dressed)
Popularity with others
Knowledge of proper etiquette

Friends

Outgrowing One's Friends

Dear Dr. Lawton:

I have some friends whom I think the world of. We've gone through high school together and shared lots of important experiences. Now we're nearing the end of high school, and I am the only one in this group who plans to go to college. I'm afraid this means that I'll grow farther and farther apart from them (especially since I'll be going out of town), and the idea of losing them makes me unhappy. I understand the importance of education, but I think keeping one's friendships is very important too. Should one continue to educate oneself even if it means the loss of close friends?

Herbert R.

Can't Be Helped If People Change

Dear Herbert:

A friend is a person with whom we share common interests and loyalties, who can be trusted with our confidences, who has our welfare at heart. But it is impossible to guarantee that a friendship, once begun, will last over a period of many years. To insure permanence, we would have to keep those involved from changing or, if they did change, to see that they changed in exactly the same ways. Whether we continue our education or not, life is a process of losing some friends and gaining others. Young people may make many vows of eternal devotion, which is very natural and understandable. Yet such pledges simply show how strong are the feelings and hopes of the friends, and not how good they are at foretelling the future.

Each one of us has many selves. In youth, it is hard to decide which of these different aspects of our personality are the dominant ones. That is why the first half of life is so likely to be one long experiment in discovering just who and what we are. Now, each of these varied selves, we often find, requires a separate friend. As we meet different people, travel, move from one neighborhood to another, change our occupation, succeed in some ways, fail in others, an alteration takes place in our tastes and point of view. Throughout life we need the approval of our equals, but, as we grow older, these "equals" may change. For the self we favored most at seventeen may not be the one we prefer at twenty-seven or thirty-seven. While some persons can make friends more easily than others, an education, if anything, is likely to increase our circle of friends because it multiplies our interests and therefore our "selves." To make young friendships permanent means we must prevent ourselves from developing. Would anyone barter maturity for friends, even if he could?

Furthermore, the friendships of our early and middle teens are followed by intense emotional relationships with the opposite sex in the late teens and early twenties. Now that another person becomes tied up with our fate, both his friends and ours have to be considered in the light of joint tastes and needs. Marriage usually means a general rearrangement of friendships, since it becomes increasingly difficult to continue friendships with persons who do not fit into the social life of the married couple. Finally, most of the friendships we have in later life are likely to develop out of our business or professional careers merely because of common interests and constant association.

If we find it difficult to continue a teen friendship into the twenties or thirties, it does not mean that our former chum is less worthy; it is simply that he no longer meets the social and intellectual needs of the different person we have become. This discovery may be somewhat painful the first few times we experience it. But we grow up, whether we like it or not, and learn to accept more gracefully the loss of an early friendship. The important thing is to have genuine friends at every age period in life, and to enjoy them as thoroughly and as long as possible. If they last for many years, so much the better. But when they go, whatever the reason, we must find others if we wish to possess one very necessary element in a complete life.

Unmatched Ages

Dear Dr. Lawton:

I go around with a crowd several years older than I am. Though I am only fifteen and a half, I look and act older. Besides, I am a senior, and somehow the boys and girls my own age seem rather childish to me. The trouble is that this older crowd smokes and drinks a bit. If I give them up I'll be lonely and miss a lot of fun. If I continue to go with them, I'll have to stand teasing or else do what doesn't seem quite right to me. What is your opinion about this?

Gladys O.

Good and Bad Points About Having Older Friends

Dear Gladys:

The simplest solution here is to find among young people one's own age those who are equally bright and mature. Another plan is to make it clear to the older group that a younger member is not especially interested in some of its activities and would rather not take part. If one says this casually, without indignation or high-and-mighty talk on the undesirability of any given practice, the others are likely to accept the decision and to refrain from teasing. But any attempt to change the habits of an older group will only make the boys and girls want to throw the critic and killjoy overboard. If the casual "No, thank you" attitude doesn't seem to work, the individual concerned must himself decide whether to go along with the crowd, keeping mum about his objections, or to quit the group.

Bright young people are often dissatisfied with those their own age. They want to rush ahead in living as they do in learning. However, we do not all acquire social experience at the same rate. Some of us at sixteen have had a good deal of practice in judging people and know our way around, so that, no matter what happens, we always land squarely on both feet. Others at the same age (or even older) may still be quite unaware of their best interests or of ways to protect these. Many boys and girls are drawn into sophisticated activities that are not wholesome for them merely because they are ashamed to appear too juvenile to their older and more experienced companions.

The young person who seeks out the company of older persons may be really as mature as they. On the other hand, he may be someone who failed to secure the attention and affection of his parents and others and is desperately trying to make up for this lack through the sense of importance which he gets when an older crowd takes him up. Such a boy or girl is making believe he has a maturity which he doesn't actually possess.

Each age has its own pleasures. A well-adjusted person is one who enjoys the experiences that belong to each successive age level. He does not anticipate activities of a later period, just as he does not hold on to those of an earlier age. A young person who tries to imitate sophisticated adult ways not only misses all the experiences that belong to one his own age but he may also lose his ability to enjoy them whenever they turn up. For the chief drawback to high-voltage pleasures is that the voltage has to be continually stepped up. After a time, we may reach a point where everything becomes tame and boring.

Richard, for example, goes about with an older group. He is the type of boy who lives only for the moment; if he has a good time today he does not care how he may feel about it tomorrow. Moreover, he is so hungry for popularity that he never asks why he is liked or what kind of people like him. He knows that with his car and generous allowance the others find him convenient to have around. But he doesn't mind, because he is flattered that they let him be one of them. He gets a great thrill out of showing his older friends that he can go them one better. And he does put on a good show for his audience. Richard never received much praise or affection at home. He doesn't like to think about his future because he doesn't feel very sure of himself, and, anyway, planning is too much like work. Richard is very popular, but he isn't at all happy.

Jane also goes with an older crowd. Her parents have given her not only a good deal of love and approval but also their complete trust. She is mature far beyond her years and is very confident of her ability to meet varied social situations. She takes part in nearly all the activities of her group, but when she decides to forego any, Jane can express herself so simply and graciously that no one notices or comments. Originally, she was teased somewhat for hanging back, but she took it like a good sport. She has fitted in so well with the crowd that it is willing to accept her on her own terms.

When Friends Prove Untrue

Dear Dr. Lawton:

Ever since I was a small kid I was pals with a boy who lived across the street. We were such good friends that they called us "The Inseparables." When we got to high school we began to pool our savings so we'd have money for camping trips, dates, and so forth. The box we kept the money in was kept in my friend's house, and we both had keys. His back door was always open, and I frequently would drop in, find no one in, and leave. One afternoon I dropped in, no one was home, so I left, as usual, but the next day when I saw my friend he acted very strange.

Well, to make a long story short, the money was gone, and my friend accused me of taking it. He not only accused me, but convicted me without proof, or judge, or jury. Naturally, I didn't take the money, but how can you prove that? What makes me sick is that I have lost my best friend through no fault of my own. I must find some way to catch the thief and prove my friend was wrong. Then he'll be sorry, and we'll be together again.

Jim R.

Go On to Seek New (and Truer) Friends

Dear Jim:

Don't go to all that trouble, Jim. The money may have been taken by a passing tramp, something almost impossible to prove, or even by your friend himself. Even if you could actually prove that, it would only make the situation worse, for he would dislike you more than ever. No, Jim, you might as well write your friend off as lost.

Two people may like and even love each other. But you can't pass a law compelling someone to *keep* liking or loving you. You can lose a friend in many ways. He may move away. Or he can marry, and you and his wife may not hit it off. Or he may die. People will do that, you know, in spite of what it may mean to those who love them.

Sometimes one friend proves himself unworthy, becomes unreasonably jealous, or makes false accusations, as in your case. And sometimes he stops liking—just because he stops liking. When we lose a dear friend we're stunned and terribly hurt. I suppose you wish you could swallow a magic pill and stop the pain. You can keep on singing "Bring Back My Bonnie to Me," but it won't work.

The main thing in friendship is mutual trust and loyalty. If you don't get it from a friend during an emergency, what good is he? The distressing thing is that your friend chose to believe you guilty without conclusive evidence.

You have been wounded badly, but you are not a dead bird yet. If you are smart you will learn from this, and your next friendship should be more satisfying. But if you are not smart, you will become a suspicious, lonely grouch. A man who overdoes this business of trusting people will often suffer, but he gets more out of life in the long run than the one who is sure everyone is a crook.

Next time you start making friends remember to put your money in a couple of different banks so that if one fails you won't go broke. Remember, also, that while friendship is something you need all your life, particular friends come and go. Sure, there are fine and splendid people in this world, plenty of them. But there are others who are "no-account," deceitful and ready to sell you out for a dime. All of us sometimes make the mistake of liking someone who is not good for us. It all adds up to this: there is no Santa Claus in this world. That is always a hard lesson to learn.

"I Do Not Like Thee . . ."

Dear Dr. Lawton:

If you know a person does not like you, how can you get them to like you? Let me explain that this person is another girl. Everyone says, "Be natural, be yourself." I tried that without any success. Then I decided to talk and act in a way that I thought would appeal to this girl, but the result was no different. This business of being liked has me puzzled. Are there any rules one can follow in making a good impression? Don't think I haven't any friends, because I have. Yet we all can have more friends, can't we? And it is annoying not to obtain the friendship you want.

Edna M. W.

"... The Reason Why ..."

Dear Edna:

There are many lists of rules for gaining the liking and approval of others. But these suggestions have to be so general that their helpfulness to any particular individual is limited. Every relationship we have with another human being is almost a rule unto itself, since each acquaintance sees a slightly different aspect of our personality and shares a different portion of our experience.

We are told that the way to create a good impression is to listen and let the other fellow do all the talking. True enough, there are times when we meet people who like to talk. That is when we should sit back and be attentive. But think of what would happen if everyone in a group wanted to be an audience at the same time! Suppose we are with a shy companion whom we try to draw out with suitable questions, but whose longest reply is "Yes" or "No." The only way to make our one-syllable friend happy is to turn on the patter and small talk.

Consider the rule, "Be yourself." But we are many selves. Which is the genuine one: the self which is gay or serious, talkative or reticent, gracious or snappy? Some of us cannot afford to behave as our first impulse prompts. In order to get along pleasantly with people, we may have to struggle constantly so that our best side stays uppermost. Perhaps this side will attract the person whose liking we desire, or perhaps it won't. If not, each of us must decide for himself whether to abandon an attempt at friendship or to play a part that may please someone else. Most of us find that even if we could keep up this deception permanently, the result does not justify all the strain.

Another drawback to a list of rules is that they make the

liking of one person for another seem entirely a matter of conscious thought and logic. However, our first reaction to a newcomer, whether favorable or not, is apt to be based on his smile, his walk, a trick of speech, etc., and not on a major quality of his mind or character. To explain exactly why we like anyone is a difficult task. It is just as hard to get down to the basic cause of a dislike, a fact well illustrated in the famous verse:

> I do not like thee, Dr. Fell,
> The reason why I cannot tell;
> But this I know, I know full well,
> I do not like thee, Dr. Fell.

Granted that we all should attempt to increase our social assets and reduce our social liabilities. Yet a boy or girl may have fine qualities and still not be liked by the particular one whose approval is sought. In fact, a person's very virtues may be the reason why he is disliked.

We all remember the neighbor's child who was held up to us as a model and how little his superiority endeared him to us. Take such an attractive quality as cheerfulness. Even this is not on every approved list. But please don't take all this as an argument against the possession of socially desirable qualities.

The need to be liked is tied up with our entire personality and outlook on the world. Yet some boys and girls can accept the fact that not everyone is going to like them and that to be disliked by certain people in given situations is really a tribute.

The more a person thinks for himself rather than with the crowd, the more positive a part he takes in his career or in the world, the greater the chance of his stirring up opposition. Not even the most tactful of persons can forever avoid a time when he must clash with someone else.

If we turn to the young person who finds his friendships unsatisfactory, we note that he often has a secret dream to be liked by everyone, the more lavish the display of interest the better. Such a boy or girl seldom pays any heed to the kind of person who likes him, what the reasons may be for the liking, and whether he himself reciprocates the feeling. Quantity is the thing here, not quality.

Yet those who are concerned about their ability to attract friends and who feel that there is little they can do to alter matters, might consider one fact, which is offered here not as consolation or as relieving them from further efforts. If few people can be universally liked, even fewer are universally disliked. There exists somewhere for every person several individuals who would approve of him exactly as he stands, if they could ever meet him.

That is why a boy or girl should take advantage of every suitable opportunity in and out of school for meeting different types of people under a wide variety of circumstances. Whether these persons are similar to us in education, interests, social background, or whether we like them, or they us, is not of chief significance. What is important is that we are building up our own standards of judging human nature, our own social skills, our own confidence.

In time we develop a flexibility in dealing with people: learning when to talk, when to listen; when to ask questions, when to answer them. We also learn when and how to be agreeable, or, should the occasion arise, when to be otherwise. You may have heard the definition of a gentleman as a person who never hurt anyone's feelings accidentally. Such surety of touch comes only from practical experience.

How to Lose a Friend

Dear Dr. Lawton:

I value friendship a great deal. As a child, it was easy for me to make friends. But now I haven't got a single one.

I go on the theory that a person either likes me right away or not at all. When I am introduced to someone with whom I think I could be friends, I can't seem to keep my real self inside me, but show my liking. This person then turns me down flat, or kids me along.

A few years ago, some fellow and I became great friends. But there was a girl who lived upstairs. Instead of coming to see me, he would go right past my apartment up to her. I wrote my friend and asked him to choose between us. He never even answered me. I actually cried because our friendship was broken.

At present, I'm in a club with four other boys. One of them is an outstanding student who thinks only of his future, and of working at something until he is good enough to earn money at it. But I think the best plan is to live only from day to day. I have no ambition to do things in which I'm not interested. I'm failing in some subjects because they don't interest me. I want to be an athletic coach, but that means finishing high school and going to college. Since those are out, I've just got to forget about the whole thing.

I think that because of my hunger for friendship I have developed an inferiority complex. When I meet people I try too hard to give a good impression. That seems to work in reverse, and I'm more alone than ever.

Art S.

Avoiding That Great Letdown

Dear Art:

I don't believe in using fancy terms, Art, but in looking at the facts. You're a funny fellow. About your No. 1 problem, your future, you go pouff, but because your friend won't give you a life contract, you break down and cry. Your problems with school and with friends are related. Solve one and you solve the other.

You live day by day because you don't trust your ability to last longer. You're saying, "Running a mile is dumb. The right distance is one yard." You're failing in school because you believe you are a failure. Without a life goal which you can accept, you look for something permanent to which you can cling. You are terribly anxious for affection and approval so that you'll feel important and have something which will fill your time and keep you from having to face your difficulties.

Suppose we look at your problem from the friendship angle. You think there is something wrong with you, and that's why others don't like you. It is doubly important, therefore, that you do well in your career—then people might admire you. But your career depends on school.

You seem to be always needing emotional first aid. Now, Art, you weren't born that way. The chances are that, from childhood on, you have assumed people looked upon you as an inferior individual. The best way to start rebuilding yourself would be to find out all the things that have happened to you that made you feel as you do about yourself. Once you understood yourself better and felt stronger, you would take things as they came and act in an easygoing manner with people.

Remember, conversation, like all living together, is a sharing of ideas, interests, feelings. Don't talk too much, and don't try to be oh, so peppy and fascinating. Neither should you be a stick of wood. How to avoid giving too much or too little of yourself is a hard lesson to learn.

Most of us start our social careers by wrapping our feelings in cellophane. After some painful experiences, we decide to reduce visibility. We shelve the line, "Be my friend (or sweetheart) forever and I'll be yours." Instead, we try waiting for a relationship to take on speed gradually. If, in time, it doesn't give us what we want, we shrug our shoulders, murmur, "No hard feelings," and go off on another scouting expedition, vowing, "Better luck next time."

Girls especially have to be cagey and wait until the boy has taken a stand. They must try not to be coquettish, and to protect themselves against the Great Let-Down.

We judge a person's true attitude toward us not by his words but by his actions. Only when two people are pretty clear about each other, or one is terribly slow to catch on, do we come right out with it.

Believe it or not, Art, even you, suffering as you do from insufficient emotional vitamins, couldn't stand having every person you met just go wild about you. A time may come, incredible as it may seem, when you will have more people liking you than you can handle. Then you'll thank the social convention which will save you the necessity of saying like an executioner, "Vanish, disappear," to some applicant for your friendship.

When you meet a person, you're so sure he will notice you are different that you plead for his liking. But even if he gives it, you wouldn't be satisfied. Instead of saving your feelings for the big emergency, you're always confessing them, getting other people to reciprocate, and then going off in search of a new scalp. You need the feeling of victory. It's a kind of daily pill that makes you feel you amount to something. You go by quantity of friends, not by quality.

Here's another shortcut for you. It is best if a man gets his sense of achievement from his work. I don't care whether you stay in school or leave. But if you stay, do the good work I'm sure you're capable of. Later you'll decide the kind of place you want to fill in the world.

How about an absorbing hobby which would bring you in contact with people where you could talk, not about your innermost thoughts, feelings, and various problems, but about something concrete and outside of you? A hobby would keep you busy and put you in a forward-looking frame of mind. In time, you would get a sense of importance, and you would have an outlet for your need to build and create, as well as for the ambition now locked up inside of you.

Your Career

"I Haven't Any Idea . . .

Dear Dr. Lawton:

How can one find out what work he is best fitted for? I am a senior in high school and feel I can't delay any longer making up my mind. I don't know what I want—except that it should be something outdoors. My father, who is a lawyer, says that if I don't want law or medicine I should be an engineer, but I don't like engineering either, and, besides, my science and math grades are not any too good. I had thought of driving a truck. A young fellow I know is getting a good salary at it, but I'm afraid that is "out." Forestry doesn't quite satisfy me.

Henry M. R.

. . . What I Want to Be!"

Dear Henry:

Were this an ideal world, all of us at a young age would display great ability and interest in one particular type of work. As soon as we finished high school or college, a job in this field would await us, and we would earn a good living at it ever after.

But this is not an ideal world, and things do not go quite this way. Probably your most practical move would be to seek out in the community someone engaged in outdoor work, whether or not you find his job appealing. Ask this person to tell you what kind of abilities and preparation are needed for success in his field, what financial return one might expect from it, what features of his calling he regards as most agreeable and disagreeable.

Try to obtain permission from this person to spend a few days going about with him, observing him at actual work, and perhaps even helping him. If you repeat this with several different types of outdoor work, you may be able to make a final choice as to which kind you prefer.

In order to carry out this "apprenticeship" idea on a large scale, some high schools have established a "Work Week" (even a "Work Month"). Through arrangements previously made with various individuals and concerns, every student at some time during his high-school course is assigned to a person in the community who is working at a particular job. The girl who wants to be a sales clerk would be assigned to watch and perhaps assist a saleslady in some store. The boy who wants to be a mechanic would work in a garage or factory. After "Work Week," students return to class and describe what they had seen and learned.

Whenever the "foster" employer has had a chance to judge the strong and weak points of his assistant, he submits a report on his findings to the teacher. This is taken up with the student in private conference. Where schools do not arrange for "Work Weeks," the individual student might devise one for himself during vacations or spare time.

That is just what Everett T. did. All one spring he had struggled to arrive at a decision concerning outdoor work. Then he went away for a summer's vacation.

Seeking some way of keeping busy, he spent his time landscaping the grounds of his parents' cottage on the lake shore. Everett now managed to spend a week with a local landscape man. This experience convinced him that he had found an occupation that would make him happy and provide a living. At present, he is taking a course in landscape architecture in college.

Many young people are likely to ignore simple jobs in favor of work requiring the greatest training. Such boys and girls sometimes may have the idea that only white-collar jobs are respectable.

There is no place in a democracy for labeling any occupation "inferior" or "superior." All honest human labor has its own dignity, no matter what it is.

Too many people still have the illusion that a college education will, of itself, lead to economic security. Consider the case of Dorothy R. Dorothy's parents wanted her to attend college because that seemed the correct thing for her to do, though neither she nor her parents were interested in any of her courses, or in additional education, for that matter. But Dorothy did have a tremendous liking and talent for hairdressing and had spent several summers in a first-class beauty salon. And this was the work she wanted to do.

After the first marks arrived, the entire family met in executive session to reconsider the matter carefully. That was how Dorothy came to drop out of college while still a freshman. Five years later she owned the latest type of beauty salon which her former sorority members were only too glad to patronize because of Dorothy's talent.

Most of us during our school years come across some occupations that attract us, and many more that repel. Whenever we suspect possible disapproval on the part of others, we may hesitate to admit our vocational preferences and aversions. We may even be afraid to admit an ambition to ourselves, because we feel sure we never will be able to fulfill it. This fear and conflict makes some of us look for a way to escape a decision.

HOW TO BE HAPPY THOUGH YOUNG

Hence we say, sincerely but inaccurately, "I haven't any idea of what I want to be."

Specialists trained in studying the relationship between personality traits and vocational preferences are often able to bring these hidden wishes and ambitions to light.

But this brings us to another big area of this general field, and I had better postpone exploring it until another time.

On Choosing a Career

Dear Dr. Lawton:

How can a girl find out if she is fitted for the particular career she has chosen? What I mean is this: I know the kind of work I want—but how can I be sure if I am right in wanting it?

Carol G.

or How to Find Your Right Job

Dear Carol:

If you have made up your mind as to the type of work you want, detailed answers to the following little test of vocational adjustment will show you whether you have chosen wisely:

1. Have you the physical strength which the future calling requires?

2. Are you seeking work which is suitable to your type of personality? For instance, are you a shy person who dreads contacts with people but who nevertheless wants to be a saleslady?

3. If you have chosen a field where success depends on the possession of many social contacts and the ability to make friends easily, as in insurance brokerage, have you this necessary equipment?

4. Is the calling you have selected one which is below or too

far above your level of intelligence? If the first, you will be discontented; if the second, you face great strain and possible failure. One's job should lie within the range of one's mental ability, but it should challenge that ability to its utmost.

5. If your choice requires a special talent, as in the case of writing, singing, or other arts, has your ability been evaluated by a professional in that field who has no particular interest in you or any reason why he should spare you the truth?

6. Do you know and can you endure all the disagreeable sides of your future vocation or do you see it through the rosy glow of daydreams? Are you like Dorothy, who wanted to be a nurse as long as she could think of herself wearing a white uniform, measuring medicine, and radiating cheerfulness, but who changed her mind when she learned she would have to assist at operations, see blood, and do disagreeable menial tasks?

7. If your profession is an overcrowded one, are you prepared to face the competition and take the chance of being eliminated before your goal is reached?

8. If your career is in a new field, are you prepared for the delay before you can earn a secure living? Have you the promotional ability and the drive necessary to push a new idea?

9. Do you want the very career that will only intensify some trait in you that should be eradicated? There is, for instance, the over-active, over-talkative boy who wanted to be a traveling salesman; he liked to be always on the go, when he needed mainly to relax. He was a tip-top salesman—while he lasted.

10. Do you want a vocation for which there is little or no demand while one is young, such as being a business executive, editor, buyer, etc.? It is fine to plan far ahead, but you must work up to your goal gradually through some other related occupation.

11. If your career requires a costly preparation, are you assured of the financial backing to see you through?

12. Are you pursuing a line of work that your parents have selected? Perhaps it is also your own choice, and so there is no problem, but you may find their selection distasteful and can think of greater success in other directions. If this is true, are you prepared to strike out for yourself and face the family music?

13. Is there any discrimination in your field which will affect you and not most others? Perhaps you are a girl who wants to be an engineer. Have you the pluck and the ingenuity with which to face this additional obstacle?

14. Some occupations require as daily tools certain academic skills. If you want to be a reporter, can you spell and construct simple, clear sentences? Are you a good observer, and are you accurate in presenting facts?

15. In order to seem modern and ambitious, some girls make a half-hearted attempt to pursue a difficult career, whereas their real interest is a home and children. While it is often possible to combine marriage and an arduous career successfully, many girls would be happier if they were honest with themselves, tried to learn something about homemaking and child-rearing and prepared themselves to become fine wives and mothers.

Granted that it is often difficult for young people to find jobs, it still remains true that the available jobs go to those best equipped for them in terms of mental ability, training, education, personality, courage, inventiveness, and social contacts (when required).

Detour or Main Highway?

Dear Dr. Lawton:

I am in a fix. Here I am, a senior, planning to study engineering. But how can a fellow tell whether a particular line of work is the one best suited for him? Is that the same as doing what you would like to do most? I've always wanted engineering. On the other hand, I could accept the first job that comes along as soon as I graduate and make some real money right away.

Bruce C.

How Can We Find Out?

Dear Bruce:

You say you like engineering. Let's stick to that for the moment. "Liking," of course, is not the whole story about any career. Success depends also on ability, ambition, emotional adjustment, health, circumstances.

We have to study the total resources of a boy or girl and compare these with the requirements of a given job. Individual analysis and what we call job analysis go hand in hand.

Let me put it this way. From now on you're not a human being, you're a car. Let's say liking or interest is the route the car takes. A few young people are lucky. From earliest years they know exactly what they want to do or else they have their minds made up for them. The more we change our route, the longer it will take us to reach a particular goal. But the taste of young people in scenery changes as they grow older, so shifting routes is very common at your age and even a little later. However, a delayed arrival is not a great misfortune if the destination is really worthwhile, and if we finally get there.

Perhaps engineering is your real interest, Bruce, perhaps not. But there are ways of discovering which kinds of work really appeal to you and which don't. A boy may say he hasn't the slightest idea what he likes, but that's not correct. Some people look mostly for security in their job and some care only for a big income. Others value mostly change and excitement, something different every day, while still others seek chiefly a chance for self-expression and artistic or intellectual growth.

Skill or ability might be considered the motor of the automobile. Now, a motor is something that can produce a certain amount of energy under proper conditions. In the same way, a bright person is a piece of machinery *capable* of doing superior work.

Of all the elements responsible for success on the job, it is easiest to rate abilities. The ordinary intelligence test estimates your chances of succeeding at academic school work. There are also measures of mechanical skill, social ability, and of special talents like the artistic, musical, etc. During World War II, for example, practically every applicant for a defense job, and every selectee, received a classification test which revealed in a broad way the abilities in which he was strongest and weakest.

Ambition or eagerness to get ahead is the fuel of the motor. Remember the fable of the hare and the tortoise? Many able people fail because they don't want to succeed hard enough. Every field is overcrowded and every career is hard—except to the person who won't take "No" for an answer.

I used to know a boy we called "Skin-and-Bones Jones." He wanted to be a fireman, but was thirty pounds under the necessary weight, and quite a bit too short. It took him five years to pass the exams, but he finally did. Then there was Bill Sylvester, who had money, social position, good looks, a place in his father's business—all the breaks. Today he is down and out: good car, but no fuel to make it go.

Emotional adjustment can be compared to a steady hand at the steering wheel. All boys and girls have moods, doubts, and conflicts. They mistake a dream for a practical possibility. They stamp out of a room, take long walks in the rain, go from wild happiness one minute to even wilder misery the next. When we grow up, however, we are supposed to know what we want, to keep an even keel as far as our moods and work output go.

We are *supposed* to know, I said. Actually there are people who all their lives and without sufficient factual reasons, change goals, quit jobs, break off relationships. It is no use to have a good motor, a clear road ahead, and a full gas tank if your style of driving lands your car in a ditch.

Health is comparable to a car's strength and endurance. Will the machine hold together or fall apart? Is it a jalopy or not? Successful men and women generally have a tremendous capacity for hard work. But while good health is an advantage, there are people who are outstanding despite illness and weakness. Their handicaps are offset by the efficient way they manage their energy and time, and by the extra work they put in.

As for circumstances, for some people the highway is perfect. There is a certain amount of luck in every successful career. For most of us, however, the road is full of bumps, detours, torn-up stretches. But obstacles don't always lead to the same results. If we are sensitive and retiring, a slight hurdle stops us. If we like a challenge and don't mind hard thinking and hard work, we go right through, over or around the hindrance.

Under the head of "breaks" we must consider prejudice. If we really practice democracy and not only talk it, we judge a worker by his ability to do a job and not by his sex, age, creed, or color. But discriminations sometimes do exist, and a young person is wise to find out what's what in particular fields.

Suppose at some given time or place we fall into a group against which there is a prejudice—should we abandon our ambition? Not necessarily. If we feel we can handle any amount of disappointment, we plan our campaign accordingly and don't take our defeats personally. But if we can't stand the gaff of struggling in a field where we think the cards are stacked against us, it is no disgrace to switch to something else at the very start.

At this point in your life, Bruce, I think you should go over the machine and check it part by part.

Which Kind of I.Q. Have You?

Dear Dr. Lawton:

My father was a lawyer—he died a few years ago—and my mother naturally wants me to follow in Dad's footsteps. But what worries me is that I know I haven't got the brainpower even to get through college. What I'd really like to do is get a job as a mechanic after graduating, perhaps in an airplane factory. I love to work with my hands. I can fix anything, from an automobile to a tiny wristwatch. But most of the fellows I know are going to college, and I think if I don't it will be an awful social come-down for my mother. If I do go, though, it might be worse for her, because I just haven't got brains enough to make the grade. Do you think I should risk it?

Ernie S.

Where Are You Strong, Where Weak?

Dear Ernie:

Which kind of brains haven't you got? For there are many varieties of brightness. Most school subjects call for only one type: the ability to handle abstract ideas. These ideas refer, not to things but to relationships and functions. Math and grammar are made up entirely of abstract ideas, a fact which causes you many sorrowful moments.

But there is a kind of intelligence which you have in great abundance, though you don't take much pride in it. *Your* brains are located in your hands. Through them you can show the world who you are and what you can do. Words aren't always necessary for communication: eyes, gestures, signals serve the same purpose. You talk with your fingers instead of with your vocal cords. When you build a model plane, you express as much as another boy might when he writes a poem.

This type of "brains" illustrates a third kind of intelligence, the imaginative or creative, a kind possessed by every true artist, inventor, or pioneer.

There is still another kind of ability—one which is essential not only to vocational success but to our personal happiness. This is "social intelligence," the aptitude for having mutually helpful and agreeable relations with other people. The successful storekeeper, salesman, or master of ceremonies has this kind of brightness in its simplest form. The most complex example of it is shown by the man who becomes a leader of other men, not through force but because he has earned their respect and confidence.

To be skilful with words, to express ourselves through the work of our hands, to make a reality of some plan or dream—all of these are fine and to be desired. But for most of us, the chief joys of life come from our relationships with other human beings. Unless we can communicate to them some part of what is inside of us, and unless we can hear a portion of what their inner voices are saying, we are apt to feel pretty lonely and thwarted at times.

Every report card, it seems to me, should have one space reserved for a mark in "Social Intelligence." Personally, I should prefer an A in this field, and a C— in French, say, than vice-versa, though I'm afraid that the student who gets a C— (or worse) in French may not be consoled by his A in Human Relations.

It wasn't so long ago that the boys and girls who went to high school were those aiming for the professions. Since they could talk and write easily, and enjoyed getting their knowledge from the printed page, they were entirely at home in the academic school.

Today we believe in a high-school education for everyone. As a result, many students are in high school at present who formerly would have been working. With an intelligence of the concrete and practical type, such boys and girls are allergic to reading and are restless in discussions of abstract and bookish topics.

Young people who are strong in academic brightness are apt to underestimate the importance of the other kinds of ability. But this snobbishness does not last once they reach the outside world. They discover that employers are not much impressed with formal schooling in itself, and that a classmate with less "school" but more "social" intelligence may get to first base ahead of them. Haven't we all met the person who has been overeducated mentally, the man who has absorbed a goodly store of ideas and facts from books but who is sunk when he tries to apply this knowledge?

The boy or girl who is truly outstanding in abstract, mechanical, or creative intelligence is likely to go far, but he will go farther if, in addition to any one (or more) of these abilities, he also rates well in social intelligence. Many industrial and business concerns today give every job-seeker a test not only of his general intelligence and the particular technical skills a job requires but also of his temperament or ability to work in a group. If a young man obtains a high score only on the general intelligence and technical skill tests he gets a particular kind of job, one which can be quite good. But if he also shows that he is not likely to blow up and upset the smooth working of a team, he has a large number of jobs to choose from, and his opportunities for advancement are not limited.

Fortunately, while the first types of brightness are largely inherited, social intelligence is in the main the result of our upbringing. We can learn at home and in school the a-b-c of teamwork, just as we learn the three R's.

Since practically every person has one ability in which he is especially strong, the problem is to find the job where this ability will be at a premium. All kinds of intelligence are needed in a democracy, and a school should consider every kind of intelligence equally valuable and equally worth training. Boys and girls should ask, not "Is this a white-collar job?" but "Does this give me a living wage and a chance to do what I can do best; is it socially useful?"

Can I Be An Artist?

Dear Dr. Lawton:

I am a senior in high school, and, like many others, I am wondering—"graduation, then what?" My ambition is to be a *good* painter. I like painting, am willing to work for it. I have talent, but painting is an art! Do you think a girl who needs financial help should study one of the arts, or should she leave it for others who can do it only for the pleasure of it? I also want very much to get away from my family, as I feel there is little chance of my being a success in this town.

Amy M. R.

How Much Do You Want To Be One?

Dear Amy:

Perhaps the best way of discussing this matter is to offer for your consideration the lives of five grownups, each one of whom solved in his own way the problem of being an artist in the presentday world.

Even in his teens, Daniel had but one purpose: that of becoming a fine artist. He was quite willing to give all his time, thought, and energies to this goal. But it was not easy for him, having been poor, to face more insecurity, to be frequently cut off from human companionship, to enter upon a lifetime of incessant hard work—all without much hope for recognition or for a real livelihood.

Daniel left his parents early, and the knowledge that he has not been able to help them is painful. He has often had to seem harsh to people who were close to him. He has refused all commercial and full-time positions because he did not want to be turned from his one purpose. Support has to come from odd jobs—not related to art—and an occasional fellowship, gift, or sale of a painting. Daniel has made many sacrifices, but he has no real regret, because he has had no choice: something within drives him on. He is happy whenever he detects a slight improvement in his work. With a deep trust in his own talent, Daniel believes that some day he will come into his own. Should he fail, no one will be able to say that he has not given all of himself to painting.

In the life of Rhoda, art was important, but so were parties and boys. Moreover, she was reluctant to deny herself the little luxuries of life. Whenever she had to decide whether to spend the afternoon with a date or to paint by herself, she chose the date. Today Rhoda paints when she can escape the cares of a large household. She now realizes that the human being and woman in her is stronger than the artist. She feels that it is better for her to be a major success as a wife, mother, friend, hostess, and only a minor success as a painter, than for her to have been the reverse.

Betty wanted to be earning a good salary as soon as she got

out of high school. Her gifts as an illustrator quickly led to an excellent advertising position, which gives her the excitement, the contacts with people, and the financial independence she has always wanted. With a husband and child, Betty's life is complete. She doesn't consider herself much of an artist any more, though she greatly enjoys spending an afternoon at an exhibit or reading about art and artists.

After having won an art-school scholarship, Howard teaches art in a high school. He would prefer to be a full-time artist but dislikes the intense grind and the financial uncertainty of such a career. He still paints in his free time and finds much satisfaction in helping develop the talent of others.

It was Allan's plan to make a great deal of money first and then, while still young, to retire and devote himself to pure art. And, sure enough, at thirty he had made a small fortune and was ready to quit business and become an artist. Though he had painted very little, his interest was as keen as ever. But the depression in the 1930's came, he lost his money, and had to start all over again. Allan admits that even with money he could not have begun serving an apprenticeship at thirty. However, he feels he has had a good time, he has made money again, and is happy if he can talk about art and associate with artists.

No one of these five lives is better or worse than the others. Each has its own plus and minus sides. For every human being has many needs. But since we can't have everything, when our different needs come into conflict, we must decide what we want most, take that, and let the rest go. Since the artist has a greater struggle to make a living, it is much more difficult for a young person to decide on an artistic career than if he selected one of the more ordinary occupations.

However, in the case of the true artist, there can be no choice. His drive is so strong that it breaks through all obstacles. Where the drive is weaker, the prospective artist is more easily kept from his goal. In the long run, whether we want to be artists or something else, each one of us gets what he has chosen.

If We CAN'T Get What We Want . . .

Dear Dr. Lawton:

First, I must explain that my family is not well off. There is no hope of my being able to attend college. Therefore, I was forced to take up the commercial course. Although I always have gotten good marks in stenography, I now find that this course was a mistake. I do not have the executive ability or sense of responsibility necessary for such a position.

The subject that has since caught my attention most is archaeology. But it is impossible for me to look into this subject further. I already have gone too far in the commercial course, and archaeology is a college subject.

How can I look forward to life with any hope when I know I am entering a career that I am not fit for?

Ann E.

. . . We CAN Want What We Get

Dear Ann:

People may be divided into those who ask no more of a job than that it pay them a living wage and those who seek, in addition to this, the satisfaction of some special interest. The first group has a problem only when employment opportunities are scarce. But the person who seeks personal gratification from his job has many hurdles to jump, even in a period of prosperity.

What happens when an ambition meets an obstacle? That

depends on the strength of the ambition and the size of the obstacle. No outsider can tell whether a young person should be able to attain some goal he has set himself. We can all point to men and women who have been able to overcome difficulties that would have defeated most other people. Laura M. is a good example.

Laura always wanted to be a doctor. But a week before graduation she learned she would have to be the sole support of the family. Acting on a definite plan, she went to a business school instead of to college and subsequently obtained a position as a secretary. In a few years she was earning a good salary. Laura then devoted the evenings and summers of the next six years to a premedical course. Afterward, she entered medical school, taking care of the family and herself the first year with her savings. The second year, Laura stayed away from school and returned to her old job. Thus alternating studies and work, she finally became a physician. Laura had given up much in the way of fun and friendships. But she had obtained what she wanted. Was it worth all the struggle and sacrifice? Perhaps not, but only Laura can decide that.

It is all very well to hear about persons consumed by a burning ambition, who achieve it in spite of every hazard. But not everyone is made of such heroic stuff. Some of us are happier when our lives take the more comfortable pace which results from satisfying a special interest indirectly instead of directly. Marie, for example, wanted to be an explorer but took a job in a museum instead; Jean became, not a bacteriologist but secretary to one; Lloyd found that teaching in an aviation high school *for him* had more advantages and fewer disadvantages than being a pilot.

There are persons who follow still another scheme of life. They prefer a routine job completely unrelated to their interests, but one which leaves them some time and energy at the end of the day for pursuing the work about which they really care. Pietro Di Donato was a brick-layer during the time he was writing *Christ in Concrete*.

Thus far we have described people who have had a dream and held on to it, if only with their fingertips. But there are men and women who seem to have lost completely the dream they once had. In the novel *The Anointed,* by Clyde Brion Davis, the chief character wants to sail the seven seas as well as to solve the mystery of the universe, but he ends up working in a grocery store and becomes engaged to a librarian. What about him and all the other boys and girls who want to be nurses, newsreel photographers, journalists? Shall we call them weaklings and pretenders because they completely abandon their ambitions and become housewives or businessmen? Not necessarily. It might mean that they finally realized what they wanted most out of life, took this, and let the rest go.

Some young people think they want one thing, when actually they want another. They often select a career without having obtained any reliable information about it. In fact, they may be interested not so much in the particular career as in the excitement and glamour which rumor has attached to it. College, for instance, instead of representing an educational or vocational opportunity, may mean only a chance to get away from home or go in for various sports and social activities. Young people often change their minds with respect to a particular occupation once they learn about the daily activities of a person actually engaged in it and discover the requirements for success in this field. It sometimes happens that a person in his daydreams has found one career enchanting and another impossibly dull, yet has made a complete turnabout when he has tried them in the real world.

Vocational success depends on a number of factors: favorable opportunity, knowing the right people, experience, native ability, etc. But the individual with the most precious qualification is the one who has a definite goal, an intense desire to reach that goal, and a profound faith in his own powers. Remember "The Flying Yorkshireman," the story of a man who believed he could fly, and did!

Sometimes a student cannot seem to find a clear road ahead vocationally. Whereupon he strikes an attitude of despair, fully expecting to maintain this tragic pose for the next fifty years or so. However, this mood is due not to the job situation outside but to the emotional situation inside. A young person who feels he is failing in his relationships with people or who finds burdensome the everyday problems of life may take refuge in overconscientious study, excessive worry about the future, etc.

A good deal of the average person's happiness depends on the kind of job he has. But our life is like a building that rests on many different supports. It is not safe to place the entire weight of the structure on one pillar: whether it be a job, a hobby, friendship, or love. Anyone who limits his ambition to vocational success is trying to obtain all his satisfactions from what, after all, is only a single part of his experience. Even assuming that one is a round peg in a square hole and can do nothing about it, life has many other satisfactions to offer, and there should be other supports to keep up the building.

Are Women as Intelligent as Men?

Dear Dr. Lawton:

I have just won a four-year scholarship in the Westinghouse nationwide science contest. Of course, I was thrilled to see my picture in the papers. But science will be a tough, self-sacrificing life, and I'm wondering whether it's worth trying to do something big in it. Sometimes I wonder whether women are really bright enough to reach as high as men in a scholarly life of abstract thinking. After all, there has been only one Madame Curie.

Dorothy S.

Depends On Who Asks the Question!

Dear Dorothy:

Your misgivings seem to have some foundation. At least the record of girls in the Westinghouse Science Talent Search, in which you yourself won distinction, is not so impressive as that of boys. Drs. Harold A. Edgerton and Steuart H. Britt, of Ohio State University, psychologists who analyzed exhaustively the results of the tests for three successive years, in which 15,000 high school seniors annually compete, found that the number of girls who made high records in the examinations, in proportion to those entering, was consistently lower than the number of boys.

There might be many reasons for this, not necessarily proving that girls are mentally inferior. They have not been accustomed, for example, to studying or developing an interest in science for as long as boys have.

One of America's leading psychologists says: "We do not have the necessary data as yet to back up this generalization, but we have more than a sneaking suspicion that the female of the species is not only more deadly, but also more intelligent than the male."

The safest conclusion today, based on the results of standard tests of intelligence, aptitude, and learning ability is that the average adult woman is mentally the equal of the average man.

At any rate, an ambitious girl has it within her to do as well as men in any intellectual field to which she devotes herself, science included. For discovering a hitherto unobserved form of the germ causing tuberculosis, Dr. Eleanor Alexander-Jackson of the Cornell University Medical School won a New York Academy of Science prize. This was the first time one of these coveted awards went to a woman. And perhaps a day will come when it won't surprise us to hear of an American woman Nobel prize-winner in science.

If it is true that men are no better than women to start with, why is it that they achieve leading rank more often in most fields of intellectual accomplishment?

One answer is that men seem to have the edge wherever creative ability and originality is called for. The great invention and discovery, the most daring imaginative departure in any field is almost always masculine. When the task calls for attention and detail and the strict carrying out of an assignment, a woman is more often as good or better than a man. Her creative nature generally is satisfied in building a home, rearing children, working for community welfare, etc. Even in occupations usually considered a woman's stamping ground, like cooking, fashion designing, interior decorating, beauty culture, the stars are male.

The explanation of superior masculine performance lies chiefly in the way boys and girls are brought up. First, there is the influence of education and tradition. History is filled with the deeds of our great men. But men write most of the books and especially the histories and biographies. If as many women as men wrote encyclopedia articles, composed epitaphs, and designed monuments, our list of earthly "Who's Who" might look a little different. Would anyone say the courage of woman in her domain is any less than that of man in his? But where are our women heroes studied?

Moreover, from the earliest years a boy is made to feel that success for him means job success, and so he can devote all his energy to his career and to his place in history. But for a woman success is twofold. Principally it means a true love relationship with a fine man, followed by a happy home life with him and their children; second, it means a vocation. A woman therefore has to concern herself with beauty aids, clothes, grooming, social skills.

Along with this, she has to train herself for a job. For some positions a woman candidate needs "more on the ball" to obtain a position than a man and will have to work harder than he to keep it. After marriage, she has to take time out to bear children, attend to their rearing, try to run a comfortable and efficient home, and still keep herself attractive to "The Man" she has taken for better or worse. Would men achieve top rank in careers as frequently as they do if they had to carry on two major roles?

Think of the way our society is organized and the equality of opportunities offered to men and women in different fields—politics, for example. What chance would you have as a candidate for mayor, supreme court judge, or President? Yet the average female aspirant for public office could easily duplicate in ability the average male. Would the world today be any worse off if women had shared its direction with men? We might have had many fewer wars.

You will be wise to take note that regardless of how you may compare with your husband in intelligence, and even though marriage should be a partnership, your mate will probably feel terribly deflated unless he *seems* to be doing most of the leading in family life. If you are realistic, you will be content to exert your point of view and perhaps even your leadership in certain spheres without seeming to do so.

You apparently possess scientific ability. If you have a truly overwhelming drive toward becoming a scientist and are able to organize your life accordingly, you are not likely to be kept back from your goal. But you should realize that you need not be great and famous in order to be happy. Sometimes a young person feels he is lacking in a quality other boys or girls possess, or he has the urgency of being "something big" constantly set before him. As a result, such a boy or girl begins to believe that only if he attains top rank in a vocation will he have "made the grade." And if he isn't a world-beater, that he has failed.

We all can't be at the head of the procession, nor would we all enjoy being there, even if we could make it. You will have done well if you get into an interesting field which gives you a sense of achievement and a secure livelihood for as long as you want it. Your real success can come only from the degree to which you feel you have been needed by immediate family, friends, and co-workers and have contributed to their satisfaction in life. In turn, you yourself will need their warm affection and respect. Also, you should have some outlet for your inner thoughts and feelings through some art or craft.

Men and women are similar not only in intelligence but in the fact that their most genuine success is what they achieve as human beings. Money and prestige are fine, but these do not fill the bill. The question you will have to answer some day is not, "Have I successfully competed with men?" but "How full of affection, interest, and usefulness has my life been?"

School

Overcoming Stage Fright

Dear Dr. Lawton:

I would like to know how to overcome my fear of giving oral reports. It is easy for me to select and prepare a talk, but when it comes to giving it orally, I feel terrible. A lump comes in my throat, my head aches, my heart feels as if it were beating out of me, and I feel as if I would forget all I have learned or memorized.

Glenn G.

By Having Something to Say

Dear Glenn:

Your dread of addressing a group is not unusual. The first step should be to talk things over with each of your teachers, who will assist you in carrying out the following plan. Start by listening attentively to the subject under discussion. Then ask questions and make comments from time to time directed not only to your teachers but to your classmates. Follow this by writing out and reading from your seat a complete speech on a topic you know well and in which you are deeply interested. Repeat this with another subject, this time reading it from the front of the room. On both occasions, allow one-third of your time for dealing with remarks from the floor. If you can make your listeners active participants, it means your own talk has been a success.

For the next step, prepare not a complete speech but merely several questions on a very debatable topic, and thereafter try to keep things moving, draw out the others, and steer opposing sides to a generally accepted conclusion. If all has gone well thus far, you will be ready for the biggest hurdle: delivering and not reading your speech. This time prepare only the briefest of notes for the body of your talk. But write out in entirety a short introduction and conclusion, since the two most difficult problems are getting started and finishing.

You will find it helpful to address your remarks to a particularly sympathetic and appreciative listener. Note his reactions and see if you can make him smile, grow serious, or become raptly attentive, whenever you so desire. Between planning your next sentence and working on the thoughts and emotions of this one-person audience, you will have no chance to worry about whether you are creating a good impression or not. When you rise to speak, remember that many of your listeners would develop the same symptoms of panic and strangulation were they in your place and that they are thanking their stars you have saved them from this fate. Remember also that probably few of your classmates could do much better than you.

Presumably this is as far as you will want to go. For attaining the final stage in a speaker's development is difficult indeed, since then you should be capable of talking, as required, on any one of a wide range of topics, without preparation and notes, before any type of audience and under any conditions. To do this requires natural ability, educational background, and years of constant practice.

In every variety of talk, the speaker must be able to arrest quickly the attention of his audience and hold it as long as *he* wishes. Assuming you have something to say, a simple, sincere, and informal approach is generally more effective than clever rhetoric or high-pressure oratory. Some speakers indulge in too much technique and fireworks for either their own good or that of their listeners. If the occupational disease of speakers is stage fright, that of audiences is exhaustion.

In preparing your talks keep in mind that all human beings have the some hopes, fears, and wishes. Each one of your listeners seeks from life what you do, and about these things he is constantly conversing with himself. A speaker, therefore, should act as if he were not really the speaker but only a member of the group he is addressing, a little more skilled than his fellows at using words which reach down to the basic human being in all of us.

You have heard the saying, "What you are talks louder than any of your words." Before one can become a speaker, he must first become a person. No manual of speech-making can make a person: only experience, reflection, and maturity. Put side by side speeches by Lincoln, Roosevelt, Churchill, and others. In each instance, can you discover a genuine person behind the words? Would you like to learn more about him? Do you think he knows what is really important in the lives of those who make up his audience? Does it seem as if he had thought and felt deeply about the subject he is discussing, and does he respect the intellectual judgment and emotional values of his listeners? An affirmative answer indicates you have found a first-rate speaker.

Many a young person secretly considers himself inferior to his companions in appearance, ability, and attractiveness of personality, though in truth he may be as good-looking, bright, and likeable as they. When such a boy (or girl) faces critical examination by others of his own age, he is sure everyone will soon discover how inadequate he really is. He is afraid not of speechmaking, dancing, parties, etc., but of exhibiting his weakness for all the world to see, a weakness—mind you—which often has not the slightest basis in fact, or which, even if it did exist, would not disturb another boy at all.

When this fear of failure in social situations is intense, the plan proposed earlier may not work. Instead, such a young person needs to learn what experiences have caused him either to set up impossibly high standards for himself or to feel he cannot achieve the same moderate degree of success as his friends and classmates. In extreme cases, outside professional assistance is required before the individual can determine the precise factors, past and present, responsible for his overwhelming sense of inadequacy.

"I'm Just No Good in Math!"

Dear Dr. Lawton:
I do very well in English and social studies in school, but when it comes to math—well, I'm just no good at it. I'm afraid I'm going to fail in it, even though I had special coaching all last term. I don't seem to be able to concentrate—that's my trouble. I suppose I could go through life without math (I plan to be a journalist), but I can't get through school without it. That's why I am appealing to you for some advice.

Dick

Neither Are a Million Others

Dear Dick:
If it's any consolation to you, there are many people with the same kind of lopsided intellectual development as yours.

Many persons possess general intelligence of a high level but do very poorly in certain specific fields, whether it's mathematics, reading, spelling, handling tools, or art. Recently I went to a gathering where a well-known surgeon, shortly after he had been introduced to a lady, whispered to me, "What is that woman's name? I can't remember names, no matter how I try." And a successful journalist at the same party confessed, "I can hardly add two and two. The balance I get in my checkbook is never the same as the balance the bank sends me." This journalist is a very bright young man who has a way with any subject or assignment that calls for imagination, the ability to use words, and the power to generalize from facts overheard.

It is rare indeed that such persons are genuinely "dumb" in a given area. Most often the condition could be corrected, provided the "sufferer" is brave enough to part with his failing.

Let's take the ability to remember. The human forgettery is as important as the human memory. Imagine what a scrap heap your mind would be if you had in it at any one time every experience, thought, or bit of information that ever had come your way. In order to deal with the world efficiently, you unconsciously had to train yourself to face life with this attitude: "Whatever will contribute to my welfare or my pleasures I will listen to and place on file for future reference. Everything else I will drop into my forgettery marked 'Gone with the Wind.'"

So we remember only what we believe it is important for us to remember. The surgeon forgot the name of the lady because he never heard it to begin with. He was thinking of himself, the impression he might be making, or of some professional matter. You can't take a picture if you don't open the shutter and expose the film. Suppose our wielder of the knife had been told by his hostess, "I want you to meet an outstanding surgeon from out of town who is thinking of moving here," would our local eminence remember the name or not? Or suppose he were told, "You will receive $1000 if you will report correctly the name of every person to whom you are introduced in the next week," what would happen? Do you forget the name of a girl you find pretty? Won't you even remember her address and phone number without pencil and paper if you have to?

You will say, "I can't concentrate. That's my trouble." Actually, you concentrate very well in the math class, though not on *math*. And so in your educational lifetime, you have really heard very little math.

You may believe you are genuinely sorry you are poor in math, but you actually like your weakness and need it. You don't really respect mathematics as a field of human endeavor, do not believe it is important to be successful there. The people you most admire are those who are good not at numbers but as journalists, news commentators, etc. The dancer looks down upon the bookworm and vice-versa. People who are good at numbers you find inferior to yourself. The horizons of such practical people are limited, you think.

Also, without your realizing it, you are getting a big kick out of the effect produced by your difficulty on other people. The attention you receive is not at all disagreeable. In fact, unwittingly you are proceeding on the theory that being a mathematical nitwit is a kind of proof or trademark that you are gifted as a fine writer and deep thinker. Don't most of us believe that an artist must dress differently from other people and be liberally endowed with "temperament?" We expect the professor to be "absent-minded," though as a vocational group professors are no more absent-minded than any other. For example, Lt. Col. Derrill Daniel had been a professor of entomology ("bugs") at the California Institute of Technology. But this didn't keep him from leading a unit of the American 1st Army in Germany.

We all take pride in our good qualities and outstanding traits. But that doesn't mean we dislike our "bad" habits. Toward them we feel a certain tender regard. Being hopeless in math is part of you, and therefore precious and fascinating to you.

Many a weakness can be overcome, but only if we are convinced through and through that the failing is a serious handicap and are *fiercely* determined to overcome it. Two things must happen if you are to change. You must find your being a dunce in the sphere of numbers as hard to bear as the inability to throw a ball or ask a girl for a date. Also, you must be persuaded that skill at mathematics is of vital importance to *you*, either vocationally, or as a human being.

"Aw, What's the Use of Studying!"

Dear Dr. Lawton:

My ambition is to learn how to run a Diesel engine. But here I am stuck in school studying irregular verbs! What good are verbs? I won't need them in my future work. I'm interested in machines, not verbs. And it seems I always have to study them just on the night I'm supposed to go to a dance. Honestly, I wouldn't mind if there was some use in studying, but it doesn't make sense—not for me, anyway.

Tom F.

No Use Sometimes; Terribly Important Other Times

Dear Tom:

Why do people study? There are various reasons, and you may think that I am conspiring with your parents and teachers in my answer, but, honor bright, any resemblance to them is entirely coincidental.

Perhaps the best way to start is to tell you about three boys I know very well. Let's take Dick Britton first. He is the kind of person who studies under compulsion, a kind of voluntary servitude. By having enrolled in school, Dick feels he has agreed beforehand to carry out orders whether or not *he* sees a reason for the immediate task. Even if the task doesn't seem to fit in with his present or future plans, it's not up to him, Dick argues, to ask why. As long as he is in school, his job is to obey.

On the other hand, believe it or not, some people study in order to learn. Here is Roy Brook. Roy is tremendously interested in math. He's active in the Math Club, spends two nights a week playing chess, and wants to design planes. Learning more and more about algebra or trig gives Roy as much satisfaction and sense of achievement as another boy or girl may get from doing the rhumba, swimming across the lake, or listening to Frank Sinatra.

Incidentally, many young people know more about Sinatra than they do about syntax, because they can see the appeal of Sinatra, but what syntax could possibly contribute is much less evident. Yet what is dull to one person—say, the study of poetry or novels—may open a new world of interest to someone else and give him a source of pleasure for an entire lifetime.

Roger Hill is another type. He studies because, even if a given assignment is dull, carrying it out makes possible some slight advance in his career. Roger doesn't ask himself if he likes each step or not. The only thing he wants to know is whether he is getting somewhere.

Roger studies irregular verbs because that means a high-school diploma, and a diploma may help him in landing a job.

Certainly it will make possible admission to college, with professional training after that, if he wants it.

You, Tom, seem to be an average American boy, with a fairly good mind and more energy than you can use. You also are the kind of person who lives entirely in the present. If what you are asked to do is pleasant and satisfies a current mood or impulse, it is good. If it is disagreeable or interferes with a current mood or impulse, it is bad. All of us have—or should have—"near" goals and "far" goals: today's job, tomorrow's final achievement. But some boys and girls are unable to see the relation of the present to what they will be doing, or the kind of person they will be, years from now.

You cannot be like Dick. You will not do things merely because you are told to do them. You cannot be like Roy—your intellectual curiosity will not be satisfied by any of your school subjects. Whether or not this is your fault is immaterial, but certainly it's a lost opportunity for both you and school. You *may* make yourself into a Roger Hill. School in that case will be a road that leads to a highway that leads to a town, where you can settle down. If you are on your way somewhere and must get there by a certain time, you keep going even if the road is full of detours, or the scenery is uninteresting, or it starts to storm.

You are not necessarily inferior to the other boys either as a student or as a person. You may do fine work in the world, but you work well only when you have the kind of job that you like and that has a direct tie-up with your immediate plans. People of your kind do well in fields where they are able to create the variety and conditions that suit them, and are permitted to do things on their initiative.

Under those particular circumstances, you may be more brilliant than your more "regular" classmates could ever hope to be. But there are thousands of places where you will never fit in. Some boys and girls find school subjects dull and useless. One student in a hundred thinks the high-school experience is almost a total waste for him. But whatever else a high-school diploma may represent, it does mean a step completed in one's life.

Perhaps you will finish school, groaning and muttering all the while. You will at least have the satisfaction of having finished something, even though, when you get out of school, you will think you are making no direct use of the subject and will believe you have forgotten it all.

I have known dozens of boys and girls who quit school: nothing could persuade them to remain at their desks or do any work. Years afterward many of these boys and girls regretted they had left. They had not changed their minds about the dullness of the subjects as they had found them, but they regretted leaving because the sense of a job left unfinished always bothered them. Other people who quit were impelled to return to school years afterward to complete their high-school work. I was one such person, and so, Tom, I know just how you feel.

No one can make you study—except you yourself. You will have to study because without studying you can't learn enough to pass your subjects. You will have to find a way to accept the dull tasks and responsibilities with which life is filled—even irregular verbs, which have no direct connection with Diesel engines. You will have to learn to study as efficiently as you can.

If you quit, I'd like to say, "Good luck and more power to you, Tom." Let's hope you're never sorry. You can always go back to school and finish up, if you want to hard enough. But it will be much easier for you to study now, rather than later in life, if you can force yourself to buckle down and get through school. (I know!) Later, there will be "Jeanie with the light brown hair"; still later, you will be married and have a family. You may think you have too much on your mind now for school, but you'll have more later on. In the long run, we all learn best by our own experience.

Do You Know How To Study?

Dear Dr. Lawton:

I study hard and get fairly good results. But I am in a position where I have to make every minute count. I have a job after school, and I also am seriously interested in my music lessons, which means lots of practicing. As you can see, that doesn't leave me much time for fun—and I like fun. By that I mean I'm only human and want to go on dates and to dances. It occurred to me that maybe I spend too much time on my homework. That is, that I don't go about it in the most efficient way possible. Have you any suggestions as to how to get the maximum results out of studying with a minimum of waste of time?

Bert H.

Streamlining Your Study Habits

Dear Bert:

Your asking about how to study reminds me of two young people we all know. One is Fred, a fellow who once took a solemn oath never to study and has kept his vow faithfully. The other is Peg who, with equal devotion, spends hours over her books, yet sees only the design of the wallpaper before her. However, this answer is not about them but about you, Bert.

Here are twenty rules of study that you might examine profitably. Of course, there are no iron-clad rules for everybody. You might take out of these suggestions whatever suits you, and if they help you I'll be very happy.

1. You can't study well unless your eyesight and hearing are good and your general physical and mental health are up to par. Have them checked.

2. It is amazing how much we can do if we operate according to a time budget. By careful planning, we can divide our time between work around the house, an outside job, school, study, good times.

3. The best studying is done not to satisfy the teacher, nor to beat a rival student, but to gain more information and skill so that we can reach some goal we have set for ourselves; to earn a living, add interest to our lives, or render others a service. Whenever you encounter a new subject or a new idea, ask yourself, "In what way can I use this?"

4. We learn to do by doing, and we lose what we do not use. Whatever it is that you study, try to apply it to practical and current situations, if possible, in your life or experience.

5. We must be ready for a particular subject and the next step within it. If previous knowledge is required, go back and get it.

6. Never begin work without knowing exactly what you are supposed to do. Students who manage to get through school with little study have a way of listening attentively when the teacher is explaining what it is essential for them to do.

7. Relate anything new you learn to something you already know. One musical instrument or language may be like another. Cross the boundaries between subjects: see whether the historical background of a novel is the true history of that period.

8. Study is not a natural human activity. Don't quit in five minutes, just because you can't get anywhere. Go through

the motions for a while longer, and the chances are you actually will be at work.

9. It is natural for our attention to wander if we find the task dull or if we have something unusually pleasant or painful on our minds. Whenever these outside thoughts cannot be denied, take a seventh-inning stretch.

10. There is a limit to which we can give any subject or task our undivided attention, a limit which varies with the interest and difficulty of the material. In learning, a change is almost as good as a rest. Keep a log of how long you can study a subject before your mind rebels. When the time is up, switch to something else and stick to that for the agreed-upon time.

One plan is to start your study with the most boring or difficult task, switch to an interesting and easy one, and alternate that way, ending with a pleasant assignment. For instance, do your math or history, then practice the piano, then take up your English homework.

Or, after having given your all to what you consider a "dull" subject, take time out, do a handspring, relax, have a jelly sandwich and milk. Then return to the faithful performance of another dull task.

11. People vary a great deal in the conditions they require for efficient study. Silence and solitude are craved by some; noise and company by others. Many young people want fast and merry radio programs when they work. One person likes the same nook, chair and pencil day after day. The next one studies wherever he is: a phone booth, a trolley car.

Conduct an honest experiment and abide by the results. Compare the quality of work turned out in a particular subject under different conditions. If you must have a particular radio program, for example, and you find it does cut down on the quality of homework, listen to the program unreservedly and do your studying at another time. If you can prove the radio helps or at least doesn't hurt your work, keep it, no matter what others say.

12. Each time you study, try to look up all the words you come across that you don't clearly understand. If you find that this means too much work, the material is probably too advanced for your particular stage of development. Efficient study is impossible without efficient reading. If you have any doubt about your ability here, see the reading expert in your school.

13. If your book is *your own personal property,* mark key sentences and make notes in the margin. But if it is not your own, jot down key ideas in a notebook. Either method helps toward a quick review.

14. Some subjects should be studied word by word. Most of one's reading, however, is rapid survey reading—"skimming." Instead of spending two hours reading several chapters of a history assignment, devote the first half hour to reading the first and last sentences of paragraphs, get someone to quiz you for the next fifteen minutes on what you have learned, and then fifteen more minutes to going back, correcting your errors, and acquiring the information you missed.

15. Some subjects consist of units that must be memorized. You can't recall a formula or a conjugation through reasoning. Big jobs of memorization should be divided into short periods and, if necessary, spread over several days. Commit the material to memory in the form in which you will use it. Since a poem will be used as a whole, learn it that way.

A series of isolated facts should be broken up and the parts learned separately, because that's the way they will be used. Whenever you can "associate" ideas instead of memorizing them, do so. Always try to understand the meaning of the material before you. Think about it a while and see if you can relate one part to another through some kind of tie-up.

16. Don't turn the page or put down the assignment until

SCHOOL

you've understood it as far as you've gone. Never think that you've learned anything if you have, as a substitute for understanding it, mechanically memorized the words.

17. While this next may sound like a squirrel chasing its own tail, one way to acquire interest in a subject you find dull (and thereby make studying easier and save time) is to try to find out more about it. We all have had the experience that the more we have learned about something, the more we wish to know.

18. Some students, especially those who can't study at home or who are not "self-starters" when it comes to studying, find it helpful to stay after school or meet in someone's house for a quiz-fest. Each student prepares the answers to certain problems, if he can, and then questions and teaches the others. Or else one person reads the question, and whoever in the group knows the answer talks up. Some young people learn better in a group of their contemporaries because all are on an equal plane.

19. Each time you study you should have a goal and a subgoal. The goal may be to obtain a fairly comprehensive knowledge of modern American history. The sub-goal may be no more than going from page 620 to 632 in your history book and making appropriate notes before getting up for the seventh-inning stretch.

20. For each of your classes, briefly write or make a talk on "How I Prepare My Work for This Class." If you will "tell all," the resulting discussion should be an eye-opener for you and your fellow-students.

Are Teachers and Pupils Natural Enemies?

Dear Dr. Lawton:

Why are so many teachers so nasty to us? Sometimes you'd think they hate us. I wonder what ever made them choose this kind of work, feeling the way they do. We have to spend so many hours in school, the least they might do is make it pleasant, but, no—they yell, order us around, make sarcastic remarks, never give us a chance to answer back when they accuse us unjustly, make threats, etc., etc., etc.

In one of our classes the other day the teacher asked us what we wanted to be when we grew up. Not one person said she wanted to be a teacher—and no wonder. They worry a lot about truancy in our school. But can you blame us when we stay away? There are days when you just can't face the prospect of looking at one sourpuss after another, or hearing their boring, scolding voices. To be fair, I know there are some nice ones among them, but the others!

Ethel M.

Are Teachers People?

Dear Ethel:

If all teachers were like those you describe in your letter, we would have had a nation-wide mutiny of school children long before this. I cannot believe all your teachers or even most of them answer to your description. Of course there are some like that, and I agree with you that they should never have become teachers in the first place. But they are extreme types. Almost equally rare is the dedicated teacher who really loves and "feels with" young people and who devotes her days and nights to inspiring them to life-long achievement.

The average teacher is not an ogre and not a saint. She is

simply a human being with the usual virtues and faults. She chose teaching as a profession in order to make a living, and she carries out her tasks as well as she can under the handicaps of low salary, tiresome extra paper work, crowded conditions, and, in many towns, if not an inferior social position, she does live in a fish bowl, where she can seldom feel free to be herself. It is unfortunate that she is also as frequently misunderstood by her pupils as she is by the community.

The only place you see your teacher day after day is behind her desk. Before school and after, as far as you are concerned, she disappears into thin air. But though she disappears from school, she doesn't disappear from life, and what happens to her at those times affects her actions as a teacher, just as your home life affects you as a pupil. If you would like to understand your teacher better and to be fair to her, you must take these factors into consideration. You've probably never met any of your teachers as a human being. Let me introduce you to one—an average teacher—I'll call her Miss Amy Bly.

Miss Amy Bly is an adult human being. She earns her living as a school teacher. Miss Bly likes young people and enjoys helping them master mathematics. She also likes to watch them grow, socially and emotionally. Miss Bly's work is not physically hard. It provides long vacation periods. It offers financial security in a regular pay check and a pension upon retirement.

But Miss Bly finds she earns less money than many of her women friends. Her work offers less variety and less reward for originality and leadership than many other fields. At times Miss Bly feels that nothing ever happens to her, that she lives in a "fish bowl." Her students graduate, go out into the world, and appear to enjoy all kinds of experience and success. Miss Bly works hard, but has to stay in the same place. Of course, she tries to have a wide range of interests and extra-curricular activities. Still, she cannot escape an occasional feeling of dull isolation.

Miss Bly wants from life what her students want. She wants a congenial job, paying enough for some leisure and a few extras, such as a car. She wants to be happy and loved, to marry and raise a family, to have loyal friendships, and to receive the approval of her associates. But, like her students, Miss Bly doesn't always get what she wants.

She, too, has her personal problems. Sometimes she leaves someone ill at home. Sometimes she comes to school after a quarrel or without breakfast. It is not always easy for her to appear relaxed before her students. Her words may sound as far away to her as they do to Jim Smith the morning after he's been "stood-up" by his girl. Suppose their two "off days" coincide! Jim won't be able to work and Miss Bly won't be patient, though ordinarily she is able to handle tough situations easily

At the end of a day, after facing one group of high-spirited youngsters after another, Miss Bly's nervous system is tired. According to a "teacher's-eye" view, a class is made up of: interested workers; constant interrupters; timid souls; an anti-school brigade; a group concentrating so hard on personal problems they can't concentrate on anything else; and, finally, the merely bored. However, Miss Bly much prefers actual teaching to the school's demand on her for endless "unessential" paper work and clerical detail.

Miss Bly faces young people who, in many cases, are blissfully ignorant of math. But she realizes this great difference in information between teacher and pupil doesn't mean a similar difference in native intelligence. She realizes math may not be as interesting to everyone else as it is to her. She knows, too, that Jim Smith may be poor in math but good in other subjects. Yet even if Jim lacks enthusiasm for math, Miss Bly knows it will help him succeed in his career. So she must be firm in her assignments.

Miss Bly has always felt that relationships with people are more important than with things. A school subject must be usable in order to become real and alive and be learned "for keeps." Miss Bly wants math to help Jim with practical problems and even contribute to his enjoyment. She also believes that the only subject anyone ever really teaches is himself.

Each year Miss Bly plans to treat the class in an informal fashion. A few students take this to mean Miss Bly is "easy," and they act accordingly. To make life bearable, Miss Bly clamps down. But then teaching becomes much less satisfying to her. Jim could help Miss Bly to be the kind of teacher she and he both prefer if he lived up to the common courtesies of group behavior, not talking to his neighbor, shouting out of turn, *ad libbing,* or acting as the class cut-up.

Like Jim, Miss Bly has a "teacher" (Supervisor) and gets report cards (Rating Schedules) based on observations of her classes. Under observation, Miss Bly often feels that she hasn't been able to show what she can really do.

Miss Bly and Jim, you see, are on the same side of the desk, both learners, but with the more advanced one leading the way. Occasionally the desk magically vanishes for both of them, and all the boring routine and petty annoyances are forgotten. That is when two minds meet and share a common understanding and enthusiasm. That is when Miss Bly says to herself: "Yes, teaching is a routine job, but a noble profession!"

Now that you've met Miss Bly, I'd like you to stop and consider what *you* are like, and how you appear to *her*. Just as you don't know Miss Bly outside the schoolroom, so she does not know you otherwise than as pupils. But since Miss Bly has had professional training in education and to some extent in child psychology, she often knows more about you than you imagine. You, too, bring your home problems with you into the schoolroom, and Miss Bly is well aware that often your strange behavior has explanations that go deeper than their surface appearance. But sometimes you try her patience beyond endurance and even average Miss Bly will fly off the handle and act like the teachers you described. Let's see what some of you are like.

Jim Smith is an average high-school student. He has heard about the "values of an education," but sometimes he can't see how a certain subject will increase his future earning power or his chances for personal success.

Jim is trying to find out what he wants from life and the vocation for which he is best suited. He also wants to know how to make a hit with his current "heart throb," how to raise the cash for a date, and how to make the fellows think he's "something."

Secretly Jim is impressed by his teachers. They have superior speech, manners, and poise. He reacts to Miss Amy Bly as he does to others in authority.

Most of his homework is done because Jim doesn't want Miss Bly to think he's a dumb-bell. He knows that Miss Bly, like his parents, has confidence in him and wishes him well.

But Jim's classmate, Dick, has an overly-protective mother. In class Dick is a timid, obedient spectator. To some he might appear "a model student." But not to Miss Bly. Dick's work is satisfactory, but it would be far better if he had learned to assert himself. In contributing something to the group he would get more out of it.

Then there is Janie. She enters into the class discussion one day and pays no attention the next. Now she succeeds; now she fails. Janie's moods may depend on her mother's habit of holding up as an example Janie's younger, brighter and more popular sister. Janie's self-confidence is wavering.

Sue is an orphan. Miss Bly understands Sue's extreme dependence on teachers but, for Sue's good, she can't accept it. Sue spends double the normal time on homework and would be glad to stay after school each day and help different teachers, if they would allow it. But Sue is another mistakenly termed "model pupil." Her desire for the affection of "foster parents," rather than a real desire for learning, urges her on to extreme effort.

Ted's father is strict with him but not with his older brother. Ted thinks his brother gets all the "breaks." In class Ted is either a rebellious hothead or a daydreamer. He doesn't care about passing math or even about graduating. He detests engineering, his father's choice of a vocation for him. Ted wants to be a swing musician.

There are other students who have ability and want to use it, but can't. They have to work after school, do all the housework, or care for the younger children in the family. Their health may be poor because of insufficient or improper diet and they are always "too tired" to study. They may not see or hear well.

School means a great deal even to those students who have convinced themselves that they're "agin it." For example, at home Ted and Dick get an overdose of opinionated ideas, family worry about money, and excited voices. An hour later they are in a light, cheerful classroom. Miss Bly is introducing them to a world where fact and logic rule. It is a welcome relief.

There are two kinds of education: one of the mind, the other of the emotions. The latter is more essential to personal happiness, but Miss Bly can do only a small part there. The job of educating feelings and attitudes is done mostly by parents.

But Miss Bly does what she can, and her students appreciate her help. They know that she doesn't pretend to be witty, learned, or charming. Neither does she pretend to be a fellow adolescent or playmate. She is merely a teacher who knows her subject and how to teach it to young people. She is patient because she knows that real learning is not easy. She gives clearly explained and workable assignments.

Miss Bly's pupils look forward to her class, whether or not they like the subject she teaches. They feel safe with her because she understands human nature. She smiles with them when they are lost in a maze of algebra equations. She doesn't "fly off the handle" at their small shortcomings. When someone is restless, goes "star-gazing," or talks to a neighbor, Miss Bly often pretends not to see. If there is a real violation of classroom discipline, she isn't sarcastic; she doesn't call names.

She knows that Ted is unhappy in the classroom because he is unhappy outside. She doesn't take his "shenanigans" personally. Miss Bly "tells him off" in a dignified way, and Ted respects her for it.

Society

Are Young People Mature?

Dear Dr. Lawton:

Our debating club recently took up a subject suggested by the father of one of the members: "Young people today are less mature and responsible than those of previous generations." The affirmative pointed to the fact that years ago boys of high-school age could be self-supporting. The negative held that our young people could be just as mature and serious if they were only given the opportunity. Would you please discuss this?

Albert B.

That Depends on Emotions, Not Birthdays

Dear Albert:

Adolescence is a term for that in-between time when a child is changing over to a grownup. However, there is no fixed date on which boys and girls turn into men and women. Young people are considered adults whenever society is ready for them. In the early part of this century, the average boy on graduating from elementary school was able to get a modest job. By the time he reached his early twenties he was in a position to marry, establish a home, and raise a family. Girls could look forward to marriage in their late teens. Until recent times, therefore, adolescence was relatively brief.

Whenever the ideas and energy of young people are needed in the labor market, they are usually permitted to assume adult responsibility at an earlier age. In a depression period, when there are no jobs, they are kept on the sidelines and told, "You are too young," for a much longer time.

Young people today, as always, want to be self-reliant and assume grownup responsibilities; they ask for a chance to prove what they can do. Yet the answer they often receive is to go back and wait a little longer. As this waiting time lengthens, so does adolescence. But nothing can stop the natural process of development. Adolescents grow up in mental ability, in emotional capacity, in the desire to enjoy the experiences and adopt the behavior of adults. Most of all, they long to become constructive members of society. Upper-termers in high school are in many respects already men and women, though still minus the complete maturity which additional knowledge and experience will bring.

Society may not be ready for young people, but life is. Out of this contradiction arise most of the problems facing adolescents. Some young people are able to make a place for themselves in the economic system at an early age as the result of thorough preparation, careful study of job possibilities, courage, and imagination. But some others, lacking work to do which society deems useful, grow confused and uncertain. Without ambition and sense of direction, such youngsters become bored and restless and turn to thrills and excitement.

We should enable young people to become adults; that is, to get jobs and marry, whenever they are mentally and physically ready. Most parents and teachers wish to respect the desire of young people to achieve independence in thought and action, and would like to give them every opportunity to take on mature responsibilities, insofar as economic conditions make this possible. Some school systems have begun to consider the problems that vitally concern growing boys and girls and are trying to answer their many questions. Such schools are attempting to give their students information about their minds and bodies, about vocational opportunities, about civic and social problems in their communities, so that young people can adjust successfully to the problems they will meet as adults. Soon, perhaps, every classroom in the land will be studying not only our national problems but their own community problems and how to meet these in democratic fashion.

Especially important is it to see the way our personal happiness depends on jobs and the chance to be socially useful. Since the American nation belongs to all its members, the help of youth in running it is required. Every opportunity should be given young people to share not merely in discussion but in the actual determination of policy, at home, in the classroom and school, and in the community. Nothing will increase the faith of young people in democracy so much as to receive evidence of its faith in them.

You're Young Only Once

Dear Dr. Lawton:
Everywhere you go you hear talk these days about juvenile delinquency. I wonder why some of us young people go straight and others go off the narrow path. I don't really know any juvenile delinquents, but there's a girl who left school, went out and got a job, and when I met her one day on the street she was dressed to kill and looked as if she wasn't passing up any

good times. There is plenty of gossip about her "morals"; even that she is being "kept" by some man. I remember when she was in school that she was sort of slow and ignored, and we all knew her home life was pretty unhappy. Now, I suppose, she feels on her own and important and grownup, and it must be quite an experience, but do you think that's enough to explain why she should take this kind of path while most of us plod along studying and planning seriously for the future? We all know other boys and girls who faced the same problems as this girl, but who didn't go her way. So I feel it must be something else.

Helen J.

What are We Waiting For?

Dear Helen:
Most young people go straight because they have a sense of security even in an insecure world, because they have something to believe in, something to cling to. If you can believe in yourself and the possibility of eventually earning a living and being of use to yourself and other people, that helps to keep the boat of life steady. Some get this feeling from their parents, some from their church; occasionally it is a bit of philosophy a teacher has offered in passing, or it may even be something inside oneself that acts as a guiding light.

Eventually, everyone must assume responsibility for his own behavior. Each one of us is the result of the world into which he was born, the parents he has, the schools he has attended.

Of course, the world should provide proper conditions for human beings to achieve a normal existence, parents should be mature and helpful, and teachers should do for their pupils all that the most enlightened educators would have them do. But suppose we don't have that set-up, what then? The answer is that we're all on our own, we are all "architects of our own fate."

What the girl you speak of in your letter probably needed was some wholesome way of having fun, some method of expressing herself and of obtaining satisfaction from life, some kind of long-distance plan for herself. Whether, having all these things, she would still have chosen the path she did is mere speculation. But not having them made it much easier for her to succumb to the lure of that slogan of the unsure and uncertain: "Eat, drink and be merry . . ." for there is no tomorrow.

One other thing to think about.

A young person needs to know the importance of listening to what the years say, not the hours. A human being has to live with his memories. He isn't one moment, one evening, one summer; he's a lifetime. He isn't one self, he's many selves. A boy or girl must be careful lest some day one part of himself will judge another part too harshly. Right now, it is hard to tell which self is most important to you. Sure, it's nice to have fun, to wear fine clothes, to put on the dog. It may seem swell to sport a car, to go places and see things, to get attention and be popular, to have someone seem to care for you. But everything in life has a price tag. The price may be too much for you later on.

If this girl were here, perhaps we would tell her not to make it too hard for a more permanent self of hers to find satisfaction. Five years from now may seem impossibly far off. But she'll be around then, and what she is now will influence the kind of person she will be then.

The secret of personal success is to live well even when life is hard, and when it is worse than hard—dull. We need a point of view which will sustain us whether the tide is in or out. We need to have some kind of regulating system—like a gyroscope—

inside of us. When there's tension outside, we must not let it carry us too far away from what we are; when things are slow, we supply our own inner excitement and interest.

Granted this girl has made a mistake. Does that mean that it's all over for her? No. For, believe it or not, all of us err plenty—even parents, even teachers. Many a grownup can point to a five-foot shelf of mistakes.

So young people have a right to a generous quota of mistakes. But the bigger we are, the more we can learn from our errors. Every person should have a special notebook called *Charged Up to Experience*, with chapters in it entitled, "What I learned from Whopper No. I, II," etc.

Why don't you try to help this particular girl by inviting her and her friends to your dances and parties? If you are afraid of what people will think of you, perhaps an entire class or group in school should do the inviting. Perhaps a school after hours should be a place for lonely young people who lack real homes. Maybe if their respectable contemporaries accepted persons like this girl more often, they could help change them. At any moment—tomorrow or right now—this girl could begin to change. It is never too late to start becoming a better person.

War Jitters

Dear Dr. Lawton:

For some time now I have found it very difficult to keep my mind on my school work, or, for that matter, to really enjoy myself outside of school. The only way I can explain it is the European situation. How can anyone plan for a job or a career if there may be another war? If civilization is going to be destroyed, what's the use of anybody trying to be anything or do anything, but if there is a chance to save it, then I want to do something about it, though I don't think I can do very much. How I'm going to make anything out of school or keep the jitters from affecting my everyday life has me worried.

David D.

Defense—Internal and External

Dear David:

Ever since the "peace," many Americans—young and old—have shown signs of war jitters. But this should not be blamed entirely on the news from Europe. Certain types of people "jitter" easily, and a tense situation simply increases their opportunities for becoming upset. There is the timid individual who, from childhood on, always has found the normal challenges of life too much for him and whose mind greatly amplifies every minor threat or danger about him. Then, too, there is the person dissatisfied with his life and work. In the worry and excitement about a war scare, he finds an escape from the usual routine, as well as an excuse for his inability to get ahead.

We are all concerned about war, but the average person does not let it take up all his thoughts or lead him permanently off the main highway of his life plan.

What actually has happened to this country? Those who have lost loved ones have suffered tragically. Young people who have returned damaged physically or emotionally also have undergone a terrible loss. The rest of us have lost some illusions. We always have taken it for granted that because we have found democracy the best form of government, every other nation must feel as we do, and, given a chance, would take us as their model. We also believed that no other country would dare think of attacking us, because of our two oceans and our greatness in size and natural resources. Suddenly we discover that there are nations who have little respect for our institutions and cultural achievements, that an attack is possible, and that our defenses may be inadequate.

We who believe in democracy have had to learn that a people may be free and advanced, that it may lead a peaceful and easygoing existence, and yet, in spite of this, may still have enemies, internal and external. Against such hostile forces democracy must actively protect itself, by means both of armaments and an intense faith in its own values.

Citizens in a democracy have no dictators to tell them what to do. They pick their own leaders and frame their own laws. Whether we have war or not, the years that lie ahead are going to be difficult ones, and we will have to make up our minds on many major policies, national and international. The United States will need, as it never has needed it before, a population that can make a wise selection from a large number of conflicting choices.

In a nation whose citizens govern themselves, young people require a special kind of education which they must not cut short if it can be avoided. As I conceive it, an education today should have several aims. It should help young people in adjusting to the problems they face in their teen years. It should also give them some background preparation for handling the chief situations they will meet as adults. This last means that a school should provide the kind of training that will be useful later on in a job. It should also equip students to make the most of their leisure time. Above all, the schools should give young people a thorough, critical understanding of our chief economic, political, social, and cultural problems. No young person ought to decide on leaving school today merely because of the possibility that war may come for us.

We cannot foretell what the future will bring. We know, however, that this world is neither a safe nor a sure place, and that it is impossible to guarantee anyone the achievement of his private ambition. War, tragic and regrettable as it may be, is sometimes unavoidable. It certainly delays the fulfilment of personal plans; it occasionally ends all planning. But then there are many other things besides war which have the same effect. Given the kind of world we have, a useful scheme to follow in mapping out one's life and future is to select not merely a single goal, but a series of goals: No. 1, the most desired; a second best, third, etc.

Sometimes a combination of persistence and good luck enables us to attain our first choice, but much more often we take a lesser one, making the best compromise permitted by circumstance and our personality make-up. The wise men of the ages all have said that peace occurs within a person, that external happenings or possessions can neither give real contentment nor take it away. One can have an orderly mind even in a disorderly world. Men have written books and composed music while bombs were falling.

Success in life depends on adaptability: knowing when to fight hard, when to accept quietly, when to take hold, when to let go. That is a difficult lesson to learn, but there are fortunate boys and girls who have acquired this wisdom early and who will make good use of it in the coming years.

Psychological Preparation for War

Dear Dr. Lawton:

How can anyone contemplate another war and atomic bombing without getting into a panic at the very thought? Sometimes I wake up at night and think about it, and I get into a cold sweat over it. Or when I hear an ambulance dashing through the night with its siren going, I imagine it's an air-raid warning all over again, and my heart starts to pound. I'm not a scary kind of person usually—in fact, I have no use for people who panic at the slightest thing. I usually remain quite calm in an emergency. That's why I am so puzzled as to why I get into such a state when I think of air raids and bombing.

Jean J.

Through Tasks and Teamwork

Dear Jean:
A severe bombing is a terrible experience. We have a legitimate right to fear it. However, normal fear is one thing and abnormal fear another. Ordinary anxiety, with its increased breathing rate and faster beating heart, may be annoying, but it provides an emergency burst of energy which can be harnessed to do valuable work.

But there can be too much of a "good thing." Chronic jitteriness makes one a mental cripple. While the sufferer may manage to offset this handicap quite well in peacetime, during a war he is a menace to himself and others.

The constant worrier is the kind of person who cannot relax or wait to get things done. Nor can he ever escape his responsibilities and ailments. If subjected to special strain, such as a failure in school, disappointment in love, or a bereavement, he becomes much more upset than the average person. He may even suddenly feel that everything around him is unreal and talk of dizziness, weakness, or approaching death, though none of this has any physical basis.

What makes this perpetual worrying machine a liability during wartime is that if there are alarming rumors afloat, he thinks he must repeat them to everyone he meets, in order to obtain reassurance that things will turn out all right. He is any war's psychological disease carrier No. 1, since he broadcasts ideas which otherwise might have died a quiet death. Every town should set up "rumor clinics" in its schools and newspaper offices, to which all large-scale gossip is brought to be tested for truth and traced to its source.

But it is during a war scare or emergency that the emotionally unstable individual is most dangerous. Incapacitated by fear, he requires special care. What is even worse, since fear is contagious, two or three frightened persons can start a panic in a crowd. This means that we must detect early the abnormally anxious person. In case of an air raid he should be evacuated to a relatively safe place. If this is impossible, he should be paired off in advance with one or more persons of proved stability who will act as psychological "insulators."

In a panic, each man or woman thinks only of saving himself, and may even turn against his neighbor to do so. Panics usually occur in large, unorganized groups, the members of which know neither each other nor where to turn for leadership. Therefore one of the most important things which air-raid or fire precaution and drill does in a school, a factory, or a community is to provide familiar leadership and organization.

It is natural for people to form a group in times of danger, because it gives the individual security he would not have alone. The group, however, must be active, and have a constructive function to carry out at all costs during the period of greatest danger. Everyone must feel that he has a share in the scheme, that he is part of a community fighting for its survival. Old people and young children should also have an assigned task to perform, no matter how simple.

This is why in the last war those Londoners who sat passively in shelters developed more nervous disturbances than those outside fighting the raids. In certain English factories, the girls during air raids joined in community singing and continued to operate their machines. Without definite tasks, people still need rehearsals in order to meet emergencies in a collected way. In a large school, older students can look after their juniors; in a small one every boy or girl can be responsible for carrying something or attending to some safety measure.

If people are trained to protect their own dear ones and possessions, they will think less about saving their own skins. Activity also diverts the individual's attention from himself, giving his fear-creating imagination no chance to get busy. A task which brings people closer into the group offers psychological protection, as well as healing power.

In every fire drill or air-raid precaution unit, the key personnel must be resourceful, quick, and decisive in action. A leader who suffers from undue anxiety will communicate it to an entire group. Such a person should never be made an air-raid warden or group leader. When the going gets rough, we expect the warden to keep his wits about him and to have planned ahead of time how to meet the various types of emergencies that may arise. He must act with authority that others recognize beforehand, must work well with people, and enjoy their respect and confidence.

This trained personnel, in order to combat insecurity, will see to it that conditions are made as normal as possible and that various activities, recreational or otherwise, can be carried on in the school or shelter.

Despite tragedy and suffering, life goes on. Should we ever be bombed, I am sure we will take it in our stride as the English did. One morning after a dreadful night raid, a London psychologist walked through the streets filled with wreckage, amazed that he could not find among all the faces he looked upon, a single unhappy one! But then the Londoners were only taking a lesson from a lowly creature, as Mary Carolyn Davies tells us in her poem, "The Cats of England":[*]

[*] Reprinted from *Voices*, by permission of the editors.

"The cats know when a bomb's about to fall.
They calmly walk to shelter, where they wait
Until the all-clear sounds, then, still sedate,
Walk back through ruins to ruined places
Which once were homes. . . . Through the sights
And sounds that stop the heart the household cat
Steps daintily, amid the newly torn
Timbers. Alone she waits, serene and still,
For her old home to be again re-born;
The god of catdom has told her that it will."

What Success in Life Means to Me

One of the most interesting of all the *Scholastic* contests was held on the subject "What Does Success in Life Mean to Me?" It was a contest crowned by the most "success," if we are to go by the great interest it awakened, the extremely large number of entries submitted, and the excellence of the contributions received.

As might be imagined, there were many different versions of what success means. Faced with such an abundance, the judges selected what in their opinion seemed the most representative attitudes of boys and girls throughout the country.

We reprint here the letters of some of the prize-winners, which include some very brief definitions of success. They came from students in the following high schools:

Hamlin Township High School, Hazel Hurst, Pennsylvania
Litchfield High School, Litchfield, Minnesota
Millcreek High School, Erie, Pennsylvania
Olds High School, Alberta, Canada.

Success Is Success in Living

To some people, success in life means success in securing material things: automobiles, trips in luxury liners, pictures on the society page, and innumerable acquaintances. To me, success in life does not consist in these, nor in having "For He's a Jolly Good Fellow" sung when I rise to speak. In fact, I don't care if I never rise to speak.

Success in life means success *in living*—a far different thing. To be a success in living you must be a real person—you must keep your self-respect; you must have convictions and the courage of those convictions; you must realize your own precious individualism and give expression to it; you must live in a give-and-take way, based on the eternal and unchanging Rights of Man.

Achievement, too, is a requisite. To aim, not only high, but rightly; to find your own groove in the scheme of things and advance along it some way to your goal, is elemental in success.

To all these must be added experience. There are some experiences that everyone should have:—the happiness that comes from a job well done; the self-respect that comes from looking at the world honestly; the love, perhaps the respect, of some others of humanity; one great love in which you may transcend yourself.

If, when the "one clear call" comes, you can say with all truth, "I have worked, I have achieved something of value, I have loved and been loved, I have found happiness in realizing myself; surely I have lived," then you have been a success in life.

SOCIETY

The Average Man's Dream of Success

I'm just an ordinary boy with neither an abundance of brains nor brawn nor have I too much imagination. I haven't much of anything, but what I have is mine. I've worked since I was quite small, helping my father do machinist's work. That was up until two years ago. Now I have a job with a prosperous gas station, working after school and during summer vacations.

Another thing I do is to save most of my money, which I'll admit isn't easy. Now, I'm not exactly stingy nor am I of Scotch parentage, but I do like to save for the bigger things in life. Last summer I bought myself a number of new clothes, including a new suit. Also, in January, I bought myself a car; I got all from being able to put a little away and not spending it on unnecessary things—girls, for example.

Now, I shall try to make clear the thing I am talking about because so far I haven't touched upon the subject of which I started to write. Concerning my putting in that seemingly useless first paragraph, I'll explain.

It all had to do with what I'd like to do and to have in the future. By this I mean success to me in the future is to have a good honest job, to save up my money for the helping of others, and yet to be contented myself. I'm intending to buy a house and have it paid for by the time I might consider marriage. The next thing I honestly intend to do is to buy a profitable gasoline station. This all takes money, I know, but I'd gladly give some of my younger life pleasures to be a success in the future.

Success Means an All-Round Happy Person

To me, success in life means happiness, faithfulness to my ideals, the friendship and love of the people I love, and the opportunity and ability to appreciate beauty in life.

You will say that the first point, happiness, seems a little vague. You will say that if I have what else I desire, then I will surely have happiness. Perhaps you are right; but I think happiness is something I must work for, just as some people work for money. I know it is possible to be happy without working for it, but this happiness is easily lost when it comes into contact with life's reality. Therefore I feel I must cultivate happiness.

When I say that I must be faithful to my ideals, I mean I will be a failure if I bargain with my conscience. No matter how successful I am in the eyes of the world, if I cannot look back upon my life without feeling ashamed, I am a failure.

If I go through life without trying to make other people happy, I will never win the friendship and love of others. I believe that it is my duty to help my fellow men and try to make their lives happier. If I do not have any friends, or do not respect and love people, how can I do this? The greatest thing a human being can give another is sincere love! Therefore, if I do not love my fellow beings, I have no claim to success.

I have seen many people budget their time without a moment for leisure and appreciation of the beauty to be found in nature, in art, in music, and in literature. People who have such a drab existence do not really live, so how can they be called successful? If ever I reach the stage where I do not feel a tremor of emotion at the sight of a green leaf, at the sound of a simple melody, then I must brand myself a failure.

Success Means Understanding Life

For me, there can be but one true success in life. I shall feel that my life is a successful one only when I have formulated a philosophy out of which will grow contentment and happiness —the sort of happiness that is reasonably stable. This philosophy will help me to understand people and conditions, to be tolerant, and to be patient.

At the present, there are two points which are clear in my mind and which I feel sure will be embodied in my philosophy of happiness. First, I must not be self-centered—a person who thinks only of himself is never happy.

A second requisite for my happiness will be that I must soon recognize what my abilities are. When I have done this, I shall not be constantly struggling to reach some goal which is inaccessible to me. However, I shall always endeavor to do my work as well as I can.

Not everyone can be highly successful in material ways, but all of us can learn the art of living suited to ourselves.

After I have acquired a definite philosophy and one that seems worthwhile to me, the next step is to *use* that philosophy —to live it!

The Universe

What Can Young People Believe In?

Dear Dr. Lawton:

We have been having an argument about some pretty important things and decided to write you a joint letter asking your opinion. I, Jerry, believe in the inherent goodness of my fellow man. I believe that some day all types of oppression will become as out-of-date as the human sacrifices of the ancients, and a wrongdoer will be treated as a sick person by a kind and intelligent society. I believe in God, and in His Divine Providence which guides and protects man and the universe. There is a famous scientist who said that the more he explores the mysteries of remote space the more convinced he is of the "Guiding Hand which has made order when chaos might be."

I, Norma, am amazed at Jerry's attitude. He must be living in a different world from me. He says human beings are fundamentally good. How anyone can believe that in this day and age is beyond me. Doesn't he read the papers? I believe in facing facts. There is more injustice and oppression today than there ever has been before. Oppression out-of-date? Don't make me laugh. As for the wrongdoer of the future being treated as a sick person by a kind society—ye Gods, one must have faith in human nature to believe that. Faith—that's something else

253

again. I used to have it, but no longer. I was deceived too often. Who's right and who's wrong, Dr. Lawton?

Jerry and Norma

They Can Believe in Their Own Ability and Courage

Dear Jerry and Norma:
I'm afraid I'll have to say something that's always unsatisfactory: you're both right and both wrong. One must trust people and believe in life, but one must also be realistic and keep one's eyes open.

You, Jerry, are too softhearted. There is a time when we all have to fight. Wrongdoers may be sick people, and we should try to cure them, but when they are threatening our safety and our happiness we may have to get tough about it, and I mean *tough*. Life is a battle between those who want to increase the range of human freedom, joy, and intelligence and those who want to limit it.

You, Norma, are mixed up because you have no faith, and without that no one can live—really. In this world you have got to be an idealistic realist. Your feet should be on the ground, but your eyes don't have to be there, too. You have been hurt, Norma, and now you are afraid to trust people, to believe in beauty and goodness and honesty. So, in order to protect your own little skin, you yell, "I won't play."

That sort of thing doesn't work. If a fellow loses a game, he doesn't say, "I'm through forever." He plays again, but this time he tries to avoid previous mistakes. You should pick your friends a little bit more carefully and avoid impossible ambitions. As long as you distrust everyone and everything, Norma, you will be confused because you are running against your own normal impulses.

Let me ask you a question, Norma. Who does the worst

things in the world?—your fellow man! But who does the best? —also your fellow man! We would all do the best if we really knew what it is and believed in it. If we don't, it is because we have received the wrong sort of training, or because we are sick, ignorant, or unhappy.

We must believe that certain things are fine and good, even if we see them kicked around. It is better to tell the truth than to lie, better to be loyal than disloyal, better to help people than to hurt them, even if we have been lied to, deceived, stepped on.

Human beings are going to be around on this planet for a long time, and what has happened during the last five thousand years will seem just like five minutes. You come around and see me a million years from now. If nations still devote their best energies to ways of destroying each other, if we still bar people from social and economic opportunities because of color or religion, if we still have crime, ignorance, poverty, ill health, why, you can call me a silly idealist.

But even if things are just as bad as they are today, I still believe that the Normas and Jerrys of a million years from now will be doing the right thing if they spend their lives struggling against the unhappiness and the injustices of that day. No one ever wastes his life who tries to study and understand, to help others, to be a good worker and a good citizen. Your life will have some meaning, Norma, if you can say, "I have always tried to and actually succeeded in increasing a person's confidence in himself and in his future." Wherever you are, Norma, there's a victim . . . of something, of someone. Find him and help him.

"Oh, World, I Cannot...

Dear Dr. Lawton:

Have you ever had a funny feeling go through you when you woke up in the morning and saw the sun shining and making the snow glisten? Only God and I know what goes on in my mind when I see such a sight. I think of hills and fields covered with trees and flowers, of horses running around carefree and gay.

I went to the country once and ever since I have been discontented with my surroundings. Every time I read a book that describes open fields and hills I would gladly change places with the characters in the book, if only this were possible. This is one reason why my scholastic record is so low. I believe I am a daydreamer or wishful thinker. I would like to know how I can overcome this obstacle.

Robert W. P.

... Hold Thee Close Enough!"

Dear Robert:

We all think our own problem unique, yet if we stretched out our hand we would touch a person who is wrestling with the very same difficulty on the very same day. And so it is here.

Perhaps you know Edna St. Vincent Millay's poem, "God's World," * whose first line we have used as heads for your letter and my reply. This poem has a conclusion which is really a cry:

> "Lord, I do fear thou'st made the world too beautiful
> this year.

---

* Reprinted from *God's World* by Edna St. Vincent Millay, Harper & Bros. Copyright 1913, 1941 by Edna St. Vincent Millay.

> My soul is all but out of me,—let fall
> No burning leaf; prithee, let no bird call."

You also may know Masefield's "Sea Fever," * with its rousing start:

> "I must down to the seas again, to the lonely sea and
>   the sky,
> And all I ask is a tall ship and a star to steer her by."

Even if we are not poets or nature-lovers, it is normal to have an interest in how the rest of the world lives, as well as to seek a chance "to loaf and invite our soul," with some lovely scenery for a backdrop. Everyone should have a generous portion of these experiences at some period in his lifetime. Students on spring days may sit in their seats with a faraway look in their eyes as they dream of mountain peaks, canoe trips, or of eating lotus-leaves in the "never-never" land.

The desire for new experience is a major human impulse and reveals itself most clearly in the late teens and early twenties. It is one of the four things that we all want, according to a famous American social scientist. Others are:

1. Response (or love and affection)
2. Recognition (or a sense of importance)
3. Security (or a livelihood, protection against danger, etc.)

I shall not reveal the order of importance that these four wishes have for most young people (or of what your parents and grandparents would do with them), though I will say that boys and girls rank them differently, and that each sex changes its preference somewhat from year to year.

The wish for new experience has consequences which are

---

* Reprinted from *Poems* by John Masefield by permission of The Macmillan Company.

both fortunate and otherwise. It makes for open-mindedness and a willingness to try out unfamiliar ideas, though not all these experiments of young people are equally successful. A boy or girl may be more impressed by the novelty of a suggestion than by whether it be worthwhile for him. Hence in our teens we find ourselves changing ideas, friends, interests—almost with the seasons. We make mistakes then, because it is hard to learn from anything but our own experience, and young people have not lived long enough to have developed the caution and stability which they will achieve later.

Were it possible for our four desires always to work together, each helping the other, life would be much simpler. Unfortunately, we often satisfy one wish at the expense of another.

Suppose we are eager for a permanent career, or seek the love of a particular person not for a semester but for a lifetime? Or suppose we want to create a reputation for ourselves in a special field? In each instance we *may* have to give up our plan to travel over the face of the globe and see all sorts of strange and fascinating sights. Probably that is why daydreaming was invented, to say nothing of verse and story-writing, because only in these ways can we get our fill of new experience without having to leave home or starve other desires.

Most people try to balance the four desires, so that all are partially satisfied. Take an individual in whom the desire for security and that for new experience seem to be the two which are most opposed. Meant for an active and outdoor life, such a young man can be happy only with a schedule which is never the same two days in succession. It would be cruel to inflict upon such a person a nine-to-five desk job.

The Martin Johnsons, explorers and adventurers extraordinary, offered an example of a couple who seemed to have attained the maximum satisfaction of all four wishes. They had a dream which challenged them, saying: "Make me real, if you can or dare!" From their life story it would seem that they met this challenge brilliantly.

We all owe it to ourselves to fight as hard as we can in order to make an actuality of a wish, providing this wish represents what we want most out of life, and if it is a wish that can and should have a place in the real world. Our final achievement may represent only a fraction of what we originally sought, but without the struggle we would not have gotten even that. And we'll always be *glad* we tried.

The vagabond impulse, then, gets all of us at times. But there is also the restlessness of the boy who, because he doubts his own powers, is impatient with responsibility and routine. Perhaps such a boy always will want to roam when he is faced with a task he dislikes. Yet it may be a task that will have to be done eventually if he is to achieve the type of success he wants.

That is why we must try to be as honest with ourselves as possible. When we say, "I want to go places and see things," is our real interest in what we are going to or in what we hope to escape from? The refugee from a conflict often finds that, no matter where he wanders, the conflict still has to be settled where it was first found.

How Can I Conquer Fear of Death?

Dear Dr. Lawton:

Recently I lost someone who meant all the world to me. I always had tried to avoid thinking about death, as something very disagreeable and morbid, but now I can't help it, because of what happened to me personally, and then when I look at the papers with the threat of war, I often wonder what is the use of all my struggling and planning to get ahead if it leads to only one result. Then I tell myself it is silly for anyone young to fear death. But still I have the fear. How can one overcome it? I also would like to know if there will ever come a time when people will stop dying? Perhaps a great scientist will find an answer to this problem some day.

Charles M.

The Great Leveler Brings Peace

Dear Charles:

You are not the only young person who has been pained and bewildered at the thought of death. There are many others just like you. But since young people seldom talk about it, each one believes only he is thus disturbed. Death is one of the major experiences of human beings. If boys and girls need help in preparing for future vocations or relationships with other people, they also need assistance sometimes in establishing a wholesome attitude toward death.

Now, it is not the mere fact of death which is upsetting. The passing away of a stranger may mean little to us. However, when someone we love dies, it is the sudden separation that fills us with insecurity, loneliness, a sense of strangeness in a strange world. Yet life is filled with other separations that we must learn to accept: a friendship breaks up, a love affair ends, we leave our school or our home town. There is also the separation from those who do not understand us, the isolation felt by the physically handicapped person, or, nowadays, by the refugee.

Separation, disappointment, and even tragedy are inescapable elements of our existence. Life involves many disadvantages and injustices. But a mature person knows where human helplessness begins and where it ends. Some losses are part of the scheme of things and are not to be altered by anger or tears.

These disappointments we must learn to meet with dignity and sportsmanship, the same kind of sportsmanship we display toward the game on the athletic field. Other evils are man-made: poverty, ignorance, prejudice, wars. Against these we have a right to rebel, since they are changeable.

Perhaps you would like some scientist to make a machinelike, feelingless human being who would never know regret, longing, or sorrow. But if he did that, he also would have to take away ambition, friendship, and love. As long as you allow human beings to form attachments for people and things, just so long must they suffer when separations come.

Man has always dreamed of ways in which death might be abolished. *Death Takes a Holiday* and *On Borrowed Time* are two modern versions of this dream which come to mind. But while all these fantasies begin by banishing death, they all end by restoring it, since natural and human society is based on the fact of death. Some years ago, a novel was written in which a scientist in an imaginary nation was able to prevent persons from dying. At first, everyone rejoiced and heaped honors upon him. But later their feelings changed, and they would have killed him—were this possible. For there was a tremendous increase in population and in unemployment. Young people could not take over the roles of adults, no one could get ahead in his vocation. There was no way to end the persistence of worn-out ideas and no escape from cruel and tyrannical rulers. Remember that death is the original democrat. It is the great leveler, treating all alike. If it removes useful and beloved persons from our midst, it also comes inevitably for criminals and dictators. Eventually our scientist found a way of bringing death back to his countrymen, who now could take up their everyday living where they had left off.

I should like to tell you how one family treated the problem of death when it came. Mr. and Mrs. X and their son and daughter were unusually close. The parents had often talked about death, especially when a pet died. This was done in a matter-of-fact way, as if they were explaining why the sea was salt or what causes thunder. They pointed out how everywhere in nature whatever is born and grows must someday pass away, to be followed by someone or something else that goes through the same cycle. Thus the young people had grown up with a normal attitude toward death. When they were in their teens, the father died. The funeral service was very brief, simple, and restrained. After it was over, Mrs. X and the children spent the day walking in the country, talking about father and the things that had interested him. Then they talked about how they might still carry out the plans he had made for them, the jobs they would have to get, the changes in living arrangements now necessary. The members of this family were not heartless; they were all deeply grieved. What they did happened to be right and satisfying for them, although to others it might have held out little meaning or comfort.

Studies made of persons who fear death show that often this fear is due to an earlier unpleasant and mystifying experience in connection with death. Such a person needs an opportunity to talk the experience over and understand it correctly. In other cases, we find that the fear of death actually represents a fear of life. When the sufferer is helped in his relationships to people, the fear of death disappears.

It is not how or when a person dies that is of the greatest significance but how he has lived, how happily and interestingly he has filled his days, how useful he has been to himself and to others. One helpful way of looking at death is to think of it as the Peace-Bringer, after the struggles and difficulties of life. Stevenson's *Requiem* is a fine example of this attitude:

Under the wide and starry sky,
Dig the grave and let me lie.
Glad did I live and gladly die,
    And I laid me down with a will.

This be the verse you grave for me:
Here he lies where he longed to be;
Home is the sailor, home from the sea,
    And the hunter home from the hill.

The Art of Breaking Bad News

Dear Dr. Lawton:

I have a very big problem. I am writing to you because there is nobody else I can go to about it. I am seventeen and I have a twin sister. My parents have been separated since I was about ten. My father remarried and has been living in another part of the country. I got a letter the other day saying that he had died. My father's new wife wrote to me about it because no one can ever say one word about my father to my mother. If I went to her she would tell me as sure as anything: "He got what he deserved."

Now, my sister Amy has always been crazy about my father and they have corresponded a great deal. She and my mother don't get on; in fact, they are quarreling all the time. Sis was secretly planning to go and live with my father as soon as she graduated from school this term. In fact, that was her one big dream. Now the problem is this. Amy isn't too strong, and I'm afraid this will be a terrible shock to her.

Some of my friends in school advised me not to tell her but to let her gradually find out for herself. After a couple of weeks, if there are no letters, she will start investigating. But I think my sister should be told, and yet I don't know how to go about it. The only people around me here are Mother's relatives, and I know if I go to them they won't be sorry at all to hear the news—quite the contrary. Neither they nor my mother are the ones from whom my sister should hear it. What do you advise me to do?

Fred G.

Calls For Words—Few, Direct, and Kind

Dear Fred:

If we could forever prevent tragic news from coming to light, a policy of concealment might be worth trying. But in this case we can't, and it is best to present the facts as straight and direct as possible. The dentist who extracts a tooth by easy stages is no friend to man. It is not the truth which does the damage in this world; it is evasion and fairytales.

When your father died, one dream of Amy's was extinguished, one edifice crashed. She must get a new dream, build a new structure, and the sooner she can get started, the better it will be for her and everyone else concerned. From infancy to old age "Life is meant to end, and meant to begin again."

Your friends, who have advised you to say nothing and let her discover the truth for herself, forget that once she begins to suspect she may discover the facts in the baldest manner possible, without having any support or consolation. She is bound to reproach you with "Why did you make me go through all this cruel suspense? Why didn't you tell me at once? I'm old enough to be told the truth and big enough to take it."

As for the mechanics of breaking bad news—the time, the place, the teller, and the exact words—all are relatively unimportant. No one would be able to stick to a set speech, and he would not be human if he could. Your glance, walk, and tone of voice, the very inability to get started, would make it all transparently clear, and no rules would be of any use. The one thing you can do is to make her feel that though she has suffered one great deprivation, her life is not a total loss, and there are other treasures left. Your love for her is still strong, though frankly a brother's love cannot help much at such a time.

One important part of our education concerns the way in which we learn to handle the suffering which is our unavoidable fate from time to time. We must not let ourselves be made giddy by joy, nor destroyed by sorrow. Sudden death is an inescapable part of the world in which we live.

Don't let the responsibility of transmitting this shock to Amy worry you unduly. Unless there is some very serious physical limitation that must keep her in cotton-wool all her life, she will probably be able to absorb the tragic news without more than temporary physical and mental distress.

The human mind is constructed for rough handling. We have been around this planet for millions of years, despite unfavorable circumstances, and we will still be around a few million years hence. In the process of natural selection, the individual who can endure the most survives to transmit these qualities to his children.

I feel sure that you will find a way to tell Amy, and she will find a way to receive and make use of a great hurt. What concerns me even more than your father's death and how to break the news is the strained feelings between your sister and mother. There are many causes for the differences that sometimes come up between children and parents, daughters and mothers. Sometimes the waters are troubled by the child; sometimes by the parent. It is easy enough to guess at the reasons for the hostility between Amy and your mother, but I would need to know much more before offering an opinion. I am sure that your mother has the chief responsibility for trying to find out what is wrong and for doing something about it. Regardless of your father's misdeeds toward your mother, he was the father of his children, and a mother should never do anything to poison that relationship. You two should try to understand your mother. Her hardness may be bitterness and unhappiness. It is possible, of course, that she continued to love your father and that she was profoundly hurt and injured by the divorce and what went before.

You had better tell your mother first. You cannot tell in advance how this news might affect her. All her bitterness, and, yes, her jealousy of the woman who took her place, might disappear now that your father is no longer alive. She might even offer to break the news to Amy herself, and might do this job with great delicacy and understanding of Amy's feelings. Do not set yourself up as a judge of your mother's real feelings about your father. Her apparent coldness may be only a cloak to protect her hurt pride.

How to handle this situation is a real test of the maturity of each one of you. You will have to manage the situation with tact, kindness, and firmness. Your mother will have her own problem facing whatever emotions this situation evokes in her. And Amy, of course, will have to make the necessary readjustments.

Amy planned for a new future, one with her father in different surroundings. It was as if she interwove with her old self a new one—exciting, beautiful, wonderful. This was her dream. But what about the reality of what she would have faced had your father not died? A stepmother who might have resented her; a father preoccupied with his own affairs with little time for Amy; the loss of her old friends and contacts; the separation from you, her twin brother; the widening of the breach with her mother, whom she surely loves despite the quarreling; and whom she needs, as all girls do on the verge of maturity. This dream of Amy's may have seemed beautiful to her, but might have meant great tragedy and disillusionment.

Now the new self that Amy built up in her imagination cannot be. Your sister must go on without her dream. It may be hard for her to believe at present, but life is bigger than any one person, bigger than any number of daughters and fathers. Amy's aim now should be to find fulfilment and happiness in whatever way is possible to her. Some day Amy may even be able to realize that there are things in life more important than death. Perhaps she will even discover the great lesson that "Pain may be the breaking of the shell that encloses our understanding." In time, Amy will reassemble the pieces of her life into a pattern different than it had been before the "news" came, and different from the one she had planned if Father had lived. Almost certainly the new pattern will be healthier and better than any she had deliberately planned.

"How Kind She Was, How True..."

Dear Dr. Lawton:

A most tragic thing happened recently in our school. Elsie R., a girl I knew well, committed suicide because she was blackballed by the leading sorority in our school. I can imagine how Elsie must have felt. Getting blackballed is a terrible experience. You don't feel as if you belonged to the human race any more. I know, because they turned me down, too, last year. I think all sororities should be abolished. They only build up prejudices and stress differences of religion and race, and sometimes result in disasters like this. Elsie would still be alive if it weren't for this sorority. I am so upset I feel like leaving this school and going some place else.

Gilda D.

That's What You'll Say Some Day

Dear Gilda:

We Americans are a nation of joiners. Bridge clubs, professional organizations, fraternal orders with special uniforms and celebrations—the number is legion. I doubt if you can or should try to abolish them, nor can you sift the good ones from the bad. To be turned down by a group with which you wish to associate yourself is always a painful experience. But most of us learn to take it. You did apparently.

About Elsie: I cannot agree with you that the sorority rejection was the cause of her suicide. But why, you ask, did Elsie take her life? Why should anyone want to take his life? It is a strange thing, isn't it? Animals do not kill themselves. Only human beings voluntarily end their lives.

Some people are unable to handle the problems of life. Other people dislike themselves intensely or have great fears. The combination of an extremely depressed, sensitive nature plus great self-contempt is not a good one, and it is from this group that many suicides occur.

Why are some people extremely sensitive; why do some people have long and profound periods of gloom or deep fears; why do some people feel they are failures, physically and mentally, when they are not failures at all? For this the students of the mind have no final answer. We do believe that probably one third of our mental make-up is inherited and about two thirds is due to the way we have been brought up.

The curious thing is that people who kill themselves are not necessarily poor, sick, or ugly. Often people who commit suicide are well-to-do, are in good physical health, are attractive-looking. Many have good marriages, are loved, etc. They have everything to live for. They are *not* failures according to the judgment of their friends and relatives, but *they* feel themselves to be failures. It is ironic that where you have the most serious physical handicaps, as in chronic-disease hospitals, suicide is a relatively minor problem.

The suicide often feels he has an insoluble problem, though he doesn't really have one, as far as any outsider can see. Some people in concentration camps killed themselves, others survived despite the most terrible experiences. The explanation lies not in what happened to them but in the attitude the person had toward what was happening.

Elsie felt herself a failure long before the sorority incident. Poor Elsie may have been foolish about her shortcomings. But to her they were real. Why she felt inadequate, why she disliked herself, I do not know. Perhaps even you or the members of her family do not know. But I am sure that the sorority incident was merely the straw that broke the camel's back. Next year, the straw might have been failure to graduate with her class; five years from now: difficulties with co-workers on the job, fifty years hence: disabling illness or loss of money.

None of these is a good reason for shuffling off "this mortal coil." There are no good reasons for suicide. People don't end their lives because of one particular reason. They may give such a reason in a farewell remark or note. When they have given us no clue to their motives, we will think back and assign a reason that seems plausible to us. But they do what they do because they have found life itself is unendurable. You can't understand this because you are not Elsie or in her mental condition. Remember that no one *at the moment of suicide* is sane.

People like Elsie always feel life is pushing them against

the wall and asking them to make impossible decisions: like accepting a life where one has been disgraced through rejection by a sorority. Elsie probably said to herself many times at tough moments: "I know a secret way of escape no one can block. Unless the game of life follows *my* rules, and unless *I* win most of the time, I won't play."

Elsie almost certainly was a person who wanted to hurt whoever had hurt her. But she was afraid to strike back, because she didn't think she was a match for her opponent. She believed her own stupidity, weakness, and unworthiness made her responsible for her own plight, as when we say: "I could kick myself for doing that." Elsie, at the end, wanted to punish herself, "blot herself out"—the word *sui-cide* itself means self-destroy. What she would have liked to do to her oppressor, to circumstances, to the "world," she did to herself.

It is true that almost every normal person at some time or other has said to himself and perhaps to others: "I wish I were dead." This does not mean anything really serious. It shows only that all of us sometimes are overwhelmed by situations from which we wish we could escape. Death, in such a case, seems to us not a final exit but a little holiday or vacation from our problems. We like life and ourselves. Things get a little too complicated and vexatious for all of us at times. That's when we want to write on our door merely "Please do not disturb," not "Gone Forever." Perfectly normal and mature people occasionally have illogical thoughts that are "wrong" and anti-social. You are not crazy, not even a tiny bit off, if a few times in your life you talked about suicide and threatened it.

Some persons who commit suicide never have said a word to indicate their unhappiness or never to the average person seemed at all upset. Other boys and girls frequently threaten to do away with themselves as a tag-line to their weekly tantrum. Such people are actors in a play. This play may be a melodrama, with a lot of sound, fury, tears, and threats. All it means, however, is that someone is unhappy and wants attention for his self-dramatizing. Think of the daydreams in which we say: "I'll go and die and then they'll be sorry they treated me so mean—they'll see me lying there all completely dead and then they'll know how I suffered." There is a little poem that ends:

> When not any wind that blows
> Shall awake me to your sighing . . .
> You will say, "How kind she was,"
> You will say, "How true she was."

What makes matters complicated is that even an expert professional cannot always distinguish between a third-rate actor or actress using psychological blackmail on "loved" ones and someone who may be merely threatening every time *except the last*. Some emotionally upset people will go to extreme limits in carrying out a threat. Even they could not tell you how far they really intended to go before they crossed the line between threat and deed.

Since it is almost impossible for the average person to distinguish between those who only threaten and those who carry out their threats, every "I know what I'll do," should be considered seriously, not as a joke. The threat rarely is going to be carried out. But it does mean the speaker is unhappy and believes he has a problem he cannot solve except by fleeing to a place where his problem cannot follow.

It would be wonderful if we could create a race of human beings who from the cradle on could handle with ease and confidence all the problems of life. Until that day arrives the emotional needs of children should be a major study for all future doctors and teachers. It should be a minor study for all prospective parents. Just as millions of people today know first aid of a physical kind, so we should know first aid of a mental kind. Many situations in life are emergencies requiring mental first aid, as much as a broken leg requires physical first aid. A person with a broken leg gets his leg fixed. He doesn't remain a cripple. So with cases of "broken" feelings or ideas.

I am assuming that your school did not have a guidance bureau. Had there been one, things might have been different. Many high schools have professionally qualified persons on their staff who have been trained to deal with educational, vocational, or personal problems. If they had found Elsie's problem too serious for them to handle, they might have suggested to the parents that Elsie go to a Child Guidance Bureau in the community or the Mental Health clinic of a neighboring hospital. Or perhaps the guidance bureau might have felt that a family physician with great understanding of young people might have been the answer.

At any rate, with the proper teamwork between classroom teacher, parent, guidance bureau and, if needed, family physician and outside psychiatric attention, Elsie would have been spotted years earlier as a child who was deeply unhappy and troubled, *or* who seemed to live in a world of her own, *or* who appeared to be holding back a great sense of hurt and injury. None of these "signs" meant that Elsie was "crazy." All they meant was that she needed help and with help could have been a perfectly normal, happy person like the rest of us.

Whether or not we have sororities is something each school should decide for itself. I can't get excited about their existence or nonexistence. But I do feel strongly about mental hygiene. Wiping out sororities would not have saved Elsie. But perhaps she might have been saved with professional aid in the school and community.

What Is Man?

Dear Dr. Lawton:

Perhaps this is a silly question, but what I can't figure out is why we are here, that is, why we were born, what the purpose of life is, and so on. If all that happens is war, quarrels at home, and trouble everywhere, what's the sense of ever having been put on earth?

Paul S.

A Bit of Dust, an Entire Universe

Dear Paul:

Each one of us needs to explain and fit together all the things, good and bad, that happen to him. The events of life are like the pieces of a jigsaw puzzle which we move about in the hope that eventually a completed picture will appear. We all must develop some kind of creed by which to live, even though it cannot always be put into words.

One of the main explanations of human existence is that since man has a divine origin and divine goal, our task is to love and worship God, live as close to Him as possible, and prepare ourselves for a more complete and perfect life in the next world.

Others believe that while we have been placed here for some definite end, what this is no puny human mind can discover. After death, however, the purpose will become gloriously clear.

Still another group of thinkers say that man is a biological accident on a planet that will return some far-off day to the nothingness from which it came. Any purpose which life has must be invented by man himself, for the human drama has a very simple plot: we are born, grow up, love, marry, have children, experience suffering, joy, adventure, discovery, and die.

According to a few specific views of human purpose, man's task is to: pursue pleasure and good times; suffer; obtain power over other human beings; secure money and fame; enlarge the boundaries of science and human knowledge; understand the universe, its structure and laws; enjoy beauty wherever it is found; do good to other human beings. Wise men always have held that real happiness comes from devotion, not to our own pleasure, comfort, or influence but to something outside of ourselves, as we see in the life of a saint or religious mystic, a social reformer, a research scientist, a philosopher, an artist.

In my own purely personal philosophy, our life has a three-fold purpose. First, each one should try to make of himself a capable worker and craftsman, and a strong human being willing to meet whatever challenges life may offer. Not that we can expect to conquer every difficulty. But we can, at least, fight hard and long and accept disappointments without whimpering. It is good to know that we have gone as far with our abilities as opportunity has allowed. However, few lives are *all* hardship and woe, unless we insist on punishing ourselves. Nearly everyone has some moments of play and fun, and some moments when he finds expression for the finest and most beautiful aspects of his nature.

Second, we go beyond ourselves and live also in our family and community. We should aim to make a success of marriage and bring to adulthood healthy and well-adjusted children. We should try to be loyal friends and good neighbors, not in a spirit of self-sacrifice or gushy sentimentality but because we want to be useful to people about us. A truly strong person enjoys creating strength in others.

Finally, we widen human purpose to include all of society.

To do this we enlist in a war against the six common enemies of all mankind: ignorance, pain, fear, poverty, intolerance, dullness. Our foe is not a particular person but any idea or custom that crushes and enslaves the human spirit, that destroys the possibility of free thinking and free living, that takes all the zest and gaiety out of life. To learn about these imprisoning customs and ideas and how liberation from them may be accomplished is an education all in itself. Whatever we enjoy of civilization today is due to the men and women who in years past fought both for themselves and for those yet unborn. Each one of us in his own limited and humble way must do the same.

To Be Or Not To Be

Dear Dr. Lawton:

I am now at the age of fifteen; probably within fifteen more years I will be married and will be starting a home of my own. The question in my mind is what kind of a world will we be living in then? How can I prepare myself for this later life? For better or for worse, for a rich life or a poor life? I do not know which.

Will my own family be confronted with the problems of unemployment and insecurity or will I have to face the tragedies of war or will my children? If in those fifteen years I do not have to face war, surely my children will, because there has been a war in every generation in the past. Will I want to bring children into the world to be killed by atomic bombs! This very thought has upset my whole sense of values. What is one to do?

Emma L. H.

HOW TO BE HAPPY THOUGH YOUNG

That Is the Question!

Dear Emma:

Man has always faced the problem of being happy in a world that constantly threatens the sources of his happiness. We moderns seem to think that life is less certain today than ever before. But when has it been more secure? Primitive man had to face disease, famine, destruction by animals and enemies. Two thousand years ago, the normal life expectancy of a newborn child was thirty years or less; today it is sixty-seven years or more. On the basis of the chance to survive we would appear to be better off.

"But," you might counter, "what's the use of knowing we can live longer than we used to if we might be unemployed a good part of that long life; what's the use of being saved from natural forces only to be destroyed by human ones, such as war?"

True enough. There has been little change except in the *type* of danger and insecurity. But remember it took us a million years to conquer the hostile forces of nature. Now we are realizing that it is worth little to overcome nature with science if we only turn around and employ this science to destroy ourselves. The trouble, of course, is not with science but with its users. Our next great task is to understand the human mind and social-economic problems as well as we do the physical world.

You don't like the kind of world in which you live. But it doesn't have to be that kind of world if you and enough other people want it different. Let us assume you are sure that certain forces threaten your happiness and that of your children-to-be. Then, instead of running away, your first job is to prepare yourself for fighting these forces in the most intelligent and effective way you can later on. Make every possible use of your educational career to help you in this preparation. Your second job will be to enlist the aid of others, including your own children, in the same fight, instead of refusing to have them—which is only another form of running away. Perhaps you are not a fighter, or are afraid of being unpopular with some people, or would rather get as much as you can from the world as it stands and let others do the worrying and changing. In that case, you can help from the sidelines.

But, after all, people do not make friends, fall in love, get married, bear children, as the result of having worked out with bookkeeping precision all the advantages and disadvantages of every move. We participate in each experience of life as we come to it because at the time that seems the most natural thing to do.

Young people often insist they will remain single, and they give all sorts of fancy reasons for this decision. At heart, however, they are bewildered by the idea of being married and a parent some day, and also a little afraid they will not prove equal to the new roles. But then they meet a suitable member of the opposite sex, and in due time they are not only willing to take a chance on matrimony and parenthood but raise a most awful fuss if anything interferes with their plans. If we are normal, the powerful drives within us overcome all obstacles, either of our own or others' making. Whoever refuses to have a child today because of the kind of world it must face should remember that this might have been said with as much or more justice at any other time in human history.

Most of us take the problems of life in our stride; some meet each new adjustment with fear and misgiving; some get across the early hurdles but are balked by later ones. Even in a world without the threat of war or intolerance, there still would exist difficulties between parents and children, disappointment in friendship and love, spiritual and intellectual defeat, sickness and death. There still would be people who felt inadequate, who went about acting as if someone had taken away their candy. Haven't you ever met a person who was most unhappy though he had all the world's gifts and goods? Confidence in one's ability to conquer life's problems, trust in the future, willingness to struggle until the last—all of this is something which a person has *in spite of* the world in which he lives.

Human beings always have suffered and objected to suffering; have known joy and wanted still more. When it comes to counting up the gains and losses in life, one group, a dauntless crew, will deem it mostly "plus." Another group, made up of pessimists, cynics, and extremely maladjusted individuals, will vote it nearly all "minus." But most of us, being optimistic realists, will just about break even: "pluses" and "minuses" balance each other. We feel "'tis better to have loved and lost than never to have loved at all," better to have married and had children than remained single or childless; better to have lived than never to have been born.

Youth Speaks for Itself

What Do Boys and Girls Really Worry About?

A contest that proved to be the "hardy perennial" of *Scholastic* contests was the one called "What's Your Biggest Problem?" After it was once launched, this contest was repeated annually for a total of five consecutive years.

Some of the prize-winning letters were later discussed in the "Live and Learn" department. Other letters, which, because of an insufficiently attention-getting presentation, did not win prizes or honorable mention, did bring up problems that deserved discussion, and a number of such letters not here will be found elsewhere in this book.

In presenting the "What's Your Biggest Problem?" contest, we asked each young person: what's on your mind; what worries you the most; what problem, whether personal, at home, in school, with your boy or girl friends, or in your community, the nation, or the world, gives you the most trouble?

Here are many of the most representative letters—received over the years—for which prizes were awarded, but which are now listed independently of original order. These letters were received from students in the following high schools:

Broadway High School, Seattle, Washington
Chandler High School, Chandler, Oklahoma

Grand Rapids Senior High School, Grand Rapids, Minnesota
North Central High School, Spokane, Washington
Olney High School, Philadelphia, Pennsylvania
Roosevelt High School, Dayton, Ohio
Walla Walla High School, Walla Walla, Washington
West High School, Minneapolis, Minnesota
West High School, Rockford, Illinois
Winfield High School, Winfield, Kansas

A Rolling Stone Gathers No———

My biggest problem is making friends. That is no easy task when you belong to a family with nomadic instincts. Since I first started going to school, I've spent no more than one year in a single school and sometimes went to as many as three schools in a year.

Friends are as much in the "scheme of things" as the food we eat, and the air we breathe. Friendship is an indefinable something which few of us are truly happy without. I am no exception. All my life I have envied other boys and girls with homes on a solid basis, growing up with brothers and sisters, sharing their joys, their pleasures, and whatever comes. Surely this is the foundation for a strong nation; not this incessant hopping from place to place, seeking and never finding, because that which is sought has never been permitted to mature.

My continuous moving about has done nothing more than to deny me these simple pleasures and make me a bit aloof from people my own age. After all, if a person tries a number of times to ascend a stairway and each time falls back before he reaches the top, then sooner or later he will become discouraged and either find another way to get to the top of the stairs or merely not bother with what is on the next floor. A poor illustration, but it expresses what I am trying to say.

So many times I have tried to make friends. So many times I have had to leave treasured friends. Now I don't care whether I make friends or not, for something in my inner mind keeps coming forth to say, "You'll be leaving town soon," or "You heard your mother say she wanted to see California." I am stopped before I even start.

Some day, God willing, I intend to have a home in a small town, be a gossiping old woman with five or ten children, and I won't leave my home, no matter what happens. That is my oath; a rebuttal to my present mode of life.

Restlessness

My greatest personal problem is a rather intangible one, as most problems go, and perhaps a somewhat uncommon one. It will be difficult to formulate my thoughts clearly; and if they seem a little incoherent in spots, my simple defense is that I am writing only what I feel.

I first became aware of this difficulty in September, when school resumed. I would come home of an evening and set out on a homework assignment with the best intentions. After only a brief period of work, I would feel a strong urge to get up and go somewhere, anywhere, just to escape from the confines of home and studies. I know I am not lazy by nature and have always taken great pleasure and interest in my schoolwork But this strange restlessness has made it impossible for me to concentrate on my studies to the best of my abilities.

I know that in this last term I should be striving to gain all the education I can, but I feel so restless, and it all seems rather futile. Nothing would please me more than to feel stable once more and to regain my old interest in school, and this restlessness and disinterest is a special problem to me because up to now I have been quite successful in my studies, and I would like to make my senior year a fitting climax to a profitable school career.

Amateur Casanovas vs. a Steady Beau

About this time last year I considered myself a very fortunate girl; I was asked to join what I considered the best girls' club in school. I was proud, and that pride gradually grew up and became a mild case of conceit.

Things started happening to me that following spring. I, who had been so indifferent to boys before, suddenly found myself right in the swing of things. My dates and friends were unlimited. I went to every dance and party given. I was having my fling, and that's all that mattered. I neglected my studies, and I paid the penalty by receiving two nicely rounded fails.

Soon this whirl of good times seemed to grow stale. All the boys I had gone with seemed superficial and shallow. I began to feel that it was just the fact that I was a good date and a good dancer that attracted boys. They certainly didn't care whether or not I had brains or ideals.

All this time I had been occasionally dating a boy I had liked and admired for over a year. He seemed older than the others, and he became an ideal companion. Our likes and dislikes were mutual; he understood me and was, therefore, considerate. So when he asked me to go steady, I said I would.

But now I am wondering whether going steady is cutting me off from other friends. Some of my friends say it is; others encourage me to continue. What am I to do, go back to these amateur Casanovas or shall I continue going steady?

Declaring My Independence

Declaring my independence has become my most vital problem. How can I make my parents realize that I am no longer a child; that I have formed my own definite opinions and ideas?

There are only three persons in my family: Mother, Father, and I. Being an "only" child has certainly caused complications.

Recently, the family decided upon my going to college. For years I have planned on getting out into the world and having the exulting feeling of being independent. During our family council I found that the folks had the college picked out and my course selected. Mom and Dad want me to be a doctor, but I dislike science immensely.

They say that teaching, my special interest, is overcrowded, underpaid in some cases, and not worth following. Maybe they know best, but I feel that I should make the choice.

Some day I plan to get married and have a happy home life. I sincerely hope my parents won't try to stop me from selecting my own husband. After all, I'm the one who will have to live with him the rest of my life.

I'm not sure that it really pays to go to college and then, after spending hundreds of dollars, get married and never make use of my education. However, education is something that cannot be taken away from a person.

Mother says parents have had more experience and should know what kind of advice to give. Perhaps this is so, but I think the motive behind their actions is that parents dread seeing their children grow up and leave home.

Parents Should Not Separate

When I was three, my father abandoned our family and set out for parts unknown. That was the little acorn from which my problem grew. All my life I have wanted a father—not a rich father nor a poor one but just the kind you run to meet when he comes home from work.

I remember when I first heard about God. My mother told me that he was everybody's father. And I remember the good feeling I used to get when I'd say those words beginning "Our Father, which art in Heaven . . ."

It's hard being reared by one parent only. Every questionnaire, whether it be for school or for a job, always inquires, "Occupation and place of residence of your father." I never can answer this; I do not know. If my father were dead, or even if my parents were divorced, it would be easier. A day seldom goes by but what someone, in entire good faith, asks me about my father. It's a bit awkward to explain, and I thoroughly detest the word "separation" or the shellacked term "estranged."

I do not believe that there is a solution to my problem, but I'd like to say to every parent, don't, *don't* separate!

I Want a Beau

Probably ninety per cent of the girls you hear from have the same problem as I have—no dates. I never have had any.

The idea is slowly becoming an obsession to me now—the idea that not one boy that I've ever known or even met gives a darn about what I do or where I go or whether or not I think he's rather nice. It's not that I mind not going out, for I love doing things with a bunch of girls. It's just that here I am a senior in high school, supposed to be having the time of my life—and I'm not. It's getting so that now people don't even bother to ask me if I had a good time at the dance Saturday or whom I had a date with on Sunday afternoon. And Friday nights, when I'm the only one without a date after club, it's awfully hard to keep the tears back.

I'm quite sure it's not my looks, and I try to read all the Listerine ads—it's just something I can't put my finger on. I get along beautifully with everyone but boys, and the minute I meet any I'm sunk. I don't know if it's what I say or how I act. Maybe it's something I'll grow out of. But in the meantime I'm a mighty unhappy girl.

Boy—Yet Part-time Maid

My biggest problem is trying to be a part-time maid and a schoolboy at the same time. I can't say that I find either part difficult, but the problem is how can I do the things required of me as a maid and still have time to study and grow to manhood? The blows my pride suffers when I am supposed to do a girl's task are really painful.

My father and mother both work and manage to keep our home regulated by remote control. Yet most of the work falls on me.

I have two younger brothers, one in the sixth grade and one in the second. It is my job to get them up in the morning, herd them to breakfast, and then, washcloth and comb in hand, get them ready for school. At noon I have to hurry home for lunch and be sure that Vernon drinks his milk and that Darrell eats something besides cake and pie.

The only housework I have to do is the breakfast and dinner

dishes, but dishwashing is my pet peeve. It isn't that washing and drying the dishes is drudgery. It is the blow to my vanity. I can picture myself years older working in the kitchen while my wife goes off to her job, for she will be sure to learn of my horrible past!

Work or School?

It all began last June thirtieth, several days after school closed. All my friends were engaged in some sort of job. After continuous persuasion, I, too, decided to work for the summer. The position proved very successful after only a week's stay. I was earning more money than my parents did at the age of twenty. Conditions, of course, were much different then.

At the end of the summer I informed the head of the department that I was leaving. He thanked me for helping out and asked me to come in on weekends or Wednesday evenings. The promise he offered me was still a good salary, with a number of other enticements. It all sounded very good at the time.

As yet I have not answered his request. School has been in session for several weeks, with me still unable to decide whether to go back or not. My employer and co-workers urge me to come back. They insist that working will do no harm. Their outlook on things is to get more help regardless of how. My teachers absolutely disagree. They think that working will harm my education. Their opinion was for my benefit, not their own.

You can readily see that I'm in what you may call "a muddle." Do you really think school and work can be managed together successfully? Is it possible to pass your school work with good grades when your mind is engaged in some other work? Do you think that little bit of money is worth throwing half your education away for? I know many students face this problem not knowing which way to turn.

Bringing Up Parents

My biggest problem is getting along with my parents. I'm sure that I am not a case for a psychologist. Nor are my parents. But we seem unable to get along as normal people should.

I'll start with my father, because there is less to say about him. Our main source of disagreement is the way he seems to think that because he is my father I should bow to his opinions on everything. I am perfectly willing to accept parental authority, but what I mean here is something different.

Recently, in an obviously harmless discussion, he said something which I somehow couldn't believe. It was something which, if it were true, everyone in the country would know or my father could not possibly. Because of this, I asked him where he got his information. When he refused to tell me, I told him I didn't believe it. This touched off an atomic explosion about what he thinks of a girl who accuses her own father of deliberately lying to her, and how, when he was a boy, children respected the opinions of their parents.

I do respect his opinions, but I feel that, since I am no longer in kindergarten, I should have a right to a few of my own. I think the world of my dad, and we have a lot of fun discussing things, but our discussions cease to be fun when this feeling enters in.

Then there is my mother. At times she is perfectly reasonable, but at other times she seems to flare up over nothing. She is always misinterpreting what I say and do into something I don't mean at all, and, when I try to explain, she won't even listen. She never believes a thing I say, but she is always ready to believe anything bad she hears about me.

She feels hurt if I don't tell her things, yet she only laughs or lectures me if I do. When I ask her something about sex, she is so "cagey" I wish I'd never asked. It seems rather unreasonable for her to expect me to unburden myself to her when she acts like this. She reads my mail, incoming and outgoing, although she should know that her actions will never inspire my confidence. Her constant harping gets as tiresome as singing commercials. I often doubt that she ever was a girl.

I love my parents, and I truly want to get along with them. I realize that I am probably as much of a problem to them as they are to me, but I don't think they realize that *they* are as much of a problem to me as I am to them.

To Be or Not to Be—Somebody

I have a lot of immediate problems, but my main one concerns what I am going to do for a vocation. What *am* I going to do? I wouldn't know. I want to be an electrical engineer but, for all I know, I may be better suited for digging ditches! For instance, I thought I was pretty good at math—until I got to advanced algebra. I can't seem to understand algebra. This is bad for a prospective engineer, when math is so essential to his work.

Another thing: In art I thought I was doing okay. But this year the teacher informed me that she had seen hen tracks with more composition than some of my drawings. After careful investigation, I found that she was entirely correct. So there I am, back in the old rut.

Now, to get down to my problem: How am I going to find out what job I am suited for? The school I go to doesn't give aptitude tests, and on bended knees I can't make them tell me what score I made on the I-Q tests, although I suspect it to be about fifty. Can you tell me what to do about this?

Does the Negro Have a Future?

I consider myself as industrious and hopeful of the future as any other American youth, but my biggest problem is in being an American Negro. My ambitions and dreams are no different than those of thousands of others of my age, but because I am an American Negro, the road to success will hold more pitfalls for me than for the average youth.

The American youth has every opportunity to become a person of worth and acclaim. If he has education, no door is closed to him, and even without it he is not destitute of opportunity to become a worthwhile citizen. I, as a Negro, have the advantage of obtaining an education—to a certain extent. My elementary and high-school education has been assured me, but as I leave this realm I am confronted with new problems. The doors of some American colleges are closed to me, and I will not be accepted in some positions, even though I may be well qualified for them.

As a student in an American school, I arise each day to pledge allegiance to the American flag. One of its phrases reads: "One nation, indivisible, with liberty and justice for all." But I am not considered an equal. The blood of Negro Americans has been shed in the protection of American "ideals." We are always talking of teaching our way of life to foreign countries. But if this way of life is no more successful in those far-off lands than it is at home in America, the world is not soon to become a better place in which to live.

How to Change From Friend to Boy Friend

In the spring a young man's fancy turns to what he has been thinking about all winter, and in the winter . . . and this I have been doing for years.

Many years ago, a family took the other floor in our two family house. In this family there was a girl my own age. We were both about ten years old then. It wasn't long before I was spending all my time in their apartment, with the parents treating me as their own son.

Whenever the daughter wanted to go out, she would tell her mother I was her "date." Mother would say, "Take care of Mae, and see that she doesn't come home too late." For two years, I have been escorting Mae to her dates, making arrangements to pick her up at a certain time and then walking around until the hour arranged for. On the way home, Mae tells me what a wonderful time she has had. But after a few dates with a boy-friend, she tells me, "I don't want to see *him* any more," and so I inform the fellow, "Mae says it is no go for you." Should she get a stand-up, Mae goes walking with me. Then we stop at an ice cream parlor, and talk about all kinds of things. As you can guess, I have fallen hard and I mean hard. To her, however, I'm a brother and an escort service. I want to be her boy-friend not her bodyguard. How do I start after all these years?

Diploma or Bigger Pay Envelope?

I am eighteen years old and a senior in high school. My father is dead. We live down at the bottom of a hill in a ruin that used to be a house.

Mother and I desire to better ourselves.

The senior year demands more money from one than the preceding years because of parties, banquets, graduation, etc., and it also demands more of my time, for I am forced to take five subjects instead of the usual four.

I have a job which takes an hour and a half of my day, the school, five hours, and my paper route two hours. Totaled up, this makes a weary end to a day, and I still have to study at home at nights; and at this rate I find it hard to study well.

My wages add up to from twenty-eight to thirty-four dollars a month. One doesn't live on wages like that; he just exists.

I have a chance to get a third job which would double my income.

With three jobs, however, my school work would suffer and my graduation would be endangered.

My problem is, should I place my schooling before all other things and suffer my mother and myself to be in privation? Or should I help us now financially and place my schooling in insecurity? The biggest factor in the problem is that if I wait I may not have the chance to give my mother the enjoyment of which she has had little.

Then, too, there's always the chance that opportunities may not be so plentiful eight months from now as they are at present, and I and many others like me will be as uprooted weeds tumbling where the winds will us to go. Would it be better to take root now? Or is a high-school diploma a more fertile rooting place?

The Man I Am Going to Marry

Have you ever wondered about your future? Everybody does, but have you ever wondered about the man you are going to marry some day? What will he be like? This question has occurred to me frequently. I have my expectations set fairly high, too high, maybe. The finding of the "man of my dreams" will be a real problem. Likely I'll end up an old maid!

For example, the man I marry must be generous, kind, and thoughtful. My comfort must be considered by him as much as his own, and not only for the first month. He must also have as much intelligence as I have. This isn't asking much, but I believe this is necessary for most successful marriages. Likewise, his religion must be the same as mine.

Then, too, my idea of a perfect husband is not only one who earns enough money for a comfortable living but one who realizes the value of money. By this I mean one who will be thrifty but not miserly, for I like a good time as well as anybody. He must also have a good sense of humor, which is necessary for any good time.

I would like my husband to have a good memory, to make up for my poor one. His would have to do double duty, but maybe I could help him in some way.

Lastly, I don't want to be in store for what my husband—if there ever is such a creature—will be in for. By this I mean I would like to eat my breakfast looking at something beautiful. My idea of perfection in this line is someone tall, with very dark, wavy hair. He must have a manly build and carriage.

I guess a man with all of these fine qualities doesn't need a wife. I had better put in my order for an angel. Maybe I'd even enjoy doing housework for him then. Don't you think I'll have a problem finding him?

The American Citizen With a Foreign Face

This world seems almost unknown to me, for there is so much for me to learn. There is a huge problem that stands before me like a stone wall. Can I work my way through to the other side and find myself in a known world?

My main problem lies in the book *From Many Lands,* written by Louis Adamic. In this book he presents the problems which confront the American citizen with a foreign face. I read particularly on the one of the Japanese American. This boy has struggled, living under harsh treatments; he was thrashed. And when seeking jobs he was turned down, not because of his lack of experience or education but because of his face.

Being a Japanese, I struggle with words and find myself constantly extracting illusive meanings from the dictionary. I must learn the hard times my colonial countrymen had to push through. So I read the novel *Northwest Passage* and see that these colonials struggled to get where they wanted. *Abe Lincoln,* by Sandburg, and other famous men's biographies will give me an idea of how the great leaders of the country led their lives. These books will show me the problems they bored through. I might find myself born to be one of these great fellows. I read these books, hoping I may clear my problem. Right now my definite problem is to find out how.

You can see that this stone wall before me is very huge and thick. I cannot get anywhere unless I read and dig into it. Another idea is that I might be able to climb over it. To do this means just as hard as battling through it.

Youth's Bill of Rights *

(A petition directed to parents, teachers, and other miscellaneous adults)

1. Stand *by* us, not over us.
    Give us the feeling that we are not alone in the world, that we can always count on you when we are in trouble.
2. Make us feel that we are loved and wanted.
    We want to love you, not as a duty but because you love us.
3. Train us by being affectionately firm.
    You really will achieve more with us through patient teaching than by punishment or preaching. Say "No" when you feel you have to, but explain your rules, don't merely impose them.
4. Bring us up so that we will not always need you.
    Teach us how to take on responsibility and become independent of *you*. We will learn this faster and better if you will let us question you, your ideas and standards.
5. Don't act shocked when we do things we shouldn't.
    It is going to take us time to learn how to grow into life properly.
6. Try to be as consistent as possible.
    If you are mixed up about what you want from **us**, why shouldn't **we** be mixed up too in what we give you?
7. Don't try to make us feel inferior.
    We doubt ourselves enough without your confirming it. Predicting failure for us won't help us succeed.

* Prepared especially for this volume.

8. Say "Nice Work" when we do something really well.
    Don't hold back the praise when we deserve it. That's the way to spur us on.
9. Show respect for our wishes even if you disagree with them.
    Respect for you will flow naturally from your respect for us.
10. Give direct answers to direct questions.
    But don't give us more than we ask for or can understand. When *you* don't know, say so, but find someone for us who does know.
11. Show interest in what we're doing.
    Even though by your standards our activities may not be important or interesting, don't reduce them in our eyes by your indifference.
12. Treat us as if we are normal, even when our conduct seems peculiar to you.
    All God's children have problems. That doesn't mean we're all problem children.
13. Sometimes all of us run into serious emotional difficulties. Should that happen, obtain for us professional counselling.
    It isn't always easy for boys and girls to understand themselves or know just what they want. That's why there are specialists in personal adjustments and vocational selection.
14. Teach us by example.
    "What you are speaks louder than your words."
15. Treat each one of us as a person in his own right.
    Children are people, not carbon copies of grownups. Treat all children in your care fairly; that is, as of equal value to you. That is how we will learn to respect the rights of other people and to treat them fairly.

16. Don't keep us young too long.

    We want a chance to prove what we can do as soon as we are ready to give proof. Don't hold us back by love which over-protects and paralyzes.

17. We need fun and companionship.

    Help us share our interests and happy feelings with groups of friends. Give us time to be with them and make them welcome when they come to visit.

18. Make us feel that our home belongs to us.

    We are *at least* as important as the furniture. Don't protect "things" at our expense by making us feel like intruding bulls in a china shop.

19. Don't laugh at us when we use the word "love."

    The need to love and be loved starts early (and never ends). Getting romantic is merely setting to soft music the eternal desire to belong to someone and have someone belong to us.

20. Treat us as junior partners in the firm.

    Democracy starts at home. If you want us to be worthy successors to you, take us into your confidence, and let us help you in managing *our* family, *our* school and *our* community.

21. Make yourself an adult fit for a child to live with.

    Prove to us "it ain't so" that parents are the worst persons in the world to have children, or that teachers are precisely the people least suited to teach. Show that home and school are not simply places where children learn how to get along with disagreeable adults.

22. Prepare us to lead *our* lives, not *yours*.

    Find out what *we* can do or *we* want to be before you force us beyond our capacity or make us become what *you* want us to become.

23. Give us the right to a major voice in our own lives.
    > Decisions that will affect our whole future should be made *with* us, not *for* us. We have a right to our kind of future.
24. Let us make our own mistakes.
    > To make wise decisions takes experience. That means we have to try ourselves out and find out for ourselves. We can only learn from our own actions—not yours.
25. Permit us the failings of average children, just as we permit you the failings of average parents.
    > Let us both break the rules sometimes. We can grow only at our own rate, which means in easy stages. We want to become the best we can become, but we would not be human if we were perfect.

Phrases to Which Young People Are Allergic *

(Arranged in order of age at which first heard)

1. My, what a big boy (big girl) you've become! (With an attempted pat on a head out of reach.)
2. Do it for mother's sake!
3. Not another word out of you!
4. You're still just a child! (With a forgiving smile.)
5. You're too young to know your own mind.
6. I don't have to tell you why, you just obey!
7. You're too old to do *that* any more.
8. You simply aren't old enough to understand.
9. Come tell mother everything.
10. I don't know what's happening to the young people today.

* Prepared especially for this volume.

11. You'll never amount to anything, if you continue to . . . (do this or that, go around with X or Y, etc.).
12. I never had the opportunities I'm giving you.
13. It's only puppy love.
14. After all we've sacrificed for you!
15. I'm nothing but a servant in my own home (To be avoided by girls when they become mothers).
16. I'm nothing but a meal ticket for my children (To be avoided by boys when they become fathers).
17. I suppose you've reached the *difficult* age.
18. I guess you must take after mother's (father's) side.
19. When I was your age I (was making X dollars a week, had finished college, had a child, ran my own home, etc.).
20. Everyone takes us for sisters.